W9-BRR-683

The
# Reference Shelf®

# Contents

# 3

## Sea Stewardship and the Cost of Neglect

# 4

## Hubris on the High Seas

# 5

## Drifting Along: The Rise of the Environmental Refugee

# Preface

## The Changing Seas

The ocean covers more than 72 percent of the earth's surface and constitutes 90 percent of all the space on Earth capable of sustaining life. All life emerged from the ocean in the distant past and is still inextricably linked to the marine ecosystem. Phytoplankton—a diverse group of oceanic photosynthesizing microorganisms—form the most basic level of the global food chain and produce more than 50 percent of Earth's oxygen. The climate of the terrestrial environment is dependent on the ocean, which removes and produces essential gases and modulates heat to produce a productive living zone where humanity and all other terrestrial life can flourish.

The oceans also constitute part of the essential structure of human culture, linking global economies through trade and shipping and providing food and resources for humans around the world. The economic impact of the ocean is immense, providing nearly $3 trillion in goods and services each year. More than three billion people live within one hundred miles of the ocean, where the economy and the environment are dominated by marine influence.

Humanity's relationship with the ocean has reached a critical juncture in the twenty-first century, as the harvest of oceanic materials is essential to the continuation of society, and yet human activity has increasingly facilitated the degradation of the marine environment to the extent that many of the world's oceanic ecosystems are on the brink of collapse. Climate change, overfishing, oceanic acidification, pollution, and other human-engineered changes in the oceanic environment threaten both oceanic life and the continuation of human society. The question of how to manage, protect, and develop the oceanic environment is therefore one of the most important environmental issues in the history of human culture.

## Oceanic Exploration

Humans have been exploring the oceans for more than seven thousand years—resulting in an incalculable wealth of knowledge and scientific, technological innovation—yet scientists estimate that less than 5 percent of the ocean has been explored. The Census of Marine Life, a ten-year exploration involving 2,700 scientists from eighty nations, estimated that there are at least a million species of multicellular marine organisms and that there may be tens or hundreds of millions of marine microbes, the vast majority of which remain unknown to science.

Advocates for oceanic exploration argue that the irreducible importance of the ocean to all life is justification enough for the continued efforts to learn as much as possible about oceanic life and ecology. From an anthropocentric perspective, scientists argue that marine animals and plants contain biological compounds and mechanisms that may provide as-yet-unknown benefits to humanity. It is estimated, for instance, that between 40 and 50 percent of all known drugs have their origin in naturally occurring plant and animal compounds. Given the diversity of the oceanic environment, scientists have estimated that it is more than one hundred times more likely that researchers will find new medications in the marine environment than in terrestrial environments. To give one example, chemicals isolated from marine animals known as sea sponges include toxic chemicals that have been used to create some of the most promising anticancer agents ever developed in pharmaceutical science.

## Development and Environmental Risk

The exploration of the ocean is not only an environmental issue; it is also linked to global economics through the many important products harvested in marine environments. Legislative and diplomatic procedures play a role in determining the portion of the ocean that is controlled by each nation and limiting economic development in the marine environment. The portion of the ocean extending two hundred nautical miles from the coast of a country comprises that country's exclusive economic zone (EEZ), an area in which the country claims sole right to economic development, including fishing rights, mining, and seafloor exploration.

The establishment of EEZs is increasingly important to the oil and gas industry, as an overall reduction in terrestrial petroleum deposits has intensified interest in offshore oil and gas supplies. For instance, there is an unresolved dispute between the United States and Canada regarding the EEZ designation in the Beaufort Sea due to the presence of the Amauligak field, a large underwater oil field discovered in 1984. In 2014, oceanic drilling produced more than a quarter of the oil used in the United States, but the increasing shortage of oil deposits that can be harvested by traditional means has increased interest in alternative methods of petroleum production, including controversial shale fracturing, or fracking, a process that involves breaking shale deposits to release natural gases or oils and is generally considered to be a far more environmentally damaging process than traditional oil drilling.

Seafloor mining is another controversial issue in marine development due to recent plans to conduct mining operations in deepwater environments surrounding hydrothermal vents. Estimates indicate that there are rich deposits of valuable materials—including manganese, cobalt, iron, and diamonds—under the ocean floor. The increasing scarcity of terrestrial deposits of these elements has intensified interest in oceanic mining. Scientists and mining corporations are developing programs and models to make deep sea mining more efficient, but environmental groups oppose many of these plans because of their potential ecological hazards. For instance, current proposals for mining involve removing portions of the sediment surrounding undersea hydrothermal vents, which are host to rich communities of organisms, many of which are poorly understood by science. Mining operations could disrupt or destroy these fragile environments by shifting sediment and removing minerals that are essential to the integrity of the ecosystem. Similarly, oil and gas drilling has well-demonstrated deleterious effects on oceanic diversity and increases pollution throughout vast areas of the marine environment.

A lack of comprehensive research makes it difficult to predict the long-term effects of oceanic development. Ironically, interest in development has provided funding for research that is otherwise unavailable in many nations and therefore has consequent benefits to marine research. The US National Ocean Policy, which began implementation in 2012, provides more stringent regulations on environmental impact research, but critics argue that current regulations are insufficient. The benefits of increasing oil and earth mineral supplies provide a powerful economic impetus to continue development, but ecologists argue that these benefits are relatively short-term compared to the long-term benefits of more aggressively protecting the global climatological role of ocean ecosystems.

## Exploitation and Stewardship

Estimates indicate that fish are a more important source of protein than beef, constituting nearly 16 percent of the protein consumed around the world. By the mid-1900s, human fishing habits were depleting stocks locally. The acceleration of commercial fishing in the 1950s and 1960s exacerbated the problem, leading to worldwide depletions in many different fish species. The commercial fishing industry peaked in 1989, with 90 million tons of fish caught around the world, and annual yields have declined since this time. In a 2006 article published in the journal *Science*, researchers argued that, if current fishing trends continue, more than 90 percent of seafood species will be unsustainable by the year 2048, virtually eliminating fishing as a viable method for providing human sustenance.

The realization that wild fish populations are reaching a critical state of depletion has intensified interest in sustainable fishing and farming of marine species. In 2013 the European Commission reported that there was a 20 percent growth in sustainable fishing between 2009 and 2013. That same year, several of the world's largest fishing powers, including the European Union, Japan, and the United States, signed a joint declaration to expand sustainable fishing programs on a cooperative basis. Marine biologists and ecologists generally agree that measures in place may postpone, but will not prevent, the collapse of the seafood industry; they argue that more aggressive measures are needed to develop sustainable fishing practices.

Fishing practices in China have become increasingly controversial in the twenty-first century, including disputes with the Philippines and the United States over fishing rights in key areas. China is the world's largest exporter, and one of the largest importers, of fish and fish products. China's fishing industry also involves higher levels of wild fishing, and China is therefore one of the primary agents in the depletion of many important marine species. While China has instituted internal measures to promote conservation and reduce depletion, these measures have had a dramatic effect on the lives of China's professional fishermen. A 2012 report on fishing in the South China Sea indicated that more than 80 percent of Chinese fishermen in that region were close to bankruptcy due to reduced yields because of overfishing. The situation in China illustrates the difficult balance between protecting the marine environment (and seafood as a human resource in general) and preserving human cultures that have been built around fishing and harvesting resources from the ocean.

## Pirates and Refugees

Piracy has been an increasing source of concern in the twenty-first century, peaking in the United States around 2009 due to the well-publicized capture of the *Maersk Alabama* cargo ship by Somali pirates. In 2013, the World Bank released an estimate that Somali piracy alone results in a loss of $18 billion annually, though this figure has been subject to debate among economic analysts. Estimates of pirate attacks are difficult to assess because many ship captains fail to report piracy due to the threat of increased insurance premiums.

Combating piracy is a complex issue, largely because pirates tend to emerge from countries that are severely economically impoverished and those who become pirates are, in part, reacting to dire situations that motivate them to take up crime. The increase in piracy off the coast of Somalia, for instance, is related to the ongoing Somali Civil War, which began in 1991 and has devastated the nation's economy, with a consequent increase in crime both within the nation and across the oceans. More comprehensive policy measures proposed to combat piracy involve increasing aid to countries with high rates of piracy, as a way to decrease the impetus for piracy, rather than simply through enhancing maritime security.

Another international issue surrounding the ocean is the rise of environmental migration, individuals moving from one location to another due to global climate change and the loss of marine habitat. For instance, when the Cyclone Nargis struck the coast of Myanmar in 2008, displacing thousands of coastal residents, scientists noted that deforestation of the coastal mangrove forests likely intensified the scale of the disaster.

The topic of environmental refugees and migration has been controversial for many reasons, one being the suggested link to global warming from some news and activist organizations. Critics of global warming sometimes argue that claims of increasing environmental migration have been exaggerated by activists. The issue intensified after 2010, due to the release of several documentary films and programs discussing the issue. While the scope of the environmental migrant problem is under debate, the underlying changes in the ocean—including deforestation of littoral vegetation and the acidification of oceanic waters due to climate change—have been demonstrated conclusively. Research demonstrating widespread oceanic degradation indicates that these various processes are accelerating and becoming more frequent, and that environmental migration, like many other oceanic issues, will likely continue to be an issue as a result.

## Demand and Decline

Population growth drives the demand for oceanic resources, which is at the root of all current issues threatening oceanic biodiversity and environmental stability. Addressing management and preservation of the ocean is an issue that transcends national identity and any single area of human enterprise and strikes at the core of the human condition. If the gravest scientific estimates of oceanic depletion and pollution come to fruition, the global environment will be altered in drastic and irreparable ways. Changes on this scale would include massive fluctuations in climate, food shortages on unprecedented scales, and the depletion of the atmosphere to dangerous, potentially catastrophic levels. Reversing current trends and addressing the core issues surrounding oceanic management will require fundamental changes in human society, and it remains to be seen whether the global community is capable of successfully addressing these challenges.

## Bibliography

"Big Threats." *International Programme on the State of the Ocean*. Intl. Programme on the State of the Ocean, 2014. Web. 24 Mar. 2014.

Bruckner, Andrew W. "Life-Saving Products from Coral Reefs." *Issues in Science and Technology* 18.3 (2002): 39–44. Print.

"A Decade of Discovery." *Census of Marine Life*. U of Rhode Island, 2010. Web. 24 Mar. 2014.

"In Deep Water." *Economist* 20 Feb. 2014: 1. Print.

Kermeliotis, Teo. "Somali Pirates Cost Global Economy '$18 billion a year.'" *CNN*. Cable News Network, 12 Apr. 2013. Web. 24 Mar. 2014.

"National Ocean Policy Implementation Plan." *White House*. US Government, 2012. Web.

"Ocean." *National Oceanic and Atmospheric Administration*. US Dept. of Commerce, 2014. Web. 24 Mar. 2014.

Pala, Christopher. "Detective Work Uncovers Underreported Overfishing." *Nature* 4 Apr. 2013: 18. Print.

"Seafloor Mining." *Woods Hole Oceanographic Institution*. Woods Hole Oceanographic Inst., 2009. Web. 24 Mar. 2014.

Welch, Craig. "Ocean-Acidification 'Refugees' Move to Hawaii." *Chinook Observer*. EO Media, 24 Sep. 2013. Web. 24 Mar. 2014.

Worm, Boris, et al. "Impacts of Biodiversity Loss on Ocean Ecosystem Services." *Science* 3 Nov. 2006: 787–90. Print.

# 1

# A New Evolution: Exploration and Development of the Ocean

© Qu Jing/Xinhua/Landov

Researchers study ocean creatures on China's icebreaker *Xuelong,* or "Snow Dragon," at Chukchi Sea in the Arctic Circle.

# The Future of the Oceans

Humanity's relationship with the seas is a historical constant—as humanity's need for transportation, food, commerce, and energy evolved, so too did the development of technology, vessels, and other tools to satisfy those needs. With significant advancements in technology in the late twentieth and early twenty-first centuries, humanity continues to learn more about the world on and under the surface of the earth's oceans. Such technology has made available a wide range of information about the landscape of the ocean floor, changes in ocean temperature, and as-yet untapped natural resources. This prevalence of information has prompted a renewed interest in how oceans can play a major role in the economy and way of life in the United States.

A number of questions have arisen with regard to the exploration and development of the ocean's resources. For some, there are questions about exactly how many heretofore undiscovered energy deposits there are within US boundaries. For others, there is a concern about which states will stand to benefit economically from offshore energy exploration and extraction operations. Still others are concerned about the impacts of such operations on the ecosystems beneath the ocean's surface and within the valleys, mountains, and canyons on the ocean floor.

## Changing Technology

The technology of the twenty-first century continues to make it possible to explore regions once considered impossible to reach. During the second half of the twentieth century, much of humanity's technological focus was directed outward into space. In the twenty-first century, however, the focus has changed, as technological breakthroughs have enabled humanity to map and study the vast depths of the world's oceans. Researchers have at their fingertips a wide array of hardware and software that can help map the ocean floor, study currents and oceanic temperatures, and analyze other surface and subsurface phenomena. Geographic information systems (GIS) technology, for example, makes it possible to create digitized, three-dimensional models of the mountains, gorges, and other formations on the ocean floor. Meanwhile, hardware placed aboard ships, airplanes, and weather satellites is increasingly making it possible to study ocean temperatures and currents.

This technology is proving increasingly valuable to those who use the oceans for economic development. GIS, for example, enables petroleum companies to conduct exploratory drilling operations in optimal grids and within legal ocean boundaries. Shipboard and aerial radar is being used to create models of ocean currents, an undertaking critical for construction of offshore rigs and even hydroelectric turbines (a field that, although relatively new, continues to develop at a rapid pace). The continuing development and application of such technologies makes oceans, once a great mystery under the surface, much more familiar and accessible for a wide range of commercial activities.

One area in which the relevance of the ocean to the American economy and way of life is evident is the pursuit of new sources of energy. The modern American economy is dependent on a wide range of energy resources, including oil, natural gas, and even so-called sustainable energies like wind—all of which are found in great volume above and beneath the Atlantic and Pacific Oceans. Scientists and engineers are even developing the technology to generate energy through current-driven turbines similar to the wind farms found throughout Europe. The United States continues to seek the most cost-efficient sources of energy, and the development of technology over the last several decades has helped locate such resources.

During the 1960s, for example, deep sea oil and gas operations off the Alaskan coast were frequently put at risk by the presence of hydrates, or methane molecules within water deposits. These hydrates would become unstable and potentially explosive once released from the stability of the high-pressure and cold-temperature ocean floor. Over the past few decades, however, energy companies have increasingly looked to extract naturally occurring hydrates themselves instead of the nearby oil and gas deposits, as hydrates have been discovered to contain much higher concentrations of usable energy. New technologies have been developed to locate hydrates and, most important, extract them safely from deepwater locations off the Pacific Northwest as well as the Gulf of Mexico.

As new sources are discovered, questions frequently arise as to the state or country to which the sites of these deposits belong. In a general sense, the federal and state governments share responsibility over permitting for certain types of offshore energy, such as wind power. There is no single federal agency governing the ocean energy arena, however, creating some confusion among the states looking to utilize ocean-based energy sources. The Commonwealth of Virginia, for example, recently looked to force the issue of whether to allow exploratory drilling off its coast by circumventing federal bureaucratic rules governing offshore exploration. Other states, wary of waiting for federal mapping of approved offshore drilling operations, are looking to follow suit.

## Environmental Concerns

Because locating and ultimately extracting these resources is not always an exact science, scientists and energy interests must launch exploratory drilling and other operations to locate the best possible sites at which to begin extraction. Offshore drilling in particular has gathered attention in the United States in recent years, particularly in the wake of the 2010 disaster at the BP Deepwater Horizon offshore facility in the Gulf of Mexico. In that incident, a well being dug deep beneath the rig began to fracture. The drilling and extraction equipment in the well also failed, resulting in a massive oil spill, an explosion aboard the rig, and the deaths of eleven people before the well was finally sealed. Years later the Gulf is still recovering from the long-term effects of the spill, and the economic impact of the disaster (including oil industry unemployment, tourism industry losses, and other factors) was enormous. The states of Louisiana, Alabama, and Florida were particularly affected by this incident, which spurred an immediate halt to expanded offshore oil exploration until a full assessment of the incident could be conducted and a subsequent set of safety and environmental protocols could be generated.

In 2013, the federal government finally released a set of strict regulations governing the safe and environmentally responsible operation of offshore oil facilities. The Department of the Interior introduced the Safety and Environmental Management System (SEMS), a comprehensive set of regulations for offshore operators. Among the seventeen criteria US operators must now satisfy in order to conduct their projects are reports on safety equipment, hazards analyses, established procedures for checking the integrity of mechanical equipment, and formal emergency training programs.

Central to the issue of the economic significance of the oceans abutting the United States in the twenty-first century are the benefits of the energy industry to the states in which they operate. According to the Bureau of Labor Statistics, the oil and natural gas industries alone employ hundreds of thousands of people to conduct exploratory operations, drill, and extract. Between 2007 and 2013, employment in these two industries increased at rates in the double digits (with the obvious exception of the period immediately following the 2010 BP disaster, when the industry was brought to a standstill pending an investigation and revised regulations). These two sectors, much of whose operations are based in the oceans, are among the fastest-growing industries in terms of employment.

The oil and natural gas arenas are not the only energy interests that provide economic benefits from operating in the waters off the United States coasts. In 2010, the federal government approved the first wind farm in the water between Cape Cod and Nantucket in Massachusetts. This farm would use 130 giant wind turbines, generating hundreds of construction and manufacturing jobs in the region. The success of Cape Wind, as it is known, would likely spur the development of other wind farms, creating thousands more jobs in order to maintain these farms.

The BP disaster and the increase in exploratory drilling projects in the oceans off US shores have also raised concerns over whether the oceans and the ecosystems therein are at risk. To be sure, technology has increasingly made possible the location and extraction of energy resources in areas that were previously unknown. In 2014, exploratory drilling is capable of digging wells in high-pressure and high-temperature spots in deep canyons and formations. Such operations may yield high returns, but the BP Deepwater Horizon incident—one of the worst environmental disasters in history—demonstrates that there are risks for which even state-of-the-art technology is unprepared.

## Developing New Policies

The growing volume of questions surrounding the exploration and development of the Atlantic and Pacific Oceans has prompted the US government to develop and implement a national ocean policy. Indeed, the United States is not alone—in 1998, the United Nations adopted a resolution declaring that period the International Year of the Ocean. In response, the federal government established the Ocean Principals Group, an ad hoc network of federal agencies to promote the conservation and sustainable development of the oceans that surround the country. In 2009, the administration of President Barack Obama launched the Interagency Ocean Policy Task Force, with which he charged the responsibility of developing a set of policies regarding the stewardship of America's oceans. In 2012, the Task Force returned with a comprehensive plan that included regulatory oversight, protocols for state sovereignty, and more effective lines of communication between local, state, and federal agencies, and researchers, interest groups, and other related organizations. President Obama also signed an executive order to create a National Ocean Council in 2010. Based at the White House, this small group was established in order to reconcile the differences between the broad range of government agencies and private organizations with interests in ocean use.

The Obama administration's ocean policies were met with mixed reviews. Many of the issues surrounding these policies are manifest in the competing interests of those who appear before the Council or seek clarification on the new regulations. For example, recreational and commercial fishermen, at odds over whether several defunct oil rigs should remain in the Gulf of Mexico or be removed, could not find a single directive from the government, as six different agencies needed to provide input. Additionally, due to the general mandates and extremely broad area of oversight (as well as the relatively small size) of the Council, opponents have argued that the inevitable delays caused by petition review processes will stall major projects, increasing costs during the delays. Furthermore, opponents complain that opposing interest groups could take advantage of the slow petition process to deliberately stall projects they seek to defeat. In the meantime, other petitions would be further delayed while these tactics are being employed, opponents claim.

In addition to the private sector concerns over the new ocean policy, the issue of developing a comprehensive national ocean policy has taken on a strong political atmosphere. In 2012, congressional Republicans held up funding for the Council until a full assessment of the Council's effectiveness and cost-benefits could be completed. Republicans also charged the Obama administration with refusing to cooperate with subcommittee requests for further information about the Council. The White House and a large group of organizations have countered such claims by welcoming what they deem a well-defined and well-informed set of policies.

Throughout history, humanity has relied on the ocean for food, transit, commerce and even fuel supplies. In the early twenty-first century, the application of new technologies to the oceans—specifically, those that help map the ocean floor, monitor currents and temperature, and even assess optimal sites for extracting natural resources—has strengthened the connection between the oceans and the nation's economy. This connection has warranted the generation of a comprehensive national policy on the use of the Atlantic and Pacific Oceans. This policy requires the inclusion of not only the federal and state governments but of the myriad of industries and organizations that gain from the oceans' economic and social benefits. To be sure, this policy is a work in progress, one that understandably has generated political debate in recent years. Nevertheless, most leaders—both in the private and public sectors—would agree that, in light of the value of the oceans' increasingly available resources to the American economy, an effective policy remains essential in the twenty-first century.

—Michael Auerbach

## Bibliography

Boswell, Ray. "Subsea Gas Hydrates Offer Huge Deepwater Energy Potential." *Offshore*. PennWell, 1 Feb. 2011. Web. 10 Apr. 2014.

Eilperin, Juliet. "National Ocean Policy Sparks Partisan Fight." *Washington Post*. Washington Post, 28 Oct. 2012. Web. 10 Apr. 2014.

Fitzgerald, Alison. "Virginia Tries to Circumvent Obama to Allow Energy Drilling." *New York Times*. New York Times, 13 Nov. 2012. Web. 10 Apr. 2014.

"Interior Secretary Salazar Approves Cape Wind Offshore Project." *Wind Energy Weekly* 30 Apr. 2010: 1–3. Print.

"Mapping—GIS." *NOAA Ocean Explorer*. Natl. Oceanic and Atmospheric Administration, 16 Apr. 2013. Web. 10 Apr. 2014.

"Ocean Current Energy." *Bureau of Ocean Energy Management*. Bureau of Ocean Energy Management, n.d. Web. 10 Apr. 2014.

"Oil and Gas Industry Employment Growing Much Faster than Total Private Sector Employment." *Today in Energy*. US Energy Information Administration, 8 Aug. 2013. Web. 10 Apr. 2014.

Shadravan, Arash, and Mahmood Amani. "HPHT 101—What Petroleum Engineers and Geoscientists Should Know About High Pressure High Temperature Wells Environment." *Energy Science & Technology* 4.2 (2012): 36–60. Print.

Taylor, Michael T., and Nickole Winnett. "Safety and Environmental Management Requirements for Offshore Operations." *EHS Today* 6.9 (2013): 74–80. Print.

United States. Congressional Research Service. "Wind Energy: Offshore Permitting." *CRS Report for Congress*. By Adam Vann. Federation of American Scientists, 17 Oct. 2012. Web. 10 Apr. 2014.

United States. Department of Commerce. "Ocean Energy and Minerals: Resources for the Future." *Year of the Ocean Discussion Papers*. Environmental Protection Agency, 1998. Web. 10 Apr. 2014.

"What People Are Saying About the Oceans Plan." *White House*. White House, 16 Apr. 2013. Web. 10 Apr. 2014.

# Accelerating Ocean Exploration

By Marcia McNutt
*Science*, August 30, 2013

Last month, a distinguished group of ocean researchers and explorers convened in Long Beach, California, at the Aquarium of the Pacific to assess progress and future prospects in ocean exploration. Thirteen years ago, U.S. President Clinton challenged a similar group to provide a blueprint for ocean exploration and discovery. Since then, the fundamental rationale has not changed: to collect high-quality data on the physics, chemistry, biology, and geology of the oceans that can be used to answer known questions as well as those we do not yet know enough to pose, to develop new instruments and systems to explore the ocean in new dimensions, and to engage a new generation of youth in science and technology. Recently, however, exploration has taken on a more urgent imperative: to record the substantial changes occurring in largely undocumented regions of the ocean. With half of the ocean more than 10 kilometers from the nearest depth sounding, ecosystem function in the deep sea still a mystery, and no first-order baseline for many globally important ocean processes, the current pace of exploration is woefully inadequate to address this daunting task, especially as the planet responds to changes in climate. To meet this challenge, future ocean exploration must depart dramatically from the classical ship-based expeditions of the past devoted to mapping and sampling.

As a first step, future exploration should make better use of autonomous platforms that are equipped with a broader array of in situ sensors, for lower-cost data gathering. Fortunately, new, more nimble, and easily deployed platforms are available, ranging from $200 kits for build-your-own remotely operated vehicles to long-range autonomous underwater vehicles (AUVs), solar-powered autonomous platforms, autonomous boats, AUVs that operate cooperatively in swarming behavior through the use of artificial intelligence, and gliders that can cross entire oceans. New in situ chemical and biological sensors allow the probing of ocean processes in real time in ways not possible if samples are processed later in laboratories.

Exploration also would greatly benefit from improvements in telepresence. For expeditions that require ships (very distant from shore and requiring the return of complex samples), experts on shore can now "join" through satellite links, enlarging the pool of talent available to comment on the importance of discoveries as they happen and to participate in real-time decisions that affect expedition planning. This type of communication can enrich the critical human interactions that guide the discovery process on such expeditions.

From *Science* 341.6149 (30 August 2013): 937. Copyright © 2013 by American Association for the Advance of Science. Reprinted with permission. All rights reserved.

Words such as "crowd sourcing," "crowd funded," and "citizen scientist" are nowhere to be found in the President's Ocean Exploration Panel report of 2000, but at the Long Beach meeting, intense excitement revolved around growing public engagement in many aspects of ocean exploration through mechanisms that did not exist 13 years ago. However, there is not yet a body of experience on how to take advantage of this new paradigm on the scale of a problem as large as ocean exploration. For example, what tasks are most suitable for citizen scientists, and how can they be trained efficiently? Can the quality control of their work be automated? Can crowd-sourced tasks be scheduled to avoid duplication and gaps?

Should any region of the ocean receive priority? Although the southern oceans are still largely unexplored, and coral reef hot spots for biodiversity are gravely imperiled by ocean warming and acidification, there was much support by Long Beach participants for prioritizing the Arctic, a region likely to experience some of the most extreme climate change impacts. An ice-free ocean could affect weather patterns, sea conditions, and ecosystem dynamics and invite increases in shipping, tourism, energy extraction, and mining. Good decisions by Arctic nations on Arctic stewardship, emergency preparedness, economic development, and climate change adaptation will need to be informed by good science. Exploration of this frontier needs to happen now to provide a useful informational baseline for future decisions.

# Expanded Boundaries and Hidden Treasures

By Robert D. Ballard
*National Geographic,* November 2013

America has had two great ages of exploration. The one that every schoolchild learns about began in 1804, when Thomas Jefferson sent Meriwether Lewis and William Clark on their epic journey across North America. The other one is just beginning. During this new age of exploration we will go farther than Lewis and Clark and learn the secrets of territories beyond even Jefferson's wildest imagination. Yet it seems safe to say that most Americans don't know anything about it.

Few realize that the single largest addition to the American domain came on March 10, 1983, when President Ronald Reagan, with the stroke of a pen, expanded the country's sovereign rights 200 nautical miles from its shores "for the purpose of exploring, exploiting, conserving, and managing natural resources." By establishing an exclusive economic zone (EEZ), Reagan roughly doubled the area within United States boundaries, as Jefferson had with the Louisiana Purchase.

Other countries have increased their jurisdiction over natural resources through EEZs and are eager to add more. Under the 1982 UN Convention on the Law of the Sea, which the United States has not joined, countries can claim sovereign rights over a larger region if they can prove that the continental shelf—the submerged portion of a continent—extends beyond their EEZ and meets certain other conditions. The United States potentially has one of the largest continental shelves in the world.

A lot is at stake. Just like the land that Lewis and Clark explored, the ocean floor contains natural resources, many of them untapped. Vast oil and gas deposits lie under the waves. So do hydrothermal vents, where copper, lead, silver, zinc, and gold have been accumulating for hundreds of millions of years. By some estimates there are more than 100,000 seamounts containing minerals critical for national defense.

That's not all that lies beneath. These watery zones encompass fisheries that nations rely on for sustenance, shipwrecks that may reveal lost chapters of history, and habitats that need to be preserved as marine sanctuaries.

Most of the U.S. EEZ hasn't been explored. In 1803, with the territory from the Louisiana Purchase newly in hand, Jefferson instructed expedition leader Lewis to "take observations on the soil & face of the country, its growth & vegetable

From *National Geographic* 224.5 (November 2013): 83–85. Copyright © 2013 by National Geographic Society. Reprinted with permission. All rights reserved.

productions . . . the mineral productions of every kind . . . volcanic appearances [and] climate as characterized by the thermometer."

Reagan did not follow Jefferson's example. To this day we have better maps of Venus, Mars, and the far side of the moon than we do of much of underwater America.

But now it's time for a new epic journey. Last June the United States' only dedicated ships of exploration launched a joint, concentrated effort to find out what lies within the country's EEZ. The National Oceanic and Atmospheric Administration's *Okeanos Explorer* mapped some of the New England Seamount chain near Rhode Island, among other places, while my vessel—the Ocean Exploration Trust's *Nautilus*—mapped portions of the Gulf of Mexico and the Caribbean. Both ships use multibeam sonars mounted on their hulls, which enable the creation of maps in three dimensions.

Lewis and Clark traveled for more than two years and had to wait until their return home to share their discoveries with an expectant nation. Although the ocean depths plumbed by these modern expeditions are more remote than the land Lewis and Clark charted, we are in constant communication with oceanographers and other experts on shore. The moment a discovery is made, scientists can step aboard either of the two ships virtually, take over operations, and share findings in real time with a plugged-in world. This is a voyage of discovery everyone can make.

# Space Exploration Dollars Dwarf Ocean Spending

By Michael Conathan
*Center for American Progress,* June 20, 2013

"Star Trek" would have us believe that space is the final frontier, but with apologies to the armies of Trekkies, their oracle might be a tad off base. Though we know little about outer space, we still have plenty of frontiers to explore here on our home planet. And they're losing the race of discovery.

Hollywood giant James Cameron, director of mega-blockbusters such as "Titanic" and "Avatar," brought this message to Capitol Hill last week, along with the single-seat submersible that he used to become the third human to journey to the deepest point of the world's oceans—the Marianas Trench. By contrast, more than 500 people have journeyed into space—including Senator Bill Nelson (D-FL), who sits on the committee before which Cameron testified—and 12 people have actually set foot on the surface of the moon.

All it takes is a quick comparison of the budgets for NASA and the National Oceanic and Atmospheric Administration, or NOAA, to understand why space exploration is outpacing its ocean counterpart by such a wide margin.

In fiscal year 2013 NASA's annual exploration budget was roughly $3.8 billion. That same year, total funding for everything NOAA does—fishery management, weather and climate forecasting, ocean research and management, among many other programs—was about $5 billion, and NOAA's Office of Exploration and Research received just $23.7 million. Something is wrong with this picture.

Space travel is certainly expensive. But as Cameron proved with his dive that cost approximately $8 million, deep-sea exploration is pricey as well. And that's not the only similarity between space and ocean travel: Both are dark, cold, and completely inhospitable to human life.

Yet space travel excites Americans' imaginations in a way ocean exploration never has. To put this in terms Cameron may be familiar with, just think of how stories are told on screens both big and small: Space dominates, with "Star Trek," "Star Wars," "Battlestar Galactica," "Buck Rogers in the 25th Century," and "2001 A Space Odyssey." Then there are B-movies such as "Plan Nine From Outer Space" and everything ever mocked on "Mystery Science Theater 2000." There are even parodies: "Spaceballs," "Galaxy Quest," and "Mars Attacks!" And let's not forget Cameron's own contributions: "Aliens" and "Avatar."

From *Center for American Progress* (20 June 2013). Copyright © 2013 by Center for American Progress. Reprinted with permission. All rights reserved.

When it comes to the ocean, we have "20,000 Leagues Under the Sea," "Sponge Bob Square Pants," and Cameron's somewhat lesser-known film "The Abyss." And that's about it.

This imbalance in pop culture is illustrative of what plays out in real life. We rejoiced along with the NASA mission-control room when the Mars rover landed on the red planet late last year. One particularly exuberant scientist, known as "Mohawk Guy" for his audacious hairdo, became a minor celebrity and even fielded his share of spontaneous marriage proposals. But when Cameron bottomed out in the Challenger Deep more than 36,000 feet below the surface of the sea, it was met with resounding indifference from all but the dorkiest of ocean nerds such as myself.

Part of this incongruity comes from access. No matter where we live, we can go outside on a clear night, look up into the sky, and wonder about what's out there. We're presented with a spectacular vista of stars, planets, meteorites, and even the occasional comet or aurora. We have all been wishing on stars since we were children. Only the lucky few can gaze out at the ocean from their doorstep, and even those who do cannot see all that lies beneath the waves.

As a result, the facts about ocean exploration are pretty bleak. Humans have laid eyes on less than 5 percent of the ocean, and we have better maps of the surface of Mars than we do of America's exclusive economic zone—the undersea territory reaching out 200 miles from our shores.

Sure, space is sexy. But the oceans are too. To those intrigued by the quest for alien life, consider this: Scientists estimate that we still have not discovered 91 percent of the species that live in our oceans. And some of them look pretty outlandish. Go ahead and Google the deepsea hatchetfish, frill shark, or *Bathynomus giganteus*.

In a time of shrinking budgets and increased scrutiny on the return for our investments, we should be taking a long, hard look at how we are prioritizing our exploration dollars. If the goal of government spending is to spur growth in the private sector, entrepreneurs are far more likely to find inspiration down in the depths of the ocean than up in the heavens. The ocean already provides us with about half the oxygen we breathe, our single largest source of protein, a wealth of mineral resources, key ingredients for pharmaceuticals, and marine biotechnology.

Of course space exportation does have benefits beyond the "cool factor" of putting people on the moon and astronaut-bards playing David Bowie covers in space. Inventions created to facilitate space travel have become ubiquitous in our lives—cell-phone cameras, scratch-resistant lenses, and water-filtration systems, just to name a few—and research conducted in outer space has led to breakthroughs here on earth in the technological and medical fields. Yet despite far-fetched plans to mine asteroids for rare metals, the only tangible goods brought back from space to date remain a few piles of moon rocks.

The deep seabed is a much more likely source of so-called rare-earth metals than distant asteroids. Earlier this year the United Nations published its first plan for management of mineral resources beneath the high seas that are outside the jurisdiction of any individual country. The United States has not been able to participate in negotiations around this policy because we are not among the 185 nations that have ratified the U.N. Convention on the Law of the Sea, which governs such activity.

With or without the United States on board, the potential for economic development in the most remote places on the planet is vast and about to leap to the next level. Earlier this year Japan announced that it has discovered a massive supply of rare earth both within its exclusive economic zone and in international waters. This follows reports in 2011 that China sent at least one exploratory mission to the seabed beneath international waters in the Pacific Ocean. There is a real opportunity for our nation to lead in this area, but we must invest and join the rest of the world in creating the governance structure for these activities.

Toward the end of last week's hearing, Sen. Mark Begich (D-AK), who chairs the Subcommittee on Oceans, Atmosphere, Fisheries, and Coast Guard, hypothetically asked where we would be today if we had spent half as much money exploring the oceans as we have spent exploring space. Given the current financial climate in Congress, we won't find the answer to his question on Capitol Hill.

But there may be another way.

Cameron is currently in preproduction on the second and third "Avatar" films. He says the former will be set on an ocean planet. No one except he and his fellow producers at 20th Century Fox really know how much the first installment of the movie series cost, but estimates peg it at approximately $250 million—or 10 times the total funding for NOAA's Ocean Exploration program. Since the original "Avatar" grossed more than $2 billion at the box office worldwide, if NASA isn't willing to hand over a bit of its riches to help their oceanic co-explorers, maybe Cameron and his studio partners can chip a percent or two off the gross from "Avatar 2" to help fill the gap.

Come to think of it, if the key to exploring the oceans hinges either on Hollywood giving up profits or Congress increasing spending, maybe we are more likely to mine asteroids after all.

# Implementing the National Ocean Policy

## Secretary Jewell Dives In

By Liza Johnson
*NewsWave*, Spring 2013

[The Department of the] Interior's new Secretary, Sally Jewell, has embraced the newly released final implementation plan for the President's National Ocean Policy for the Stewardship of the Ocean, Our Coasts, and the Great Lakes. "As the new Secretary for one of the federal departments most involved in implementing President Obama's National Ocean Policy, I look forward to working with the National Ocean Council to build on its collaborative accomplishments and its new plan to improve our ocean, coasts, and Great Lakes," said Secretary Jewell. "As stewards of millions of acres of marine and coastal national parks and wildlife refuges, as well as 1.7 billion underwater acres of the Outer Continental Shelf, the Interior Department praises President Obama's foresight in planning for the management of the oceanic and coastal treasures that are so important to America's environment and economy."

The Secretary of the Interior and other Cabinet officials are members of the National Ocean Council—charged with implementing the President's National Ocean Policy established by Executive Order 13547 in 2010.

On April 16, 2013 the White House, on behalf of the National Ocean Council, released the final National Ocean Policy Implementation Plan that addresses national priorities for a strong ocean economy, safety and security, coastal and ocean resilience, local decisions and choices, and the science and information needed to inform society in priorities and support decisions. The Plan was developed with significant input from national, regional, and local stakeholders and the general public following release of the draft plan in 2012. Interior's bureaus were actively involved in the development of the Plan, and are committed to implementing the actions within the Plan. Interior has over 80 specific actions, second only to National Oceanic and Atmospheric Administration.

Below are a few examples that highlight Interior's role in the broader interagency effort.

## Ocean.Data.Gov

Ocean.data.gov is a web portal that includes data, information, and decision-support tools for a wide variety of users. Interior leadership and support have been

From *NewsWave* (Spring 2013): 1+. Copyright © 2013 by U.S. Department of the Interior. Reprinted with permission. All rights reserved.

instrumental in developing and contributing data to, as well as maintaining, the interagency data framework. By 2015, all federal non-classified geospatial data and information will be available through ocean.data.gov.

## U.S. Coral Reef Task Force

Interior serves as the co-chair of the U.S. Coral Reef Task Force, which includes federal agencies and state and territorial members. The task force is undertaking several actions in the Implementation Plan, including coordinated projects in targeted locations to reduce impacts of land-based pollutants on coral reefs through its Watershed Partnership Initiative, creating reef resilience and adaptive management strategies, and developing a reference handbook for managers as they assess, mitigate, and restore coral reef ecosystems.

## Offshore Energy

Interior supports a number of offshore energy actions that contribute to the national economy and national safety and security as well as ensuring that the development of these energy sources contributes to coastal resilience and ecosystem health. Through coordinated approaches, the Plan will help streamline the permitting process but does not affect any statutory or regulatory obligations. Specific actions related to oil and gas are focused on preventing spills in the Arctic including technological developments that minimize risk and improve response, containment, and support infrastructure and planning in the challenging Arctic environment. These actions bring together federal agencies, industry, academia, and international partners and rely on completing scientifically based field or test tank experiments and tests of response tools for U.S. Arctic marine waters. These actions are also designed to improve resilience to risks associated with increased shipping activity through the Arctic waters.

Actions related to renewable offshore energy activities include compiling available and relevant climate, water, wind, and weather data; environmental models of seasonal and extreme conditions; and other information to support the development of the nation's coastal and offshore renewable energy, including wind, ocean thermal, and hydrokinetic (e.g., waves, tidal energy) resources.

Additionally, the plan calls for analyzing economic contributions and impacts (including job creation) of emerging ocean uses on the communities and regions dependent on marine and coastal resources. These include renewable energy, aquaculture, and biotechnology. Programs like these require Interior to play a leadership role in implementing the Plan, supporting regional decisions and supporting the larger vision of the National Ocean Policy: "An America whose stewardship ensures that the ocean, our coasts, and the Great Lakes are healthy and resilient, safe and productive, and understood and treasured so as to promote the well being, prosperity, and security of present and future generations."

# National Ocean Policy Creates More Red Tape, Hurts Economy

By Doc Hastings
*Sea Technology*, January 2013

The oceans are an integral part of the U.S. economy, supporting millions of jobs throughout the country. It is important to protect and properly manage the oceans through a balanced, multiuse approach that recognizes the need for both environmental stewardship and responsible use of resources. Unfortunately, President Barack Obama has imposed new regulations that counter this balanced approached to ocean management.

The administration's National Ocean Policy creates a massive new federal bureaucracy with unprecedented control over our oceans, Great Lakes, rivers and watersheds that could negatively impact nearly every sector of the U.S. economy in significant ways.

## Additional Bureaucracy

President Obama enacted the National Ocean Policy by issuing an executive order, meaning this drastic change in ocean management was done without Congressional authorization. To date, no bill has passed the U.S. House of Representatives to implement similar far-reaching ocean policies.

The executive order creates a web of bureaucracy that includes dozens of new policies, councils, committees, planning bodies, priority objectives, action plans, national goals and guiding principles. Rather than streamline federal management, the president's initiative will instead add layers of new red tape and create a top-down approach.

For example, federally-controlled regional planning bodies will be tasked with creating zoning plans for each region without input or representation from local stakeholders or affected industries. All relevant federal agencies, states and regulated communities will be bound by the plans, which will be used to make decisions on regional permitting activities.

## Job and Economic Impacts

Although marketed as a common-sense plan to develop and protect our oceans, the National Ocean Policy will inflict economic harm and uncertainty on America's job creators. Imposing mandatory ocean zoning could place huge portions of our oceans

From *Sea Technology* 54.1 (January 2013): 40. Copyright © 2013 by *Sea Technology*. Reprinted with permission. All rights reserved.

and coasts off-limits, curtailing energy development, commercial fishing and recreational activities.

The reach of the policy goes beyond the oceans. It gives the regional planning bodies authority to regulate as far inland as necessary. This could impact all activities occurring on lands adjacent to rivers, tributaries or watersheds that drain into the ocean.

A multitude of industries could be affected, including agriculture, fishing, construction, manufacturing, mining, oil and natural gas, and renewable energy. These industries support tens of millions of jobs and contribute trillions of dollars to the U.S. economy.

The policy also involves vague and undefined objectives that would create uncertainty for businesses and job creators, and open the floodgates for litigation. According to testimony received by the House Natural Resources Committee, this uncertainty will likely increase costs to private landowners and businesses, cause companies to cut back on investment and job creation, and limit American energy production both on- and offshore.

It is also unclear how much this initiative will cost taxpayers, how it is being funded and if it will take money away from existing agency budgets at a time when budgets are already being cut.

## Congressional Oversight

The House Natural Resources Committee held a series of oversight hearings to better understand the policy, but the Obama administration has failed to answer questions on the funding for this initiative, the breadth of its reach and the impact it will have on jobs, the economy and energy security.

This led to a bipartisan vote of the House in May 2012 to pause funding for the president's initiative until its job and economic impacts are known. This effort was supported by more than 80 organizations, including the U.S. Chamber of Commerce, American Farm Bureau Federation, National Association of Homebuilders, American Forest and Paper Association, and National Fisheries Institute.

## Going Forward

The House Natural Resources Committee will continue conducting oversight on the implementation and impacts of the National Ocean Policy.

The administration can and should require executive agencies to work in a more coordinated manner, share information and reduce duplication. However, the initiative goes far beyond this common ground. Instead of the administration's top-down approach that imposes new bureaucratic restrictions and costs jobs, the U.S. needs a balanced policy to take into account local, regional and national interests to ensure the responsible and sensible use of our oceans.

# National Ocean Policy:
# Plan, Schedule, but No Muscle

By Pietro Parravano and Zeke Grader
*Fishermen's News*, June 2013

In mid-April (2013) the Obama Administration released its long-awaited National Ocean Policy Implementation Plan. The plan is a scaled down version of last year's draft developed following a set of regional hearings held in 2009 by the Council on Environmental Quality, the National Oceanic and Atmospheric Administration (NOAA) and other federal agencies, followed by the President's National Ocean Policy Executive Order of 9 July 2010 (EO 13547) that, among other things, created the National Oceans Council.

The release of the Plan and its Appendix, setting out a schedule for implementation, garnered the expected responses. The big ocean conservation groups applauded it. Many industry types and the more moderate recreational fishing groups were circumspect. There were shrill statements from the House majority leadership and some radical sport fishing groups, who labeled it as top-down Washington micromanagement. And, for us, it was—"Is that it?"

## Background

This year marks the 10th anniversary of the issuance of the Pew Oceans Commission's report on the plight of the nation's oceans and resources, coupled with a set of recommendations for improving the health of the oceans and their dependent economies. The US Commission on Ocean Policy released its report the following year. Both reports called for a national ocean policy, among their numerous recommendations, and helped spur the action begun by the Obama Administration in 2009.

As the demands on the ocean have grown beyond transportation routes and a place for food gathering, it was clear to many of us that some form of planning and coordination among government entities would be necessary in the future. It seemed obvious that to avoid conflict among uses as well as to protect ocean resources (e.g., protecting fish stocks from non-fishing activities) where existing authorities lacked jurisdiction (e.g., fishery agencies have no authority—excepting perhaps, under the Endangered Species Act—over land based activities impacting ocean resources) some form of coordinating entity was needed. Hence, the call for a National Ocean Council and/or regional ocean councils.

From *Fishermen's News* (June 2013). Copyright © 2013 by Philips Publishing Group. Reprinted with permission. All rights reserved.

Both ocean reports were criticized by regional fishery council officials who felt somehow the ocean councils would meddle in fishery management. We, frankly, saw it as just the opposite.

Here was an opportunity for the regional councils to make the case for fish conservation over activities those fishery bodies had no authority over. The ocean councils could become a "super bully pulpit" for the fishery councils to address non-fishing threats to our fish stocks. In retrospect, that was perhaps mistaken. While the regional fishery councils can be bully boys at pushing around small-boat fishermen and other fishery interests they don't like, they've always been timid when it comes to speaking up against powerful interests—such as agribusiness, hydropower, or oil and gas—and there was no reason to believe they would now use the new ocean councils to suddenly step outside of their allocation role and become advocates for conservation.

Our other nagging concern that has grown since a national ocean policy began getting traction in 2009 was that many uses that quite frankly don't belong in the ocean would be allowed to start or expand, including open-ocean finfish aquaculture and offshore drilling, to the detriment of ocean resources and traditional uses such as maritime transportation and fishing. We have provided extensive comments on the issue in past *FN* columns.

## Motherhood

Reviewing both the Implementation Plan and its Appendix, there is really little the fishing community can find fault with in most of the goals set forth. Who doesn't want better seafloor mapping, better access to data, the reduction of coastal wetland loss, or protection of ocean habitats (fishermen can't do it by themselves)?

But instead of identifying specific "who's" and "how's" of accomplishing the goals set out there, the document begins looking like a bureaucratic planner's sandbox with lots of process, analysis, memorandums of understanding (MOUs), pilot and demonstration projects. Indeed, to avoid the rancor of states, many in Congress and their business patrons, the whole thing is mostly voluntary—meaning don't expect much to happen.

## Where's the Beef?

With apologies to Walter Mondale, we're wondering if this Implementation Plan and its Appendix is what General McClellan would have devised had he been ordered by Lincoln to protect the oceans, instead of defending the Union. There just doesn't seem to be any beef, or muscle anyway, in the document.

One example is water quality. With the exception of a brief discussion of Clean Water Act (CWA) 310 grants, there is no mention of enforcement of existing CWA authority to improve water quality. Moreover, it completely misses the fact that estuaries (which affect ocean resources) depend on freshwater inflows. There is absolutely no discussion of enforcing the CWA for "flow impaired" waterways, yet we know that in the San Francisco Bay/Sacramento-San Joaquin Delta freshwater extractions upstream are affecting the health of the estuary and species such as chinook salmon. Earthlaw's Linda Sheehan has made this point repeatedly. The recent drought in the Midwest has had similar effects on the Mississippi River Delta. Yet nowhere is there any discussion of utilizing existing CWA authority in pursuit of improved river flows and, thus, better ocean health.

Another example is the discussion of job creation. NOAA and the regional fishery councils' aggressive promotion of individual fishing quotas (IFQs) or "catch shares" is reducing employment in fishing through fleet consolidation. Some job losses were expected as overfishing and stock rebuilding began to be addressed, but much of the actual job loss has been excessive and unnecessary.

Added to this problem, the pay to remaining captains and crew in IFQ fisheries will be affected wherever shares are held by third parties, when approximately 25 percent of the value of the catch from captains, crewmen and the fishing community is siphoned off into the pockets of non-fishing "armchair captains," processors, NGOs, bankers, or hedge fund managers. Nowhere does the Plan address this oceans job issue, nor does it even touch on possible solutions such as development of community fishing associations (CFAs).

## Just Say No

The Plan extensively discusses climate change and its closely related problem of ocean acidification. But while a lot of attention is given to "adapting" to climate change, the authors don't appear to discuss its causes or prevention.

Current levels of offshore oil and gas extraction are allowed for, and new development is even anticipated under the Plan, instead of looking toward a phase-out of oil and gas extraction in the ocean and elsewhere and an aggressive phase-in of non-greenhouse gas producing renewable energy. Offshore oil and gas, of course, is not just a problem from the standpoint of climate change. Spills and seepage into the environment threaten fishery resources, as does the seismic testing utilized in offshore oil exploration.

The Plan is to be lauded in much of its discussion of aquaculture development, particularly in regard to shellfish. However, it does not draw the line at shellfish mariculture expansion in the ocean, but would permit open-ocean finfish farming, which is problematic for a variety of reasons from pollution, spread of disease and parasites into the wild, escapes, and the navigation hazards created by ocean pens and cages. Instead of calling for finfish farming in closed containers onshore where this form of aquaculture belongs, the Plan seems to endorse these operations offshore, for example, in its mention of the Gulf of Mexico aquaculture plans.

## Show Me the Money

Another troubling part of the Implementation Plan and its schedule is lack of any discussion of how all of this is to be paid for. We're not arguing against the Plan because of money, but there needs to be an honest discussion about where the funding is going to come from, other than just CWA 319 grants. True, some things such as coordination between the states (e.g., the West Coast Governors' Agreement on Ocean Health) are not costing the federal government anything, and some of the actions don't have any substantive federal cost associated with them or are paid for from other sources, but a lot of new money will also be needed.

Both of the ocean commission reports called for the establishment of an Ocean Trust Fund to financially support oceans conservation work. That concept is not to be found in this document, yet it needs discussion if we're serious about protecting our oceans and the economies, such as fishing, that depend on ocean resources.

In fact, the document fails to even mention in its discussion of ports that Congress is refusing to turn over monies from the existing Harbor Maintenance Trust Fund (funded from a fee on goods coming into US ports) back to local ports for such things as maintenance dredging. This is particularly critical at this time for smaller, coastal fishing harbors, where we're about to lose the economic activity and jobs these ports create.

## Not Ready for Prime Time

Our quibble is not with the many things the Plan mostly sets out to do, nor its goals. At present, however, it is just skeletal—and not a perfect skeleton at that. At best, it's a 90-pound wimpy weakling.

It needs money—something we've discussed in this column at length regarding fishery science. But it'll take more than money—we don't want just a pile of flab.

The Plan needs to include strong measures—even at the risk of offending some in Congress and the Chamber of Commerce—such as enforcing existing Clean Water Act provisions. It also needs some obvious fixes, such as its current language on offshore oil and aquaculture, if this Administration is serious about climate change and the protection of our oceans. What we need is a lean ocean plan with muscle. This one is not yet there.

## What the Plan Says about Commercial Fishing

Commercial fishing is an important part of America's history and economy, and contributes healthy local food to our country. The commercial fishing community relies on healthy coastal and ocean resources, and safe access to those resources.

The National Ocean Policy Implementation Plan identifies specific actions federal agencies will take to spur our ocean economy, strengthen security, and improve ocean health.

Commercial fishing will continue to be managed exclusively by the relevant state and federal fisheries managers and Regional Fishery Management Councils or Commissions.

Federal agencies have committed to actions in the Implementation Plan that will benefit the commercial fishing industry, including:

- Protect, restore, or enhance 100,000 acres of wetlands, wetland-associated uplands, and high priority coastal, upland, urban, and island habitat.

- Conduct targeted research and disseminate findings to address valuable information needs related to the direct and indirect impacts of climate change, ocean acidification, and other stressors on coastal economies, and key species, habitats, and ecosystems.

The Implementation Plan also supports voluntary regional marine planning, which brings together ocean users to share information to plan how we use and sustain ocean resources. Neither the National Ocean Policy nor marine planning creates or changes regulations or authorities.

### *Excerpts from the Implementation Plan:*

"Commercial fishermen will be better equipped to meet our Nation's growing demand for healthy seafood through improved science that supports increased sustainable fishing opportunity."

"Restoration activities provide direct economic opportunities, and healthy natural systems support jobs in industries such as tourism, recreation, and commercial fishing. Agencies will coordinate to protect, restore, and enhance wetlands, coral reefs, and other high-priority ocean, coastal, and Great Lakes habitats. Agencies will also establish a National Shellfish Initiative with commercial and restoration aquaculture communities to identify ways to both responsibly maximize the commercial value of shellfish aquaculture and achieve environmental benefits such as nutrient filtration and fish habitat."

# New Federal Ocean Policy Bodes Ill for Alaska

By Charisse Millett
*Anchorage Daily News,* May 11, 2013

Alaskans today have tremendous potential opportunities that can provide lasting benefits for decades to come. Plentiful energy and mineral resources, new Arctic shipping lanes, vibrant fisheries, and a bustling tourism industry are but a few of the areas that could all combine to usher in a new era of unprecedented economic and societal prosperity for the people of Alaska and beyond.

Unfortunately, prospects for this bright future could potentially be delayed if not derailed as a result of President Obama's issuance of the July 2010 National Ocean Policy Executive Order and the recently-released National Ocean Policy Final Implementation Plan.

Most troubling is the requirement that federal entities implement a national ocean zoning plan known as Coastal and Marine Spatial Planning to "better manage" a host of commercial and recreational activities and reduce what are said to be conflicts among incompatible human activities. The Interior Department has noted that the Coastal and Marine Spatial Plans "will serve as an overlay for decisions made under existing regulatory mandates" and "assist the [Bureau of Ocean Energy Management] . . . in making informed decisions."

New government-staffed "regional planning bodies" overseen by a 54-member White House-led National Ocean Council, are to develop "marine plans" by 2017 that may determine who gets to do what where on the water and even on land. Even though Alaska has chosen not to participate, the federal government has already proceeded ahead with plans to create a regional planning body for the region, having last year identified seven officials from the U.S. Department of the Interior alone to participate in CMSP activity in Alaska.

Policy supporters and the final implementation plan itself assert that the initiative does not introduce any new regulations. Yet, in addition to the zoning plan, the recommendations that were adopted in the Executive Order plainly state that effective implementation will "require clear and easily understood requirements and regulations, where appropriate, that include enforcement as a critical component."

Furthermore, the final plan requires federal agencies to take actions including the adoption of Ecosystem-Based Management (EBM) performance measures and incorporation of EBM into federal environmental planning and review processes,

From *Anchorage Daily News* (11 May 2013). Copyright © 2013 by *Anchorage Daily News*. Reprinted with permission. All rights reserved.

reactivation and repopulation of the National Marine Sanctuary Site Evaluation List, and the protection of millions of acres of federal lands.

Other developments indicate that the policy is already impacting prospects for energy development in Alaska. The administration's offshore oil and gas leasing program for 2012–2017 delays previously proposed lease sales offshore Alaska until at least 2016 and calls for "targeted" rather than area-wide leasing in the Alaskan Arctic.

Few economic sectors are as important to Alaska as energy. Alaska's offshore waters hold an estimated 27 billion barrels of oil and 132 trillion cubic feet of natural gas, and drilling in these waters could generate an estimated average of 55,000 new jobs, $145 billion in new payroll, and $193 billion in government revenue over the next fifty years. The continued viability of the Trans-Alaska pipeline is dependent on access to these resources, as well as onshore deposits located in areas such as the National Petroleum Reserve-Alaska and ANWR.

At a time when efforts here in the state have been re-doubled to move energy and economic development forward, the National Ocean Policy may emerge as the latest regulatory tool for those opposed to such progress to stand in the way.

The National Ocean Council itself has acknowledged that the undertaking "may create a level of uncertainty and anxiety among those who rely on these resources and may generate questions about how they align with existing processes, authorities, and budget challenges." In addition, it has recognized the "complexity of organizing, managing, and implementing the National Ocean Policy."

When Alaska first became a state 53 years ago, the federal government made promises to relinquish lands that it subsequently failed to keep. With another potential land grab on the horizon, Alaskans must now unite and urge leaders in Washington to hit the brakes on this policy before it is too late. Nothing less than the future and well-being of our state may be at stake.

# Advocates Push for New Atlantic Offshore Drilling

By Emery P. Dalesio
Associated Press, December 26, 2013

Southern politicians and energy industry groups are increasing the push to allow drilling off the U.S. Atlantic Coast for oil and gas deposits that could be puny or mean big cash to a part of the country where it's now largely absent.

Although drilling, refineries and the jobs that could accompany them are at least a decade away, the Obama Administration is weighing a decision expected to be announced in the next three months on whether to take an important early step: to allow seismic testing of the sea bottom. The tests could firm up estimates of how much hydrocarbon deposits may be out there.

Also next year, the Obama administration is expected to ramp up work preparing the country's 2017–2022 ocean energy exploration plan. Companies that specialize in deep-water drilling want the roadmap to include selling leases that allow companies to explore, saying thousands of new jobs, economic growth and reduced foreign imports would follow.

"This is an area that's been off limits to oil and gas exploration and production for over 30 years," said Randall Luthi, president of the National Ocean Industries Association, a trade group.

But a big burst of jobs created by exploration and drilling could take a long time.

Unlike the Gulf of Mexico, where a massive network of undersea pipelines course oil and gas onto land, that would all need to be built to deliver Atlantic energy, said Gary Gentile, a senior editor for oil news at *Platts*, a trade publication.

"You're talking about having to build up a massive amount of infrastructure to support any kind of offshore development. So now we're talking a decade or two into the future before realistically any of that oil can be tapped, if it's there," Gentile said.

Conservation concerns led to congressional and presidential roadblocks to Atlantic development beginning in 1982 until they were removed in 2008.

Environmentalists still say oceans and sea creatures would be harmed by drilling or even seismic testing. Public hearings over the past two years in New Jersey, South Carolina and elsewhere by the U.S. Bureau of Ocean and Energy Management attracted opponents to testing with undersea air guns they say can harm whales, dolphins and fish.

From Associated Press (26 December 2013). Copyright © 2013 by Associated Press DBA Press Association. Reprinted with permission. All rights reserved.

"The industry wants to paint the picture that the Atlantic is oil nirvana, that we can exploit the resources and the states will become rich, unemployment will be solved, and it will do everything but take out the garbage," said Derb Carter, North Carolina director for the Southern Environmental Law Center.

If Atlantic tracts are opened up, current estimates are that drilling with the best technology now available could yield a total of between 1.3 and 5.6 billion barrels, the Bureau of Ocean Energy Management reported earlier this year. The agency's mid-point estimate of 3.3 billion total barrels of oil is roughly equal to what Saudi Arabia's state-owned oil company pumped last year alone.

Atlantic drilling's advocates contend that new testing will reveal more oil and gas deposits than decades-old tests believed.

Bringing Atlantic fossil fuels to market is better than leaving them buried, even if the finds don't much change America's overall supplies, said David McGowan of the North Carolina Petroleum Council.

"We are not saying that the Atlantic is going to be the largest part of U.S. production. Rather, it will be one piece of the larger U.S. oil and gas pie," he said.

Luthi's group and the American Petroleum Institute this month unveiled job projections they said would flow from a new East Coast offshore energy industry.

North Carolina juts east almost to the Gulfstream and near likely drilling grounds, has a long coastline and two ports, so it should expect the greatest job creation, followed by South Carolina, the groups said. The groups see the offshore industry creating about 20,000 jobs in North Carolina in 15 years if exploration is allowed starting in 2017, with thousands more jobs resulting as those paychecks circulate through the economy.

Still more thousands of jobs would come along the entire East Coast and inland states as the influx of black gold and natural gas courses onshore, led by mining, manufacturing, administrative and scientific fields, the groups said.

The industry's job projections don't consider the environmental costs to all and economic costs to tourism businesses, the law center's Carter said.

The industry report marks an effort "to lay the groundwork for reconsideration of opening the Atlantic," Carter said. "It's all on the positive side as if there's no adverse impacts of putting an industry of this nature in an area that it doesn't exist—that depends on clean beaches, tourism, fishing. A full analysis would at least take that into consideration. There will be costs associated with this that should also be considered."

Luthi and other advocates say the only way to really know if oil and gas are below the ocean floor is by drilling. The first step to that is seismic testing with underwater equipment that fires compressed air that generates intense sound waves. Researchers study the echoes to map potential oil and natural gas deposits.

A 2010 Congressional Research Service report said research studying the impact of seismic surveys on fish and marine mammals produced mixed findings.

The drilling decision is a trade-off between financial gain and the environmental costs since oil spills do happen, and they obviously result in environmental and economic harm, said Andrew Hoffman and Tom Lyon of the University of Michigan's Erb Institute for Global Sustainable Enterprise.

Offshore oil isn't likely to drive down prices for U.S. consumers because oil is in demand worldwide. Producers will sell wherever they can fetch the best price and are unlikely to discount it for the American market, the two business professors said.

"It will still mostly be substituting domestic oil production for foreign oil imports," Lyon said.

# Proposed Energy Exploration Sparks Worry on Ocean Canyons

By Paul Greenberg
*Yale Environment 360*, January 21, 2013

*The Atlantic Canyons off the Northeastern U.S. plunge as deep as 15,000 feet and har-bor diverse and fragile marine ecosystems. Now, the Obama administration's plans to consider offshore oil and gas exploration in the canyons are troubling conservationists.*

"Your jaw's gonna fricking drop," the guy fishing next to me said, "when after, like, three minutes, you still haven't hit bottom." These words were spoken to me last September as I dropped a three-pound weight and two globs of clam bait over the side of the party fishing boat *Viking Star* into an abyss few people know exist—an abyss that is re-emerging as a battleground in the fight for the world's dwindling natural resources.

I was fishing 150 miles off Long Island in a bioregion commonly referred to as "the Canyons"—a latticework of 70-odd, 1,000–15,000-foot deep trenches that fili-gree the periphery of the continental shelf from North Carolina to Maine. Some of the canyons were formed relatively recently during the last Ice Age when sea levels were lower and the passage of ancient rivers carved out channels. Others may be older and may have come about as the result of the underwater equivalent of ava-lanches.

But whatever their age or provenance, the canyons abound with life. Golden tile-fish, the oddly named knob-headed creature I was hoping to entice to eat my clam gobs, create pueblo-like burrow villages in the canyon walls and floors. Deepwater coral that can live for over a thousand years prosper in and around these structures. Meanwhile, further up the water column, broadbill swordfish work the "tempera-ture breaks" that form when warm water eddies break off the Gulf Stream and mix with the canyons' colder water. All this is topped off at the surface by spotted dolphin, tuna, marlin, mahi mahi, and myriad other pelagic species. Many of these creatures are extremely vulnerable and slow to rebuild if disturbed by humans.

But in spite of the incredible diversity and fragility of these ecosystems, the Obama administration, with a renewed appetite for domestic sources of oil and natural gas, is on the verge of jumping into the abyss—it is now considering allowing oil and gas exploration in the canyons as soon as this year.

This policy is a marked change from that of the last half century. Though oil companies drilled 51 test wells throughout the Atlantic shelf in the 1970s and found

From *Yale Environment 360* (21 January 2013). Copyright © 2013 by Yale University. Reprinted with permission. All rights reserved.

the presence of more than seven million barrels of oil and trillions of cubic feet of natural gas, the U.S. government repeatedly blocked fossil fuel exploration there, and in 1990, President George H. W. Bush signed into law an outright moratorium on continental shelf drilling. But since 2008, when George W. Bush rescinded his father's executive order, the federal government has been edging closer and closer to at least trying to accurately assess the value of what's down there.

Speaking in Norfolk, Virginia last March [2012], U.S. Secretary of the Interior Ken Salazar stated, "As part of our offshore energy strategy, we want to open the opportunity . . . to conduct seismic exploration . . . so we can know what resources exist in those areas." Salazar called it "a critical component to this Administration's all-of-the-above energy strategy."

The beginning of continental shelf energy exploration is seismic testing. John Filostrat, a spokesman with Interior's Bureau of Offshore Energy Management, told me in an email that an environmental review is now underway "that could support approval of new seismic and other survey activity in the mid- and south Atlantic planning areas as early as 2013."

And while full-on Atlantic shelf development is still at least four years away (the current leasing plan does not include the Atlantic and expires in 2017), contractors understand that offshore prospecting is a long but potentially very profitable haul. John Young, a retired ExxonMobil seismic exploration expert who now consults for the Florida-based Continental Shelf Associates, says that "environmental impact statements are already being prepared and seismic companies are getting ready to submit permits. The chances are pretty good that at least some areas of the north and mid-Atlantic will soon be opened to exploration."

Environmental organizations see seismic testing as a slippery slope. Brad Sewell, a Natural Resources Defense Council senior attorney, calls this kind of exploration "the gateway drug to full-fledged oil and gas development." And though the public focuses on accidents such as BP's Deepwater Horizon spill, Sewell and others worry that the seismic testing phase, which is done well before any drilling, poses considerable risks all by itself.

In seismic testing, guns filled with compressed air are dragged over a target area and fired repeatedly. These mini explosions create high-impact sound pulses that echo deep into the earth's crust, giving oil and gas prospectors an acoustically derived image of the deposits below. While this may be good for the prospectors, saving them many millions on test wells, the noise from seismic testing can reach 230 decibels, well above the threshold of 180 decibels that federal researchers have set as a safe level for marine mammals. "Imagine dynamite exploding in your living room every 10 seconds for days, weeks or even months on end," Oceana's president, Andrew Sharpless, wrote in a recent *USA Today* editorial.

To be fair, the scientific literature on the long-term effects of seismic testing on both marine mammals and fish is sparse, and perhaps the environmental reviews being commissioned by the government will add some scientific clarity. But Sharpless noted that the testing plan is rushed, given that "technologies that will significantly reduce the impact of seismic surveying aren't far off." Indeed, in time, an emerging technology called marine vibroseis, which uses a transducer to spread out the acoustic probing at a lower intensity over a longer period, could become a much more common tool in the bottom cartographer's toolbox.

New technologies or not, Sharpless indicated, Oceana and other conservation groups would be digging in their heels in the years to come. "The current five-year plan for offshore drilling does not allow drilling activities until at least 2017," he said. "We intend to fight to maintain and ultimately extend that prohibition."

Fossil fuel exploration and drilling represent only one potential threat to the Atlantic Canyons. The other is commercial fishing. Until now, the deeper portions of the Canyons have been spared the impact of bottom trawling, and no one has yet to drag canyon walls where tilefish make their burrows. Yes, recreational anglers like myself have plied the depths, and draggers and long liners in some canyons have worked areas down to about 1,500 feet. But the essential ecological integrity of the very deep parts of the canyons is relatively untouched. In addition, better catch limits instituted in the 1990s have led to much improved fish stocks.

But reforms to U.S. fishing rules may change how fishermen seek their prey. Previously, fishermen were limited to a prescribed number of days at sea, the idea being that restricting fishing time limited the amount of fish a boat could catch. In the last decade, however, fisheries managers have decided that limiting overall catch instead of time at sea would be a better fulcrum against overfishing. But under this new regime, should fishermen not fill their quota on traditional fishing grounds, they now have unlimited time at their disposal. They could conceivably "go prospecting," as NRDC's Sewell puts it, in hopes of filling their quota in nontraditional places, like, for example, the deeper parts of the canyons. Even if they don't catch anything in the abyss, just the effort of trying could be a big negative.

"You're talking about slow-growing, vulnerable organisms down there," Peter Auster, a marine biologist with the Mystic Aquarium and the University of Connecticut told me. "A small disturbance can last a long, long time."

Many biologists and advocates believe that areas of the canyons need to be set aside now as protected zones before fishermen or fossil fuel prospectors can become dependent on them. "You want to do this now," Sewell said, "not just because the damage hasn't been done yet, but because there's no economic reliance yet. You have your best chance of protecting an area when no one wants to go into it."

Funding should be available through several federal agencies for continued exploration and survey of the mid-Atlantic and Northeast canyons over the next three years. But once the research is done and environmental impact statements have been drawn up, a stark choice will have to be made. "Based on a modicum of science and a clear path toward economic gain," Auster wondered aloud, "will we have the political will to set these things aside?"

For the moment, though, the competing interests that have so affected areas like the Gulf of Mexico have yet to arrive at the Atlantic canyons. The fishing remains extraordinary. The moment my gobs of clams touched the bottom of Atlantis Canyon off Montauk a series of violent yanks tilted my pole down. Pulling up, I felt the inexorable yaw of the bottom and cursed, fearing I'd hung up on the canyon floor.

But as I pulled and pulled, I felt the mud burrows give way. All at once pop!—whatever I had been yanking was suddenly pulled free. And it had been heavy; my arms had become Jell-O hauling whatever it was I'd hooked 1,000 feet up from the deep.

Ten minutes later, I saw the reason for the difficulty. This time, I had caught not one but two big golden tilefish after less than 15 seconds of contact with the mysterious bottom of the canyon. And all at once it occurred to me how tilefish might have gotten their name. The unknown sea floor down there must be fricking tiled with them.

# 2

# The Exploited Seas

© Ismail Zitouny/Reuters/Landov

The Bouri oilfield, Libya's biggest offshore field, is seen 81 miles north of Tripoli.

# From Collapsing Fisheries to Oil Spills

## The Toll of Ocean Exploitation

Humans have harvested the bounty of the ocean since time immemorial and over the centuries came to treat the sea as a source of limitless abundance. But as the population grew and industrialization developed, this conceit eventually ran aground. It took well into the twentieth century before people began to grasp that the ocean was a finite and fragile resource, one that would have to be managed to ensure that it continued to yield its benefits. Even so, adjusting to that realization has been problematic at best, while the toll of centuries of abuse has not been so easily fixed.

For countless generations the ocean was principally a source of food. Fishermen were limited by their technology, however, due to their basic tools—sailboats, small nets, and baited lines—and did not have a significant effect on populations. This created a sense that the ocean's resources were unlimited and populations could be replenished. Steam-powered trawlers were soon deployed, easing fishermen from their dependence on the winds and tides. Following World War I, fishing boats were outfitted with diesel engines, further increasing their speed and range. After World War II, new innovations that served the war effort—radar and sonar, for example— were adopted by fishing fleets. Now instead of searching for their catch through trial and error or intuition and experience, fishermen could track them with technology. Whereas fog and darkness might have impeded their efforts in the past, they could now navigate without visibility. Refrigeration increased fishing efficiency as well, allowing catches to be preserved more effectively. In the 1960s, fishing boats started to use flash freezing. Soon vast, factory-like trawlers were built and began capturing unprecedented amounts of fish.

Meanwhile, as their mobility and tracking and preservation technology improved, fishermen were also making advances in how they pulled in their catch. Chief among these was bottom trawling. In this procedure, a massive net with weights attached is dropped into the ocean, often falling all the way to the seafloor. The trawler then drags the net for miles, scooping up the sought-after fish as well as untargeted bycatch, all the while stirring up the ocean floor and damaging marine ecosystems.

These new technologies led to soaring fish harvests. In 1950, the global wild catch was less than twenty million tons. By the late 1980s it had risen to nearly ninety million. But the spiking hauls hid the underlying tension and fisheries were under severe stress. The northern cod fishery off the Atlantic Coast of Canada and the northern United States demonstrated the threat. Historically the cod fishery was one of the richest in the world and had been a reliable source of food for hundreds of years. But by the late 1960s it was clear that the cod were not replenishing themselves. So in 1970, the International Commission for the Northwest Atlantic Fisheries (ICNAF) instituted catch quotas limiting how much fishermen could bring in. But it was not enough. By the 1990s, the situation had reached critical mass. In the thirty years from 1962 to 1992, estimates of the stock of northern cod capable of reproducing had fallen from 1.6 million tons to between 72,000 and 110,000 tons. Fearing that cod were about to be fished to extinction, the Canadian government issued a moratorium on fishing the Grand Banks off Newfoundland in July 1992, slashing the catch quotas. In the United States, similarly drastic measures were instituted as well. Since then, the quotas have been adjusted and revised, but the fishery has yet to return to sustainability let alone where it was in its heyday.

The state of the cod fishery is not an isolated case. Everywhere, fisheries are under stress and many are in danger of complete collapse. In a landmark analysis published in the journal *Nature* in 2003, marine biologists Boris Worm and Ransom A. Myers studied the condition of saltwater fisheries. Their findings served as a dire warning, noting that there had been a 90 percent decline in large predatory species. Unless something was done, they predicted, the ocean could be empty of wild seafood by 2048. The United Nations (UN) Food and Agriculture Organization (FAO) released its analysis of the world's fisheries in 2012. The report concluded that in 2009, 57 percent of ocean fisheries were fully exploited, meaning that they have reached their maximum sustainable yield; 30 percent were deemed overexploited. The study confirmed the scientific consensus that fisheries are buckling under the weight of overfishing and other threats.

But as concerns about the sustainability of wild seafood were growing more pronounced, another form of fishing was becoming increasingly common. Though practiced for upwards of two thousand years, fish farming, or aquaculture, has enjoyed exponential growth over the past several decades. In aquaculture, seafood is raised commercially, whether in tanks or enclosures. Though heralded by some as a way to ease the burden on fisheries, aquaculture is not without its risks. If the farm is raising carnivorous seafood—salmon, for example—it may depend on wild-caught fish for feed, further taxing wild fisheries. Much like livestock farms on land, aquaculture can create excess amounts of waste that may pollute the surrounding environment. Also farm-produced stock, confined in close proximity to one another, is more susceptible to disease. Fish can escape from their enclosures and may then prey on or breed with the native fish population, creating potential ramifications for the health of the fishery. But these shortcomings notwithstanding, farm fishing is not going anywhere. By 2018, the FAO predicts humans will consume more farmed seafood than wild caught.

But fishing is just the oldest and most traditional means through which humanity has exploited the ocean. While advances have made the practice exceptionally more efficient, taxing the ability of fisheries to sustain themselves, that is not technology's only impact on the ocean. Indeed, technology has created entirely new methods of accessing the sea's resources. The ocean is now tapped for energy in the form of oil and natural gas and soon vast mineral wealth from the seafloor may be extracted through deep-sea mining. The means of harvesting these commodities, in the latter instance, has already led to catastrophe, as demonstrated most recently by the Deepwater Horizon oil platform disaster in April 2010, which sent over two hundred million gallons of oil spilling into the Gulf of Mexico.

The first offshore saltwater oil wells were drilled off the coast of California, near Santa Barbara, beginning in 1896. These wells were connected to the shore by long piers. More were dug elsewhere in the ensuing years, though for decades they were never built out of sight of land or to especially deep depths. As drilling technology improved, however, wells went out further from shore. In 1947, a well was dug 10.5 miles off the coast of Louisiana. Barge drilling also developed around this time. The forerunners to the massive offshore platforms seen today, these barges—mobile-drilling platforms—could be towed to multiple sites, drilling one well after another. In 1954, American production of offshore oil accounted for 133,000 barrels per day, about 2 percent of total production. By 1971, daily offshore production had climbed to 1.7 million barrels a day and 20 percent of the total in the United States.

Throughout the expansion of offshore drilling, there were periodic environmental disasters. The very first wells off Santa Barbara were eventually left derelict and leaked oil, contributing to polluted beaches and ocean habitats. A blowout at another well off Santa Barbara in 1969 spilled eighty thousand barrels. This led to a temporary moratorium on new drilling near California's coast as well as increased regulation. By 1981, American offshore production had fallen one-third from its 1971 peak. In 1990 it stood at only 1.1 million barrels. Even as production stalled off American shores, advances in drilling and seismic technology had vastly expanded the depths at which oil and natural gas could be accessed. Whereas the first wells were confined to shallow water, today ultra-deep drilling units—those that operate at five thousand feet and below—have extended their reach to depths of twelve thousand feet and can bore an additional twenty-eight thousand feet beneath the seafloor. Thanks to these and other developments, by 2009, nearly two million barrels of oil per day was acquired off the US coast.

Deep-sea fracking has also become another controversial tool in offshore energy exploration. When done onshore, fracking involves injecting a mixture of sand, water, and various chemicals underground during the drilling process to better access the natural gas contained therein. There are a number of environmental concerns associated with it, including that the process may contaminate groundwater, release harmful gases, and even cause earthquakes. Offshore fracking is meant to optimize the performance of underwater wells rather than get at otherwise difficult-to-reach gas deposits. The process is the same, however, though it involves considerably less sand and chemicals. Proponents maintain that offshore fracking is safe, however, few if any impact studies have been conducted and regulations and oversight are still in their infancy. There are widespread fears that the practice may contaminate the surrounding environment or lead to Deepwater Horizon–caliber catastrophes.

Meanwhile, deep-sea mining operations may soon open up a lucrative new frontier in ocean exploitation. Improvements in mining, drilling, and other technology combined with the rising prices of precious metals have made such projects increasingly feasible. Companies are especially interested in mining massive sulfides, mineral-rich underwater formations created by hydrothermal vents—underwater geysers—that spew up steam and other material from inside the earth's crust. While some claim that deep-sea mining may in fact have less of an environmental impact than onshore mining, scientists are worried about the potential for long-term harm to ocean resources. Given humanity's history of damaging marine ecosystems in the course of extracting the sea's bounty, such concerns are understandable. Indeed, the underlying lesson of the fishing crisis—or the various oil spills that have occurred over the years—is that ocean resources are both delicate and limited. Their misuse can lead to disaster for both the environment and humanity's ability to sustain itself, and once tapped out, they are not easily replenished.

—Paul McCaffrey

## Bibliography

"Big-Fish Stocks Fall 90 Percent Since 1950, Study Says." *National Geographic*. Natl. Geographic Soc., 15 May 2003. Web. 4 Apr. 2014.

Carroll, Chris. "End of the Line." *National Geographic* 211.4 (2007): 90–99. Print.

Dennin, Mark, and Shiva Polefka. "Fracking Goes To Sea: California Regulators Startled To Learn Of Offshore Hydraulic Fracturing." *ThinkProgress*. Center for Amer. Progress, 24 Oct. 2013. Web. 15 Apr. 2014.

DeNoon, Daniel. "Salt-Water Fish Extinction Seen By 2048." *CBS News*. CBS Interactive, 2 Nov. 2006. Web. 15 Apr. 2014.

Higgins, Jenny. "Cod Moratorium." *Newfoundland and Labrador Heritage Web Site*. Memorial U of Newfoundland, 2009. Web. 4 Apr. 2014.

Jarvis, Brooke. "Deep-Sea Mining—Bonanza or Boondoggle?" *PBS*. WGBH Educational Foundation, 25 June 2013. Web. 16 Apr. 2014.

Levitt, Tom. "Overfished and Under-protected: Oceans on the Brink of Catastrophic Collapse." *CNN*. Cable News Network, 27 Mar. 2013. Web. 4 Apr. 2014.

McCloskey, William, and Bryan Alexander. "Fished Out." *International Wildlife* 23.3 (1993): 38–43. Print.

Myers, Ransom A., and Boris Worm. "Rapid Worldwide Depletion of Predatory Fish Communities." *Nature* 15 May 2003: 280–83. Print.

Roney, J. Matthew. "Taking Stock: World Fish Catch Falls to 90 Million Tons in 2012." *Earth Policy Institute*. Earth Policy Inst., 19 Nov. 2002. Web. 14 Apr. 2014.

Sielen, Alan B. "The Devolution of the Seas." *Foreign Affairs* 92.6 (2013): 124–32. Print.

Velasquez-Manoff, Moises. "Nowhere to Hide: The Onslaught of Fishing Technology." *Christian Science Monitor*. Christian Science Monitor, 10 June 2008. Web. 14 Apr. 2014.

Vince, Gaia. "How the World's Oceans Could Be Running Out of Fish." *BBC*. BBC, 21 Sept. 2013. Web. 4 Apr. 2014.

# Deep Sea Mining: Coming Soon to an Ocean Near You

By Carlos Duarte and Sophie Arnaud-Haond
*The Conversation*, September 24, 2013

The depletion of resources on land together with the increase in resource demand and the parallel development in technologies for deep sea exploration have brought the issue of deep-sea mining to the forefront of political, industrial and scientific debate.

Shallow submarine mining is already a reality in coastal areas, such as the De Beers Marine diamond mining operation in Namibia, in depths up to 150 meters. The current challenge is to move these operations to the deep sea, which contains vast resources of minerals, including manganese, iron, nickel, copper, cobalt, rare earths and gold, often associated with areas of volcanic activity. Whereas nations are sovereign to regulate seabed mining within their economic exclusive zones, the access to resources in the seabed and ocean floor beyond these national jurisdiction waters, referred in United Nation Convention on the Law of the Sea (UNCLOS) as "the Area", is organized and controlled by the autonomous international organization called "International Seabed Authority" initially established under UNCLOS.

To date, the International Seabed Authority has entered into seventeen 15-year contracts for exploration for polymetallic nodules and polymetallic sulphides in the deep seabed with thirteen contractors. Eleven of these contracts are for exploration for polymetallic nodules in the Clarion Clipperton Fracture Zone in the Pacific, with two contracts for exploration for polymetallic sulphides in the South West Indian Ridge and the Mid Atlantic Ridge.

These contracts allow the contractors to explore specified parts of the deep oceans outside national jurisdiction, giving each contractor the exclusive right to explore an initial area of up to 150,000 km². Russia, China, Korea, Germany and France are the nations involved in most of these contracts, which include contracts for small nations, such as Nauru, Kiribati and Tonga, whom would likely open them up to tender by international companies.

Indeed, at a summit on Deep-Sea Mining in London [July 2013] Mark Brown, Minister of Minerals and Natural Resources of the Cook Islands, announced that the Cook Islands is embracing deep-sea mining as a pathway to multiply the country's gross domestic product by up to 100 fold, as they assessed that the Cook Islands' 2 million km² exclusive economic zone contains 10 billion tons of manganese

From *The Conversation* (24 September 2013). Copyright © 2013 by The Conversation Trust. Reprinted with permission. All rights reserved.

nodules, which contain manganese, nickel, copper, cobalt and rare earth minerals used in electronics. Negotiations are under way between the Cook Islands and companies in the UK, China, Korea, Japan and Norway, towards granting the first tenders within a year.

These facts suggest that we may soon face an underwater gold rush, but in most citizens' minds deep-sea mining is still something for sci-fi movies. Much to the contrary, the technology for deep-sea mining is not something of the future but it largely exists. A deep-sea mining operation consists of a mining support platform or vessel; a launch and recovery system; a crawler with a mining head, centrifugal pump and vertical transport system; and electrical, control, instrumentation and visualization systems. Companies such as Lockheed Martin, Soil Machine Dynamics, IHC Mining and Bauer or Nautilus Minerals are developing vehicles for deep-sea mining, pledging they are in the position to readily develop techniques to operate down to 5,000-meter depth. Indeed, the submarine vehicles required are already in existence and their operations are described in compelling animations.

Besides direct removal of parts of the sea floor during mineral collection, increased toxicity and turbidity is expected in the water column due to sediment resuspension during the extraction (i.e. near bottom) and tailings rejection after minerals are sorted on the floating platform (i.e. near the surface) resulting in clouds of particles forming plumes. Waste will represent 90% of the volume of materials pumped to surface and, thus, seabed operations will deposit massive amounts of waste at the sea floor. This waste can, in turn, release massive amounts of metals and other elements to the surrounding water, impacting on the ecosystems that thrive near these deep sea mining sites. While near bottom resuspended sediment may cause a major threat to local communities, surface plumes generated by tailing may have a wider impact by affecting larger areas.

Here is, however, where the main problem lies. Deep sea communities are very poorly characterized and mapped, and even where a reasonable taxonomic knowledge could be claimed and communities mapped over accurate scales, their sensitivity to these impacts is unknown. Despite these uncertainties, there is little doubt that losses of fragile deep-sea communities during the operations will be unavoidable, and the focus of industry and scientists is placed in the ecological restoration of the deep sea from impacts of mining.

The International Marine Minerals Society has developed a voluntary Code for Environmental Management of Marine Mining that recommends that plans for deep sea mining include at the outset procedures that "aid in the recruitment, reestablishment and migration of biota. . ."

The first impact assessment for a deep-sea mining project has now been produced. This was commissioned by Nautilus Minerals Inc., incorporated in Canada but also present in Australia (Queensland). Nautilus was granted the first mining lease for polymetallic seafloor massive sulphide deposits at the prospect known as Solwara 1, in the territorial waters of Papua New Guinea, where it is aiming to extract copper, gold and silver. The company, which is likely to be the first one to implement deep-sea mining is also looking at operating in the exclusive economic zones and territorial waters of Fiji, Tonga, the Solomon Islands, Vanuatu and New Zealand.

A workshop, promoted by Nautilus Minerals Inc., was held in Sète (France) in November 2012, including one of us (S.A.-H.) to consider the feasibility of ecological restoration of the deep sea following mining operations. The outcomes of the workshop are reported in a paper, including coauthors from Nautilus Minerals Inc, published in the journal *Marine Policy* (Van Dover et al. 2013). This exercise indicated that most of the direct costs (80%) for a deep-sea mining restoration program would be associated with ship use, including use of remotely operated and autonomous underwater vehicles. The experts attending this workshop concluded that deep-sea restoration will be expensive, but that cost alone should not be a reason for inaction and that restoration should be included in project budgets. They concluded that where restoration costs are prohibitive, offsetting options can be explored but that neither restoration nor rehabilitation objectives or commitments should be taken as a "license to trash."

A record of disasters in the offshore oil and gas industry, as well as deep sea fisheries, shows that there is a high price to pay in allowing industry to move offshore faster than scientific research does, yet only a handful of nations—which do not include Australia—are sufficiently equipped for deep sea scientific exploration to keep pace with industry. The basic knowledge (taxonomic inventories, habitat mapping, characterization of faunal assemblages and dynamics of deep species interactions) of deep sea ecosystems and the evaluation of their vulnerability, recovery time scales and processes is a matter of urgency, but this goal cannot be met without significant investments in capabilities for deep-sea research. Providing the immediacy of deep-sea mining, the investment in scientific infrastructure and research to provide the scientific underpinnings for the safe and sustainable mining operations in the deep-sea is an imperative.

## Bibliography

Van Dover, C. L., J. Aronson, L. Pendleton, S. Smith, Sophie Arnaud-Haond, D. Moreno-Mateos, E. Barbier, D. Billett, K. Bowers, R. Danovaro, A. Edwards, S. Kellert, T. Morato, E. Pollard, A. Rogers and R. Warner. 2013. "Ecological restoration in the deep sea: Desiderata." *Mar. Policy*, http://dx.doi.org/ 10.1016/j. marpol.2013.07.006

# Will Deep-Sea Mining Yield an Underwater Gold Rush?

By Meghan Miner
*National Geographic*, February 1, 2013

*Some environmentalists say the lure of precious minerals threatens ocean life and local cultures.*

A mile beneath the ocean's waves waits a buried cache beyond any treasure hunter's wildest dreams: gold, copper, zinc, and other valuable minerals.

Scientists have known about the bounty for decades, but only recently has rising demand for such commodities sparked interest in actually surfacing it. The treasure doesn't lie in the holds of sunken ships, but in natural mineral deposits that a handful of companies are poised to begin mining sometime in the next one to five years.

The deposits aren't too hard to find—they're in seams spread along the seafloor, where natural hydrothermal vents eject rich concentrations of metals and minerals.

These underwater geysers spit out fluids with temperatures exceeding 600°C. And when those fluids hit the icy seawater, minerals precipitate out, falling to the ocean floor.

The deposits can yield as much as ten times the desirable minerals as a seam that's mined on land.

While different vent systems contain varying concentrations of precious minerals, the deep sea contains enough mineable gold that there's nine pounds (four kilograms) of it for every person on Earth, according to the National Oceanic and Atmospheric Administration's (NOAA) National Ocean Service.

At today's gold prices, that's a volume worth more than $150 trillion.

## Can an Industry Be Born?

But a fledgling deep-sea mining industry faces a host of challenges before it can claim the precious minerals, from the need for new mining technology and serious capital to the concerns of conservationists, fishers, and coastal residents.

The roadblocks are coming into view in the coastal waters of Papua New Guinea, where the seafloor contains copper, zinc, and gold deposits worth hundreds of millions of dollars and where one company, Nautilus Minerals, hopes to launch the world's first deep-sea mining operation.

Last year, the Papua New Guinean government granted the Canadian firm a

From *National Geographic* (1 February 2013). Copyright © 2013 by National Geographic Society. Reprinted with permission. All rights reserved.

20-year license to mine a site 19 miles (30 kilometers) off their coast, in the Bismarck Sea in the southwestern Pacific Ocean. The company plans to mine the site, known as Solwara 1, by marrying existing technologies from the offshore oil and gas industry with new underwater robotic technologies to extract an estimated 1.3 million tons of minerals per year.

Samantha Smith, Nautilus's vice president for corporate social responsibility, says that ocean floor mining is safer, cleaner, and more environmentally friendly than its terrestrial counterpart.

"There are no mountains that need to be removed to get to the ore body," she says. "There's a potential to have a lot less waste. . . . No people need to be displaced. Shouldn't we as a society consider such an option?"

But mining a mile below the sea's surface, where pressure is 160 times greater than on land and where temperatures swing from below freezing to hundreds of degrees above boiling, is trickier and more expensive than mining on terra firma.

Nautilus says it will employ three remote-controlled construction tools that resemble giant underwater lawn mowers to cut the hard mineral ore from the seafloor and pump it a mile up to a surface vessel.

That vessel would be equipped with machinery that removes excess water and rock and returns it to the mining site via pipeline, an effort aimed at avoiding contaminating surface waters with residual mineral particles. The company would then ship the rock to a concentrator facility to remove the mineral from the ore.

## An Unknown Impact

At least that's the plan.

But the ocean floor is still a mysterious place, seldom visited by humans, compounding the known difficulties of working at sea.

Scientists weren't even able to prove the existence of underwater hydrothermal vents until 1977.

That year, an expedition of geologists, geochemists, and geophysicists from the Woods Hole Oceanographic Institute, Oregon State University, the Massachusetts Institute of Technology, Stanford University, and the U.S. Geological Survey proved their existence in the Galápagos rift with cameras and a manned dive in the submersible *Alvin*.

The animal-rich landscape and huge temperature shifts came as a surprise.

"When the first people went down there, and saw these things, they had no idea," says Mike Coffin, a geophysicist and executive director of the Institute for Marine and Antarctic Studies at the University of Tasmania in Australia. "The submersible had windows that could melt at temperatures lower than what was coming out of the vent."

And, in contrast to the desert-like landscape that the scientists expected, it turns out that hydrothermal vents are home to lots of life: snails the size of tennis balls, seven-foot-long (two-meter-long) tubeworms, purple octopi, and all-white crabs and skates.

It turns out that, far from the sun's life-giving light, the same minerals now eyed by the mining industry support lively communities.

Now some researchers fear that deep-sea mining could jeopardize those communities by altering their habitats before the systems have been fully explored and explained.

"We're still just grappling with this reality of commercialization of the deep sea," says Cindy Van Dover, director of Duke University's Marine Lab. "And scrambling to figure out what we need to know."

Van Dover was aboard the first manned biological exploration of the hydrothermal vents in 1982 and was the only woman to pilot the submersible *Alvin*. Despite the strides that have been made in understanding the deep sea, she says, it's still a young science.

When it comes to the impacts of mining on any deep-sea life, "there's a particular type of research that needs to be done," she says. "We haven't yet studied the ecosystem services and functions of the deep sea to understand what we'd lose."

"We don't yet know what we need to know," Van Dover says.

Conservationists also say they want to know more about the vent ecosystems and how they will be mined.

"The whole world is new to the concept of deep-sea mining," says Helen Rosenbaum, coordinator of the Deep Sea Mining Campaign, a small activist group in Australia that campaigns against mining the Solwara 1 site.

"This is going to be the world's first exploitation of these kinds of deep resources. The impacts are not known, and we need to apply precautionary principles," she says. "If we knew what the impacts were going to be, we could engage in a broad-based debate."

Rosenbaum says some communities in Papua New Guinea are raising concerns about the sustainability of local livelihoods in the face of mining and say they aren't receiving the information they need.

The Deep Sea Mining Campaign is especially concerned about the impacts of toxic heavy metals from the mining activities on local communities and fish. The group claims that the Environmental Impact Statement for the Solwara 1 mine hasn't effectively modeled the chemistry of the metals that would be stirred up by the mining process or the ocean currents that could transport them closer to land.

"The Solwara 1 project is scheduled to be a three-year project," Rosenbaum says. "The mining company thinks they'll be out of there before there are problems with heavy metal uptake. We might not see the effects for several years."

A report released in November 2012 by the Deep Sea Mining Campaign ties exploratory pre-mining activities and equipment testing by Nautilus to "cloudy water, dead tuna, and a lack of response of sharks to the age-old tradition of shark calling."

Shark calling is a religious ritual in which Papua New Guineans lure sharks from the deep and catch them by hand.

Another concern for Deep Sea Mining Campaign: Papua New Guinea's government has a 30 percent equity share in the minerals as part of a seabed lease agreement with Nautilus.

The company and government are currently involved in a lawsuit over these finances, but the Deep Sea Mining Campaign says government investment could compromise its regulatory efforts.

## Mining for Dollars

Nautilus' Smith insists that the company has taken a careful and transparent approach. "The biggest challenge the company faces," she says, "is funding."

Fluctuations in commodity pricing, the high cost of working underwater, and financial disagreements with the Papua New Guinean government have been setbacks for Nautilus.

Last November, the company announced that it had suspended construction of its mining equipment in order to preserve its financial position. Smith says that Nautilus is still committed to finding a solution for its work in Papua New Guinea, and that the company could still extract minerals as early as 2014.

Other companies around the world are also exploring the possibility of mining throughout the South Pacific.

The International Seabed Authority, which regulates use of the seafloor in international waters in accordance with the United Nations Convention on the Law of the Sea, has granted 12 exploratory permits to various governments—including India, France, Japan, Russia, China, Korea, and Germany—in roughly the last decade.

And as long as the promise of riches await, more firms and governments will be looking to join the fray.

"It's economics that drive things," says the University of Tasmania's Coffin. "Tech boundaries are being pushed, and science just comes along behind it and tries to understand what the consequences are. Ideally, it should be the other way around."

# Why Arctic Ocean Oil Drilling Is a Risky Choice

By Rick Steiner
*The Ecologist*, October 19, 2011

*It's not a question of "if" a major spill will occur in the Arctic, but "when and where", says conservation biologist and oil industry expert Rick Steiner.*

As we enter the end of the age of oil, it is clear that most of the world's easily accessible oil has already been produced. Oil companies are now moving offshore into the last hydrocarbon frontiers—deepwater and the Arctic Ocean.

The dangers of deepwater drilling came into sharp focus in 2010 with the BP Deepwater Horizon disaster, where 200 million gallons of oil spilled into the Gulf of Mexico over a 3-month period. Another high-risk environment is the Arctic Ocean, which geologists suggest may be the last significant oil and gas frontier left. As decisions are made on oil and gas drilling in the Arctic Ocean, we need to understand and acknowledge the risks.

First, even if nothing goes wrong, there would be unavoidable impacts from each phase of oil development in the Arctic Ocean—seismic exploration, exploratory drilling, production platforms, pipelines, offshore and onshore terminals, and tankers.

Offshore oil development will include airplanes, helicopters, support ships, drill ships, platforms, artificial islands, icebreakers, waste streams from ships and rigs, lights and noise, extensive coastal infrastructure construction (ports, roads, causeways, staging areas), subsea pipelines, geotechnical coring, and noise from underwater seismic surveys. These industrial activities will add significant disturbance in an Arctic ecosystems already suffering terribly from warming.

The acoustic disturbance to marine mammals from offshore oil development is of particular concern, as underwater noise can affect communication, migration, feeding, mating, and other important functions in whales, seals, and walrus. As well, noise can affect bird and fish migration, feeding and reproduction, and can displace populations from essential habitat areas. Some of these impacts can be reduced or mitigated with lease stipulations, but most cannot.

And of course, beyond these unavoidable operational impacts, there is the very real risk of a large oil spill from exploration drilling, production, pipelines, terminals, and tankers. While government and industry ritually understate the risk of oil spills

From *The Ecologist* (19 October 2011). Copyright © 2011 by Ecosystems Ltd. Reprinted with permission. All rights reserved.

and overstate their preparedness, for high-risk environments such as the Arctic Ocean, we should assume that a large marine oil spill will occur.

In fact, for development off Alaska's Arctic coast, U.S. government authorities project the risk of a major spill at about 30–50 percent, and that a worst-case blow-out could release some 1.3 million barrels (58 million gallons) of oil.

So if drilling proceeds in the Arctic Ocean, then everything possible to reduce risk should be required. The risk reduction standard for the Arctic should go well beyond industry's preferred standard of "As Low As Reasonably Practicable" (ALARP), to "As Low As Possible" (ALAP), regardless of cost.

This highest safety standard would include best available and safest technology for all components of an offshore drilling program—blowout preventers with redundant shear rams, well design and integrity verification, proven seabed well capping equipment, independent well control experts on rigs, rigorous cementing and pressure testing procedures, dual well control barriers, immediate relief well capability on stand-by, state-of-the-art seabed pipeline design and monitoring, tanker traffic monitoring, strict seasonal drilling windows allowing sufficient time for response to late-season spills, robust spill response plans, rigorous government permitting and inspection, and Citizens Advisory Councils to provide effective citizen oversight. As well, financial liability for offshore oil spills in the Arctic should be unlimited, thereby motivating companies to incorporate the highest safety standards possible.

## Not "If" but "When" a Spill Will Occur

But regardless how safe we make offshore drilling in the Arctic, there will still be a significant risk of a major oil spill, and policy makers and industry need to be honest about this. People will make mistakes, and equipment will fail. It's not a question of "if" a major spill will occur, but "when and where."

A major spill will travel with currents, in and under sea ice during ice season, and it would be virtually impossible to contain or recover. Even with robust oil spill response capability, in most scenarios far less than 10 percent will be recovered, and a major spill could easily become a transnational event.

A large spill would undoubtedly cause extensive acute mortality in plankton, fish, birds, and marine mammals. As well, there would be significant chronic, sub-lethal injury to organisms—physiological damage, altered feeding behavior and reproduction, genetic injury, etc.—that would reduce the overall viability of populations.

There could be a permanent reduction in certain populations, and for threatened or endangered species, a major spill could tip them into extinction. With low temperatures and slow degradation rates, oil spilled in the Arctic would persist for decades. And a major oil spill in the Arctic Ocean could severely damage subsistence harvest opportunities, and forever change the lives of coastal peoples.

Put simply, oil drilling in the Arctic Ocean cannot be done without risk and serious impact. There will be chronic degradation, and there will be spills. So the policy question is whether we wish to expose the Arctic Ocean and its people to such risk.

## Short-Term Profit Motives

To many, offshore oil drilling in the Arctic Ocean represents the classic fallacy of "suboptimization": maximizing one component of a complex system to the overall detriment of the system as a whole.

For a few decades, there may be billions of dollars in profits earned, and billions of barrels of oil and gas equivalent in energy supplied. But the overall long-term cost to the region and global biosphere as a whole could be exorbitant, far outweighing the short-term benefit. Regardless of how safe we conduct offshore drilling in the Arctic, we would simply be doing in the best possible way something that we shouldn't be doing at all.

And therein lies society's fundamental choice with the Arctic. Do we continue our industrial expansion into one of the last wild and extreme areas of the world, extract and use the billions of tons of fossil carbon energy here, further degrading the environment of the region and world, and further delaying our necessary transition to a sustainable energy economy? Or, do we choose another, kinder and sustainable future for this magnificent place? Our choice here will tell us a lot about who we are, our selfless vs. selfish nature, and what our long-term future will be. Let's hope we choose wisely.

# No More Offshore Drilling: Clean Energy Needs to Be Our Goal

By Jacqueline Savitz
Oceana, March 12, 2013

Any discussion about modern energy policy must be set against a climate change backdrop. Our reliance on fossil fuels has put unprecedented amounts of carbon dioxide into our atmosphere, with global impacts that are increasingly hard to deny. They range from the acidification of our oceans to the increased frequency and severity of storms. Sea level rise is beginning to force residents of small island nations out of their homes, and changes in rainfall and other weather patterns will cause famine and drought in some places. The only way to change course is to make clean energy our goal. That means moving away from fossil fuels, not expanding our focus on them, and reducing offshore drilling, not expanding it.

If the United States were a company it would need a smart business plan complete with goals, timelines, milestones and a strategy for meeting them. Our CEO would analyze the competition and the business environment. To address climate change, we would set a clean energy development goal: to build a clean energy industry that provides half of our needs by a set year, and hopefully all of our needs at a later date. This goal would reduce the risks and costs associated with fossil fuel production as well as the attendant risks of climate change.

The projections show we can do this. There are a variety of clean energy solutions on the horizon, and many of them are already proving to be useful here and abroad. Investors like John Doerr see the tremendous potential in clean energy. Doerr called clean energy "the next great global industry," and argued that green technologies could be the biggest economic opportunity of this century. But, he points out that we may be missing out because of our "competitiveness crisis," where countries like China are lapping us on clean energy. How can that be?

They are ahead of us because the "All of the Above" approach to energy, which has been advocated by some in the fossil fuel industry and adopted by President Obama in his first term, simply doesn't work. It sets the clean energy sector up with a losing proposition: compete against the richest companies in the world, which are heavily subsidized and have accumulated tremendous power in Congress over more than a century, and see how you do. Clean energy companies must compete with wealthy fossil fuel companies for investments, labor, talent, parts, and access to resources, just to name a few critical needs. This drives up the costs and reduces our net on our goal.

From Oceana (12 March 2013). Copyright © 2013 by Oceana. Reprinted with permission. All rights reserved.

We need new energy policies that stop favoring the fossil fuel industry. Clearly, we can't stop all drilling immediately. But we can decide to stop issuing new leases, and not to start drilling in areas that are high risk, or low return, like the Arctic and the Atlantic, respectively. New drilling will not lower the price at the pump. Oil is traded, and its price is set, on the global market. The gas prices fallacy is proffered by the oil and gas industry for its own benefit and we all know it's not true.

What is true? Offshore drilling is dirty and dangerous, the BP oil disaster laid to rest any doubts about that. Congress has failed to pass a single bill to improve offshore drilling safety. And offshore drilling in the Arctic is extremely misdirected as Shell is clearly demonstrating.

Before we expand oil drilling any further, we need to ask ourselves (those of us that are not in the oil and gas business, that is) where do we want to be in 2030 or 2040? Do we want to watch more footage of oil gushing into our oceans, watch the climate crisis unfold for our children and shift our energy dependence from the Middle East to China? Or do we want to cash in on a climate saving investment that prevents those outcomes and achieves our goal? If the answer is the latter, then we should stop expanding offshore drilling and get to work on energy policy that is favorable to clean energy.

# California Finds More Instances of Offshore Fracking

By Alicia Chang and Jason Dearen
Associated Press, October 19, 2013

*State officials discover use of oil production technique is more widespread than estimated.*

The oil production technique known as fracking is more widespread and frequently used in the offshore platforms and man-made islands near some of California's most populous and famous coastal communities than state officials believed.

In waters off Long Beach, Seal Beach and Huntington Beach—some of the region's most popular surfing strands and tourist attractions—oil companies have used fracking at least 203 times at six sites in the past two decades, according to interviews and drilling records obtained by the Associated Press through a public records request.

Just this year in Long Beach Harbor, the nation's second-largest container port, an oil company with exclusive rights to drill there completed five fracks on palm tree-lined, man-made islands. Other companies fracked more than a dozen times from old oil platforms off Huntington Beach and Seal Beach over the past five years.

Though there is no evidence offshore hydraulic fracturing has led to any spills or chemical leaks, the practice occurs with little state or federal oversight of the operations.

The state agency that leases lands and waters to oil companies said officials found new instances of fracking after searching records as part of a review after the AP reported this summer about fracking in federal waters off California, an area from three miles to 200 miles offshore. The state oil permitting agency said it doesn't track fracking.

As the state continues its investigation into the extent of fracking—both in federal waters and closer to shore—and develops ways to increase oversight under a law that takes effect in 2015, environmental groups are calling for a moratorium on the practice.

"How is it that nobody in state government knew anything about this? It's a huge institutional failure," said Kassie Siegel, an attorney with the Center for Biological Diversity. "Offshore fracking is far more common than anyone realized."

Little is known about the effects on the marine environment of fracking, which shoots water, sand and chemicals at high pressure to clear old wells or crack rock

From Associated Press (19 October 2013). Copyright © 2013 by Associated Press DBA Press Association. Reprinted with permission. All rights reserved.

formations to free oil. Yet neither state nor federal environmental regulators have had any role in overseeing the practice as it increased to revitalize old wells.

New oil leases off the state's shores have been prohibited since a 1969 oil platform blowout off Santa Barbara, which fouled miles of coastline and gave rise to the modern environmental movement. With no room for physical expansion, oil companies instead have turned to fracking to keep the oil flowing.

The state launched an investigation into the extent of offshore fracking after the AP report in August. California officials initially said at the time there was no record of fracking in the nearshore waters it oversees. Now, as the State Lands Commission and other agencies review records and find more instances of fracking, officials are confused over who exactly is in charge of ensuring the technique is monitored and performed safely.

"We still need to sort out what authority, if any, we have over fracking operations in state waters; it's very complicated," said Alison Dettmer, a deputy director of the California Coastal Commission.

Nowhere is the fracking more concentrated than in Long Beach, an oil town with a half-million residents and tourist draws such as the *Queen Mary*.

The city's oil arrangement stems from a deal drawn up in 1911, when California granted the tidelands and other water-covered areas to the city as it developed its harbor. When oil was discovered in the 1930s, the money started coming in.

Long Beach transferred $352 million of $581 million in profits to state coffers in fiscal year 2013 from onshore and offshore operations, according to the city's gas and oil department. Most of the oil recovery comes from traditional drilling while fracking accounts for about 10 percent of the work.

The department says fracking is safe. It has a spill contingency plan and monitors pipelines. Well construction designs are approved by state oil regulators. The designs can be used for conventional drilling and fracking. And the oil industry says offshore fracks are much smaller operations than onshore jobs, involving only a fraction of the chemicals and water used on land.

City oil officials see themselves as partners with Occidental Petroleum Corp.—not regulators—though officials participate in the company's internal audits and technical reviews by the state.

Occidental and the city briefly took a fracking timeout after passage of the state's new rules. Long Beach oil operations manager Kevin Tougas said there are plans to frack again later this year. Occidental spokeswoman Susie Geiger said in an email that the company doesn't discuss its operations due to "competitive and proprietary reasons."

No one is tracking the amounts or precise composition of any fracking chemicals that enter the marine environment, though in September the state passed a law that starting in 2015 would require disclosure of agents used during the procedures.

Fracking fluids can be made up of hundreds of chemicals—some known and others not since they are protected as trade secrets. Some of these chemicals are toxic to fish larvae and crustaceans, bottom dwellers most at risk from drilling activities, according to government health disclosure documents.

Myriad state agencies that oversee drilling, water quality and the ocean said they did no monitoring of fracking chemicals during offshore jobs.

Don Drysdale, a spokesman for the California Department of Oil, Gas and Geothermal Resources, said the new regulations will include "extensive protections" for groundwater.

The industry estimates that about half of the fluids used during fracking remain in the environment; environmentalists say it is much higher. Long Beach says it uses a closed system and there's no discharge into the water. Instead, fluids are treated before being re-injected deep under the seafloor.

The Long Beach Water Department, which monitors well water quality annually, said there are no known impacts to residents' water from fracking.

"It's our hometown," said Chris Garner, a fourth-generation resident who heads the gas and oil department. "We have a vested interest in making sure the oil operations have been without harm to the city."

# The Empty Oceans Act: House Offers Draft Bill to Gut Protections for Fisheries and Fishing Economies

By Alexandra Adams
*Switchboard*, January 17, 2014

If destroying livelihoods and depleting fish populations around the country is the goal, then I've got a proposal for you. The draft bill recently proposed by House Natural Resources Chair Representative Doc Hastings is a virtual roadmap to reversing all of the success we've had in rebuilding depleted ocean fisheries around the country and turning back the clock to the era of boom and bust fisheries management.

The Magnuson-Stevens Fishery Conservation and Management Act governs how we conserve and use our nation's fisheries. This bill was amended in 1996 and 2006 with strong bipartisan support to include provisions to end overfishing and rebuild depleted fish populations. The late Senator Ted Stevens of Alaska was a leader of these reforms, working to ensure a legacy of healthy U.S. fisheries and fishing economies.

Senator Stevens' legacy proved strikingly successful. In the early 1990s, many important fish stocks, such as the iconic New England cod, suffered large declines or collapses. Today, while challenges remain, many of these stocks have been brought back. NRDC's "Bringing Back the Fish" report documented how nearly two-thirds of fish stocks put in rebuilding plans since 1996 have either rebuilt to healthy population levels, or have made significant rebuilding progress, resulting in increased gross commercial revenues of $585 million—92% higher (54% when adjusted for inflation) than before the rebuilding plans.

Given these benefits to coastal communities, fishermen, and ecosystems, Representative Hastings' interest in dismantling the law that made it possible is very puzzling. The Hastings draft would take us back to a time before the success of the Magnuson-Stevens Act and to when fish populations—and the fishermen that depended on them—were in dire straits. This proposal adds loopholes, waters down legal standards, encourages costly delays, and reduces transparency and accountability. The draft guts the rebuilding requirements that forced managers to make tough decisions that allowed our stocks to rebound, including by removing requirements for rebuilding timelines. This was doubtlessly done in the name of "flexibility." But the current law already has sufficient flexibility: although there is a general requirement for a 10-year rebuilding time period (scientists have demonstrated that

From *Switchboard* (17 January 2014). Copyright © 2014 by Natural Resources Defense Council. Reprinted with permission. All rights reserved.

most stocks can be rebuilt in this time period), the Magnuson-Stevens Act also provides certain exceptions and time for rebuilding plan development. In fact, with flexibility under the current law, the average time period in rebuilding plans to date has been 19.6 years.

The theme of this draft bill is definitely flexibility: the flexibility to fish until there is nothing left. The proposal lowers the standard for what constitutes a healthy or re-built fish population. It limits the authority of scientists to set science-based annual catch limits, a requirement that Congress added to the law in 2006. The proposal allows even the most depleted fish populations to continue to be subject to overfish-ing for as long as another seven years. It exempts "non-target, incidentally harvested stocks of fish" from annual catch limits and accountability measures, which means much less accountability for the catch of hundreds of stocks that aren't "targeted" by fishermen but are caught anyway.

As if these attacks on modern-era fisheries management weren't enough, the draft bill also goes after open and transparent government. The proposal would make a wide range of information secret and unavailable to the public, including the results of cooperative research funded by taxpayer dollars and data collected by government-funded biologists used to inform how we manage fish populations. The proposal exempts many types of fishery information from public disclosure under the Freedom of Information Act, undermining our nation's fundamental commitment to open government. This bill even denies states and federal agencies (outside the National Marine Fisheries Service) access to any data that would be used to make better decisions about where to locate new ocean industry, such as offshore wind, in order to minimize impacts to the environment and existing uses, like fishing.

Finally, Representative Hastings' proposal attacks vital bedrock environmental laws such as the National Environmental Policy Act (NEPA) and the Endangered Species Act (ESA), as well as the National Marine Sanctuaries Act and the Antiq-uities Act (by which national monuments are created). Compliance with NEPA is eliminated entirely, which will allow fisheries managers to act without adequately analyzing effects on the marine environment, without considering alternatives or ways to minimize impacts, and to further limit stakeholder and public involvement. The Hastings draft bill would undermine the ESA by putting the industry-dominat-ed fishery management councils in charge of recovering endangered marine mam-mals, sea turtles, and other vulnerable marine animals. The councils would also be put in charge of fisheries-related activities in national marine sanctuaries and national monuments.

After years of sacrifice by fishermen to rebuild our fisheries and with the U.S. now the model for fisheries management around the world, Representative Hast-ings has proposed that we turn back the clock. What a mistake that would be.

# Ocean Grabbing:
# Plundering a Common Resource

By Michèle Mesmain
*Slow Fish*, April 26, 2013

Oceans and coasts have always occupied a privileged space in our imagination, cultures, customs, economy and way of life. People have lived along the shore and used marine resources for tens of thousands of years, and are doing so in increasing numbers. Currently more than 60% of the world's population lives in coastal areas, leading to a corresponding increase in pressure on natural resources, through fishing, pollution, tourism, resource extraction and the like.

Many coastal communities around the world are finding themselves caught between increasing pressure from the land and depleting marine and coastal resources. Within this context of scarce resources and growing demand, environmental awareness and speculative capitalist dynamics applied to common goods, a sharper focus is being turned on our marine resources and their subjection to different forms of ocean grabbing. Not only is ocean grabbing affecting food security in developing countries, but the privatization of marine resources, another form of ocean grabbing, often touted as an environmentally friendly option, is in fact impacting negatively on both small-scale fishers, coastal communities and the ecosystem.

## Ocean Grabbing and Food Security

One form of ocean grabbing is linked to food security, as seafood is being massively harvested in the global south by foreign fleets and exported, leaving local fleets without enough resources for the local populations, many of which largely depend on fish as a protein source. In the words of Olivier de Schutter, Special Rapporteur for the United Nations on the Right to Food, " 'Ocean-grabbing'—in the shape of shady access agreements that harm small-scale fishers, unreported catch, incursions into protected waters, and the diversion of resources away from local populations—can be as serious a threat as 'land-grabbing.' " In Africa, this diversion of resources is mainly perpetrated by large vessels from the EU, China and Russia. Even when fishing is legal and documented, most fleets are heavily subsidized and externalize the costs of overfishing and resource degradation, making fishing a highly profitable industry that threatens the right to food of millions.

New European regulations will demand that fleets from member states apply the same rules that apply within the EU, so they will have to fish within the Maximum Sustainable Yield (MSY) limits. This will prove difficult, since in many cases

From *Slow Fish* (26 April 2013). Copyright © 2013 by Slow Food. Reprinted with permission. All rights reserved.

there is not enough data to determine a stock's MSY, but also, that alone is not a solution, as a large fleet could be fishing within MSY limits, and still leave smaller fleets with limited capacity unable to catch their share.

Also, while a few bilateral trade agreements state that part of the financial compensation has to be devoted to coastal infrastructure, which should benefit local fleets, many do not. Or the infrastructure put in place only serves large operations, making it even harder for smaller fleets to access ocean resources. "In Mauritania, we are seeing fish meal factories built by the Chinese springing out of the ground at an alarming rate," says Nedwa Moctar Nech, coordinator of the Slow Food Imraguen Women's Mullet Botargo Presidium. "They will transform tons of smaller and juvenile fishes plundered from the oceans," she says.

## Fisheries Privatization

Though nothing new, this may be the form of ocean grabbing about which the general public is least aware. Dominant economic theories have promoted the privatization of fishing access to maximize profits for more than four decades, following similar patterns to agriculture. Privatization involves redefining access rights or privileges to open, common or state-owned fisheries by increasing the level of private allocation of, and control over, public resources. Recently, this trend has embraced environmental concerns about the ocean's health, with claims that widespread privatization is a solution, leading to some degree of public support. The phenomenon, often called rationalization or catch share management rather than privatization, is coming to dominate many policy discussions and implementations over the world.

This is how it goes: Building on the narrative of the tragedy of the commons, in which if the seas belong to all, they belong to no one, fishers are seen as doomed to act as self-interested, competing actors, forced to race for resources, making it impossible to avoid degradation. This logic sounds natural and commonsense, as does the "rational" solution of privatization. A Total Allowable Catch (TAC) is defined for each fishery and divided among the individuals of the fleet according to "historical" fishing records, usually over the past five years, during which the most informed fishers have been "racing for quota," catching as much as possible and targeting strategic species. Hence, access rights to a common resource become private property rights, called Individual Transferable Quotas (ITQ) or Transferable Fishing Concessions (TFC) among many other names, and are transformed into a tradable commodity.

This twinned economic and environmental narrative for privatization, largely spread by the media and lobbyists, has found it a wide range of powerful proponents, promoting a situation in which, increasingly, fish become the property of a generation of wealthy owners, most of whom did nothing more than fish in the right place at the right time to get a stake.

The latest step in this process has been the creation of the Global Partnership for Oceans, initiated by the World Bank at Rio +20, which seeks to unite states, companies, research institutes, foundations and environmental organizations to protect the oceans, but with no involvement of fishing organizations and clearly promoting a widespread program of privatization. In a compelling "Call on Governments," the World Forum of Fisher Peoples and the World Forum of Fish Harvesters and Fish Workers denounced the global push for the introduction of private property rights as a tool to manage the ocean's fish resources. Instead, the organizations are appealing to governments to look towards a human-rights-based approach.

The privatization narrative overlooks the fact that overfishing is more the result of industrial processes that have modernized and developed fisheries in recent decades, than the human propensity for individual greed. Also, there is no clear link between privatization and conservation. In fact, privatization encourages a logic of speculation, rewarding those who have invested in fisheries financially, rather than with their labor. It leads to property rights migrating from rural to urban owners, and to leasing practices where those who fish are not those who own the rights, among many other phenomenons that favor wealth accumulation through these processes of dispossession. "Up to 80% of the landed value of my fish goes to lease the fishing right," explains Dan Edwards, a fisherman from Vancouver Island, where catch share programs have been in place for more than a decade. "It's the elephant in the room," he continues. "It's easy to get desperate, and also, there is no economic margin left to invest in modernizing your own boat, let alone in local infrastructure. The money goes to someone who doesn't fish any more, and might be living on the other side of the planet."

Today, 35 nations have restructured major fisheries, implementing nearly 400 privatization access programs to manage over 850 species. In most cases, local fleets have shrunk and become concentrated. Fleet numbers in the Bering Sea have decreased by up to 30% from their original numbers, and in New Zealand, more than 80% of fishing rights are held by less than a dozen companies. "Of the 1,400 boats we originally had in Iceland, half were crushed by bulldozers only 44 months after implementing catch share programs," recounts Arthur Bogason, co-president of the World Fisher Forum.

Most communication over these issues has been framed so that resisting privatization does not sound like resisting a dominant economic logic that promotes the commodification of fishing rights to maximize profit, but sounds more like resisting the fight for a better marine environment and management of resources.

The logic of privatization also obscures the many examples of successfully managed commons worldwide, some of which are the subject of Nobel Prize winner Elinor Ostrom's studies on governing the commons, where fishing communities have formed their own bottom-up institutions, to share and manage local resources, even in a context of changing technology and culture. Such is the case of the prud'homies in the French Mediterranean, a local institution with over a millennium of history.

## Privatization's Wider Implications

Ocean grabbing does not stop with the privatization of fisheries, which is just the first step of a systematic attempt to control the whole marine ecosystem and benefit numerous other industries, like tourism, oil and gas extraction, aquaculture, pharmaceutical extraction, marine transportation and bioenergy, among others, and in some cases, military activities.

In Mexico, the Terra Madre San Mateo Del Mar Ikoots food community inhabits a semi-desert area in Oaxaca, making its living mostly from fishing. The community members are opposing a wind energy project set directly on the lagoon, which would destroy their livelihood. In Sri Lanka, the members of NAFSO, a local organization that includes 30,000 fishers and their families, have been fighting against the appropriation of their lagoon for tourism purposes. Women harvesting seaweed in Tamil Nadu were expelled from their ancestral grounds because of the creation of a huge Marine Protected Area, set up without stakeholder involvement. These are just a few examples. Even in Europe alone, looking at the map of oil and gas marine extraction is enough to see what is at stake. Meanwhile, aquaculture is being heavily promoted worldwide. The European Union, for example, plans a growth by 40% over 10 years, with no mention of limiting it to closed-contained or land-locked farms or non-carnivorous fish.

## Towards a Different Model

Olivier de Schutter has called on governments to rethink what fishery models they support, highlighting the fact that small-scale fishers actually catch more fish per gallon of fuel than industrial fleets, and discard fewer fish.

A new model must put the emphasis on local co-management of ocean resources, in ways that involve the small-scale fishers and other local stakeholders who depend on the oceans, helping them participate fully in the value chain while refraining from undertaking large-scale development projects that adversely affect their livelihoods. Fisheries and small-scale fishers must also be made an integral part of national right-to-food strategies.

In the hopeful words of the Special Rapporteur: "It is possible and necessary to turn these resources away from over-exploitation, and towards the benefit of local communities."

## Bibliography

"Fisheries Privatization and the Remaking of Fishery Systems," Courtney Carothers and Catherine Chambers, *Environment and Society: Advances in Research*, Volume 3, Number 1, 2012

*Governing the Commons*, Elinor Ostrom, Cambridge University Press, 1990

"Neoliberalism in the oceans: 'rationalization,' property rights, and the commons question," Becky Mansfield

"Property and fisheries for the twenty-first century: seeking coherence from legal and economic doctrine," Seth Macinko & Daniel W. Bromley.

# Fish 2.0: Investing in Sustainable Oceans and Fisheries

By David Bank
*Impact IQ*, January 30, 2013

The sorry state of the world's oceans is creating investment opportunities in a range of enterprises that are pioneering the sustainable fishing industry of the future.

The Pacific bluefin tuna population is down 96.4 percent. More than 85 percent of fisheries are being fished at or over their capacity. More than 100 species of fish are threatened with extinction.

Such indicators point to the threat to the $390 billion global seafood market, but also to openings for investments in stock recovery strategies, fishing fleets and processing equipment, management systems and certifications and marketing of sustainable brands, one of the fastest-growing segments of the industry.

In the coming months [2013], *Impact IQ*, along with our partner SOCAP, the social capital markets conference, will be exploring opportunities and tracking investments in promising ventures advancing sustainable oceans and fisheries.

Already, a group of investors looking for such opportunities is offering $75,000 in cash prizes and the prospect of investments and loans of between $100,000 and $10 million to support small and medium fishing businesses implementing sustainability strategies.

The Fish 2.0 contest, launched this week, is intended to help fishing businesses pitch their plans to impact investors seeking to support sustainability of local communities and ocean resources with financially sound investments. The deadline for initial submissions is March 31.

"Seafood plays a key role in the food system, and we're looking to invest in business owners who have promising ideas for growing their enterprises and breaking into new markets," says Taryn Goodman, director of impact investing at RSF Social Finance, one of the backers of Fish 2.0. Other sponsors include Charly and Lisa Kleissner's KL Felicitas Foundation in Silicon Valley, A-Spark Good Ventures in the Netherlands, and Social-Impact International, which operates in India and Vienna.

Investing in sustainable fisheries has lagged other food and natural resource investment segments, such as timber and agriculture. The thousands of species caught in particular conditions and geographies means a disaggregated market and fragmented supply chain, in sharp contrast to, say, poultry and beef. There's often a culture clash as well. Business owners find many investors don't understand the industry; investors struggle to find businesses that meet their investment criteria.

From *Impact IQ* (30 January 2013). Copyright © 2013 by *Impact IQ*. Reprinted with permission. All rights reserved.

"With the right capital investments, businesses in the sustainable seafood sector could be growing faster," says Monica Jain of Manta Consulting in Carmel, Calif., the organizer of the Fish 2.0 competition and author of "Financing Fisheries," a primer on investment opportunities in wild fisheries.

The potential opportunity is huge. Of the $390 billion global seafood market, $168 billion is in "wild capture" (as opposed to aquaculture and other segments), and of that, $94 billion is the value when the fish or seafood is pulled out of the ocean. (Another $74 billion is added along the supply chain.) Asia represents by far the biggest share of demand; the U.S. seafood market is about $13.5 billion.

Global seafood demand is expected to double by 2050 to 230 million tons. The seas can't produce that much under current practices.

The World Bank estimates sustainably managed fisheries could increase harvest yields by up to 95 million tons, worth up to $72 billion. That shows up in increased revenues for fishing vessels, ports, processors and others, creating opportunities to make equity investments and loans.

Good ideas are out there. A recent study in *Science* magazine found the right management tools could increase the abundance of fish by up to 40 percent from current trends. For example, a system known as catch shares aligns incentives for fishermen with the replenishment of depleted stocks and is showing impressive results in both population growth and economic growth, according to the Environmental Defense Fund, which implemented catch shares among red snapper fishermen in the Gulf of Mexico.

Based on their own catch in previous years, the fishermen were allocated a share of the total allowable catch. Having a percentage of the total fishery gave each fishing operation a stake in rebuilding fish populations.

"Fishermen and investors tend to live on opposite ends of the spectrum, with each not understanding the other," says TJ Tate, who heads the Gulf of Mexico Reef Fish Shareholders Alliance. Bringing the two camps together, she adds, means "both our businesses and our fisheries prosper."

A handful of funds and institutions have been making fishery investments for years. For example, the California Fisheries Fund is a nonprofit revolving loan fund that invests in fishermen, fishing businesses, ports, communities and others to advance both environmental conservation and economic stability in port communities. Some community development finance institutions, such as Coastal Enterprises Inc. in Maine, make loans to harvesters, processors and other players in the seafood supply chain. CEI claims that its more than 200 loans totaling $14.3 million have created more than 1,500 full-time jobs.

Foundations and other social investors are increasingly interested in the intersection of sustainable fisheries and oceans, food security and economic development. Confluence Philanthropy is sponsoring a series of roundtables for foundations considering mission-related investments in fisheries. The Marine Fisheries program of the David and Lucile Packard Foundation sponsors a range of sustainability initiatives, including Future of Fish, which has identified a host of innovative sustainability strategies.

# 3

# Sea Stewardship and the Cost of Neglect

© Erik De Castro/Reuters/Landov

Fishermen prepare to fish amid floating garbage off the shore of Manila Bay during World Oceans Day in Paranaque, Manila, June 8, 2013. In December 2008, the United Nations officially designated June 8 each year as World Oceans Day.

# Pollution, Climate Change, and Beyond

There are two varieties of threats to the ocean from humans—direct exploitation and indirect damage. In the case of direct exploitation, humans engage in the extraction of certain natural resources from the sea, be they fish, energy, or mineral resources. The consequences of these pursuits are often immediately apparent, whether in the environmental and economic degradation wrought by overfishing and fishery collapse, or in the tragedy of an exploding offshore platform causing millions of gallons of oil to spill into vital marine ecosystems. Though direct exploitation does do severe damage to the ocean and the resources therein, it may be that humanity's more indirect excesses are even more detrimental to the health of the sea. These phenomena do not arise out of human efforts to take something from the ocean. Rather, they most often occur when people wittingly or unwittingly put something into the ocean. Pollution, climate change, ocean acidification, invasive species, and even sonar- and noise-related damage to marine habitats all result from humanity's more unintentional influences on the ocean.

For millennia, humans treated the ocean as both sewer and garbage dump. Lulled by the sea's vast size, most believed that humans could never pollute it enough to do any serious damage. But as populations grew and industrial and chemical wastes were added to the mix, the cost of contamination became more and more clear.

Agricultural waste can have a particularly deadly impact on the world's oceans. For example, nitrogen- and phosphorus-rich fertilizers, used by farmers to sustain their crops eventually end up in the ocean after washing into rivers and streams. There, the fertilizer runoff can catalyze the growth of giant algae blooms. These algae blooms and their subsequent decomposition use up most of the oxygen in a given area of water, creating so-called dead zones that are, more or less, incapable of sustaining any marine life within their perimeter. There are hundreds of dead-zone systems throughout the world's oceans, covering hundreds of thousands of square kilometers.

Climate change is another example of how human action indirectly impacts the ocean. Human consumption of fossil fuels is leading to rising air and ocean temperatures. Greenhouse gases have already trapped enough heat in the atmosphere to increase global temperatures about 1.53 degrees Fahrenheit between 1880 and 2012, according to the Intergovernmental Panel on Climate Change. A 2013 study conducted by researchers from Columbia University, Rutgers University, and the Woods Hole Oceanographic Institute and published in the journal *Science*, found that this, in turn, has caused ocean temperatures to spike by about 0.32 degrees Fahrenheit. This increase in temperature has two major implications, each of which disrupts ocean ecosystems. As the temperature of their habitat rises, marine organisms change their behavior, often migrating elsewhere or succumbing to the elements.

But these trends are not climate change's only influence on the sea. One major side effect of climate change—ocean acidification—is especially damaging to marine ecosystems. Scientists have estimated that about half of the carbon dioxide emissions from humans has been absorbed into the sea. Over the last two hundred years, that amounts to about 550 billion tons of carbon dioxide. This has helped mitigate surface climate change that would have occurred had the carbon dioxide stayed in the atmosphere; the absorbed carbon dioxide is also, however, altering the chemistry of the ocean. As carbon dioxide is taken on by seawater, carbonic acid is created, raising the overall acidity of the water, especially near the surface. In fact, in the twenty-first century the ocean is now 30 percent more acidic than it was prior to the Industrial Revolution. Scientists estimate that it will be 100 percent more acidic by the end of the twenty-first century.

What does this mean for marine life? Among certain fish, this elevated acidity is believed to inhibit reproduction. In addition, a number of marine organisms, from shellfish, to corals, to phytoplankton, rely on calcium carbonate as part of a chemical calcification process through which they form their shells and skeletons. The higher acidity inhibits this shell/skeleton growth and causes seawater to become more corrosive, contributing to the deterioration of these shells and skeletons. Researchers see this as a potentially catastrophic situation. Marine ecosystems rely on the health of shellfish and coral reefs to support the food chain. If the health of these organisms is compromised, the fundamental framework of the food chain could be disrupted, affecting creatures of all kinds, even humans.

Climate change also contributes to another phenomenon endangering marine ecosystems: invasive species. These organisms originated in one location but have found their way to another, frequently via human means. When an alien species is introduced to a new environment, it is often incapable of adapting, and soon dies off. In other instances, however, the organism might acclimate exceptionally well, upsetting the balance of the new ecosystem, and sometimes threatening native species. As water temperatures have risen due to climate change, nonnative species have migrated to habitats that were previously unsuitable for them, often with unanticipated consequences. Helen Davidson for the *Guardian* (5 Aug. 2013) reported on a study that found that rising ocean temperatures are "pushing species towards the poles" at a rate of seven kilometers per year, sending reverberations through countless ecosystems.

But climate change is just one factor contributing to the invasive species problem in marine habitats. One of the principal modes of transporting nonnative species is through maritime shipping. Boats transporting goods across the ocean can be the unwitting carriers of organisms from one end of the earth to another. Such sea life is often transported in a ship's ballast water—seawater that is held in ballast tanks in the hulls of ships. Ballast water helps weigh vessels down, so that they float lower in the water, helping to provide stability. The ballast can be adjusted by pumping water in or out, depending on how much cargo a ship is carrying or what the weather and sea conditions are. This means that seawater—and sea organisms—can be pumped into a ship's ballast tank off the coast of China, for example, and be released in the Caribbean, potentially injecting alien species into fragile marine ecosystems. Indeed, according to estimates, ten billion tons of ballast water is moved across the planet by cargo ships every year.

Among the especially problematic invasive species spread via ballast water over the years is the sea walnut, an organism similar to a jellyfish. Its natural habitat is off the Atlantic coast of North and South America, but in the early 1980s, sea walnuts turned up in the Black Sea and soon after the Caspian Sea, where they devastated local fisheries by eating the zooplankton that fed the local fish. Sea walnuts have since spread to the Mediterranean Sea, the North Sea, and beyond.

But ballast water is not the only means of nonnative species transmission. Invasive species can attach themselves to boats or even trash that then circulates throughout the planet via ocean currents. People also sometimes adopt exotic aquatic pets and then release them into nonnative habitats.

Last, sonar—sound navigation and ranging—and general human-made sound have also proven a threat to marine life. Sonar is a process by which sound is used to detect objects. There are two principal forms. Passive sonar is when listening devices are used to detect other objects. Active sonar is when noise pulses are emitted in order to listen to the echoes and thereby measure the size and distance of other objects. It is the latter form that has been found to have a negative effect on marine life.

Whales and dolphins are especially sensitive to this type of noise. Such species communicate through sound to locate one another, find food, attract mates, and otherwise interact with the world. Human-made noises interfere with that communication. This can lead whales and dolphins away from resources or even lead to injury or death.

Beaked whales have particularly sharp hearing, and sonar has taken a demonstrable toll on them. In a 2009 study published in the journal *Aquatic Mammals*, researchers analyzed all documented incidents of beaked whale mass strandings—when the animals beach themselves on the shore in large groups—between 1874 and 2004. Out of the 136 incidents, all but 10 occurred after 1950, when modern sonar was first deployed, and the technology is believed to have played a role in a significant number of the strandings.

Additional experiments demonstrate that hearing sonar causes whales to change their behavior, often drastically. In a recent experiment in Southern California, researchers outfitted Cuvier beaked whales with devices to measure the noises they were exposed to. Then, the scientists simulated the sound of military sonar. At first, the whales stopped feeding and swimming. In fact, some ceased eating altogether for between six and seven hours. But after first hearing the noise, the whales made efforts to elude it, either swimming away, or performing deep dives.

Other human-made noises may be negatively affecting marine life, too. A mass stranding of one hundred melon-headed whales off the coast of Madagascar in

2008, for example, was blamed on seismic surveys conducted on behalf of Exxon-Mobil in the course of oil explorations.

The lesson from all these phenomena is clear. Some of the most essential human activities, even those seemingly unrelated to the ocean—from energy consumption to farming—all tend to have some form of runoff that eventually finds its way into the sea. Frequently this runoff results in considerable and even fundamental contamination of ocean ecosystems, and harsh and deadly implications for marine life. But inasmuch as such activities are integral to human life, finding ways to mitigate, let alone counteract their damage, will be an ongoing struggle for years to come.

—Paul McCaffrey

## Bibliography

Bruno, John F. "The Impact of Climate Change on the World's Marine Ecosystems." *Huffington Post*. TheHuffingtonPost.com, 18 June 2010. Web. 9 Apr. 2014.

Carrington, Damian. "Whales Flee from Military Sonar Leading to Mass Strandings, Research Shows." *Guardian*. Guardian News and Media, 2 July 2013. Web. 9 Apr. 2014.

Davidson, Helen. "Climate Change Pushing Marine Life towards the Poles, Says Study." *Guardian*. Guardian News and Media, 5 Aug. 2013. Web. 9 Apr. 2014.

de Melker, Saskia. "Coral Reefs and Shellfish Battle Acidifying Oceans." *PBS NewsHour*. MacNeil/Lehrer, 5 Dec. 2012. Web. 9 Apr. 2014.

Diaz, Robert J., and Rutger Rosenberg. "Spreading Dead Zones and Consequences for Marine Ecosystems." *Science* 15 Aug. 2008: 926–29. Print.

"Marine Invasive Species." *National Geographic*. Natl. Geographic Soc., 2014. Web. 9 Apr. 2014.

"Ocean Acidification." *National Geographic*. Natl. Geographic Soc., 2014. Web. 9 Apr. 2014.

"Sea Temperature Rise." *National Geographic*. Natl. Geographic Soc., 2014. Web. 9 Apr. 2014.

Smithsonian Environmental Research Center. "5 Invasive Species You Should Know." *Ocean Portal*. Smithsonian Inst., n.d. Web. 9 Apr. 2014.

Spector, Dina. "Our Planet Is Exploding With Ocean Dead Zones." *Business Insider*. Business Insider, 26 June 2013. Web. 9 Apr. 2014.

# Climate Change to Cause "Massive" Ocean Damage by 2100

*Environment News Service,* October 18, 2013

By the year 2100, about 98 percent of the oceans will be affected by acidification, warming temperatures, low oxygen, or lack of biological productivity, and most areas will be hit by a multitude of these stressors, finds a new study of the impacts of climate change on the world's ocean systems.

These biogeochemical changes triggered by human-generated greenhouse gas emissions will not only affect marine habitats and organisms, but will often also occur in areas that are heavily used by humans, concludes the international team of 28 scientists.

"When you look at the world ocean, there are few places that will be free of changes; most will suffer the simultaneous effects of warming, acidification, and reductions in oxygen and productivity," said lead author Camilo Mora, an assistant professor at the Department of Geography at the University of Hawaii at Manoa.

"The consequences of these co-occurring changes are massive—everything from species survival, to abundance, to range size, to body size, to species richness, to ecosystem functioning are affected by changes in ocean biogeochemistry," said Mora.

Mora and Craig Smith with U-H Manoa's School of Ocean and Earth Science and Technology worked with a 28-person international collaboration of climate modelers, biogeochemists, oceanographers, and social scientists to develop the study, which is published in the scientific journal *PLOS Biology.*

The human ramifications of these changes are likely to be massive and disruptive, the scientists predict. Food chains, fishing, and tourism could all be impacted.

The study shows that some 470 to 870 million of the world's poorest people rely on the ocean for food, jobs, and revenues, and live in countries where ocean goods and services could be compromised by multiple ocean biogeochemical changes.

The researchers used the most recent and robust models of projected climate change developed for the Fifth Assessment Report of the Intergovernmental Panel on Climate Change to inform their analysis.

They quantified the extent of co-occurrence of changes in temperature, pH, oxygen, and primary productivity based on two scenarios—a business-as-usual scenario wherein atmospheric carbon dioxide, $CO_2$, concentrations could reach 900 ppm by 2100, and an alternative scenario under which concentrations only reach 550 ppm by 2100.

From *Environment News Service* (18 October 2013). Copyright © 2013 by *Environment News Service (ENS).* Reprinted with permission. All rights reserved.

The scientists said this second scenario would only result from a concerted, rapid $CO_2$ mitigation effort, beginning today.

They discovered that most of the world's ocean surface will be simultaneously impacted by varying intensities of ocean warming, acidification, oxygen depletion, or shortfalls in productivity.

Only a very small fraction of the oceans, mostly in polar regions, will face the opposing effects of increases in oxygen or productivity, and nowhere will there be cooling or pH increase.

"Even the seemingly positive changes at high latitudes are not necessary beneficial. Invasive species have been immigrating to these areas due to changing ocean conditions and will threaten the local species and the humans who depend on them," said co-author Chih-Lin Wei, a postdoctoral fellow at Ocean Science Centre, Memorial University of Newfoundland, Canada.

Co-author Lisa Levin, a professor at Scripps Institution of Oceanography at the University of California, San Diego, warns, "Because many deep-sea ecosystems are so stable, even small changes in temperature, oxygen, and pH may lower the resilience of deep-sea communities. This is a growing concern as humans extract more resources and create more disturbances in the deep ocean."

The researchers assembled global distribution maps of 32 marine habitats and biodiversity hotspots to assess their potential vulnerability to the changes.

As a final step, they used available data on human dependency on ocean goods and services and social adaptability to estimate the vulnerability of coastal populations to the projected ocean biogeochemical changes.

"Other studies have looked at small-scale impacts, but this is the first time that we've been able to look at the entire world ocean and how co-occurring stressors will differentially impact the earth's diverse habitats and people," said co-author Andrew Thurber, a Scripps alumnus and now a postdoctoral fellow at Oregon State University.

"The impacts of climate change will be felt from the ocean surface to the seafloor. It is truly scary to consider how vast these impacts will be," said co-author Andrew Sweetman, who helped to convene the original team of investigators and now leads the deep-sea ecosystem research group at the International Research Institute of Stavanger, Norway. "This is one legacy that we as humans should not be allowed to ignore."

# Ocean Acidification: The Other Climate Change Issue

By Ashanti Johnson and Natasha D. White
*American Scientist,* January/February 2014

*Carbon dioxide from the atmosphere reacts with coastal water to increase the acidity of the ocean, a trend that threatens many marine ecosystems.*

Within Earth's vast oceans exists a diverse population of beautiful creatures that depend on a delicate balance of chemistry to remain viable. The tiniest animals are often the most important and underestimated species in any environment; they also are among the most vulnerable.

In the frigid waters of the Southern Ocean, off the coast of Antarctica, one such creature is the pteropod, *Limacina helicina antarctica*. These pea-sized marine snails, popularly known as sea butterflies because they appear to be using two "wings" when they swim, serve as a major food source for commercial fishes such as pink salmon. Yet this crucial resource is on the wane, as increasing levels of acid in the ocean threaten to dissolve its aragonite shell and impair its normal development.

More than 200 years ago, people developed a variety of machines to accomplish tasks traditionally completed by hand. These great advances in technology, however, have come at a steep price: the industrial and agricultural activities that drive our global economy have added significantly to the levels of carbon dioxide in the atmosphere. Most carbon dioxide remains in the air, but as much as 25 percent is absorbed by the world's oceans, according to the National Oceanic and Atmospheric Administration (NOAA). Once in the water column, carbon dioxide ($CO_2$) reacts with water ($H_2O$) to yield carbonic acid, which releases hydrogen ions ($H^+$), effectively increasing acidity.

Since the start of the Industrial Revolution, the pH level of the world's oceans has dropped by 0.1 unit, which amounts to a 30-percent increase in acidity. Estimates based on business-as-usual scenarios from the Intergovernmental Panel on Climate Change (IPCC) suggest that if current trends persist, oceanic pH could drop by another 0.5 unit by the end of this century. That is a huge change: a 150-percent increase in acidity. Such an alteration in the marine environment could have devastating results both for ocean organisms and for the people who depend on them.

From *American Scientist* 102.1 (January/February 2014): 60–63. Copyright © 2014 by Sigma Xi Science Research Society.

## Bioavailability of Metals

Metals occur naturally in many coastal and estuarine environments and are essential for the growth and survival of microorganisms that live by means of photosynthesis. A balance of trace metals, such as iron, nickel, copper, zinc, and cadmium, is crucial. If trace-metal concentrations fall too low, photosynthesis falters; if they rise too high, the excess of metal may prove toxic. For any given substance (metal, nutrient, or even a contaminant), the amount that may be readily metabolized is known as *bioavailable*.

The potential of ocean acidification to influence the bioavailability of metals comes down to basic chemistry. Increasing influxes of $CO_2$ cause a decrease in pH, which results in an increase in $H^+$ and thus a decrease in hydroxide and carbonate ions in most surface waters. Normally, both hydroxide and carbonate form strong complexes with divalent and trivalent metals, effectively sequestering those compounds from uptake by photosynthetic organisms; under acidified conditions, however, hydroxide and carbonate remain as free metals that are bioavailable.

Recent environmental models suggest that hydroxide and carbonate ions will decrease consistently—as much as 82 and 77 percent, respectively—by the end of the century. Such a decrease is expected to change the speciation of a number of metal ions. Most organic macromolecules in seawater are negatively charged; therefore, as a result of lowered pH, the surface of the organic macromolecules is less available to form complexes with metals.

A number of studies have predicted that ocean acidification might exacerbate the potential effects of other anthropogenic stressors, thereby raising the bioavailability of environmental contaminants, particularly that of waterborne metals. Acidification also modifies the interactions between marine organisms and metals. Ambient trace-metal concentrations in the open ocean are low; marine organisms have evolved efficient mechanisms to compensate for this, many of which are yet to be characterized. Not surprisingly, small increases in the concentration of normally scarce metals often prove toxic.

Individual metal species have different fates and cause varied impacts, depending on their function in the environment. For example, should ocean acidification increase the available concentration of free ionic copper, productivity in photosynthetic organisms may decrease. The resulting increase in free ionic copper in the environment can cause physiological damage to some aquatic species. Copper affects the activation of olfactory receptor neurons by competing with natural odorants for binding sites; such an effect has been shown to impair the sense of smell in juvenile coho salmon (*Oncorhynchus kisutch*). These fish depend on olfaction to find food, avoid predators, and migrate. According to one study, even low levels of copper produced a physiological stress response, characterized by hyperactivity, elevated blood levels of the stress hormone cortisol, and an increase in the synthesis of metallothionein, a metal-detoxifying protein.

On the other hand, antagonistic (decreased) toxicities have been observed between carbon dioxide and free ionic copper in a small coastal crustacean, *Amphiascoides atopus*. Metal toxicity was likely antagonistic because of the presence of increasing $H^+$ and the competition for binding sites between $CO_2$ and copper for $H^+$.

Alternatively, the observed antagonistic effect could be due to the animal's suppressed metabolism, which would reduce its rate of metal transport. If acidified conditions should cause the concentration of dissolved iron to rise, this may stimulate photosynthesis, giving rise to a negative feedback mechanism. This mechanism has a potential positive effect: Ocean acidification may actually make more iron bioavailable, thanks to both the increased fractionation of dissolved iron and elevated iron ($Fe^{2+}$) concentrations in coastal systems.

## Effects on the Food Web

The effects of ocean acidification fall not just on certain species or particular regions, but throughout the food webs of the globe. According to the NOAA Ocean and Great Lakes Acidification Research Plan, changes in ocean chemistry probably exert several indirect effects: shifting predator-prey interactions, increasing the prevalence of invasive species, modifying the distribution of pathogens, or altering the physical structure of ecosystems. Naturally, some organisms are expected to experience greater effects than others. Among those most likely to take a hit are the calcifying organisms, such as corals, clams, scallops, oysters, and other shellfish. Conversely, some photosynthetic zooxanthellae (the symbionts that live on coral and provide its nutrition) or shallow nearshore seagrasses may be individually stimulated by an increase in carbon dioxide. Their stimulation is expected to change the dynamics of the ecosystem by disrupting nutritional transfer from zooxanthellae to corals and by interfering with the efficient use of carbon by thriving seagrasses, leading to overpopulation.

Initial studies focused on the negative effects of decreased calcium carbonate ($CaCO_3$) saturation and on the inability of calcifying organisms to produce protective shells; more recent studies show that acidification may also take a toll on species growth, behavior, and survival. Noncalcareous species such as fish have shown impaired development and decreased olfactory ability, as well as some evidence for changes in body composition and a decrease in growth rate. Bacterioplankton may also be affected by acidification, exhibiting longer bloom times, increased growth rate, and increases in nitrogen fixation. A secondary impact for humans and wildlife may arise from the extended bloom of certain bacterioplankton, which can secrete substances that are toxic to some humans and wildlife.

When carbonate concentrations decrease in the oceans and bivalves become less able to extract it effectively, they form thinner shells that make them more susceptible to predators. A computer simulation of future ocean conditions showed that three ecologically and commercially important bivalve species—the hard clam (*Mercenaria mercenaria*), the bay scallop (*Argopecten irradians*), and the Eastern oyster (*Crassostrea virginica*)—would suffer delayed metamorphosis and reduced growth in response to lower levels of carbonate. The impaired ability of each species to form a calcified skeleton appeared likely to translate into prolonged predation on the more vulnerable species and a decrease in the survival rate of their larvae.

Within the marine environment, the sea butterfly is an indicator species currently threatened by the pH changes taking place both in deep water and near the ocean surface. Among the first ecosystems to be identified as vulnerable, of course, were the coral reefs. In addition to the vulnerability of the coral species themselves, coralline algae, calcareous benthic foraminifera, and other reef-building species may be affected. One review estimates that by the middle of the century, corals and calcifying macroalgae will calcify 10 to 50 percent less than before the Industrial Revolution. This steep decrease will take a toll not only on the coral's functioning but also on other ecosystem dynamics (such as the interaction between coral and its symbionts) and on the architectural complexity of the reefs the corals construct. In one study, researchers postulate that the loss of architectural complexity will decrease habitat diversity, which in turn will drive down biodiversity. This decrease, together with the loss of coral reef species through bleaching, disease, and overexploitation, threatens the persistence of coral reef and fish communities and of the sustenance fishers who depend on them.

If ocean acidification continues as expected, can evolution offer a key to the health of marine organisms? Not all species can adapt rapidly to changing environments; those that have this capability, however, show that rapid evolution can alter responses to environmental change, ultimately affecting the likelihood that a population will persist. During the Paleocene-Eocene thermal maximum, a brief warming spell that occurred about 55 million years ago, animals that evolved lighter skeletons were able to remain in areas where calcium carbonate is relatively difficult to obtain.

The capacity for organisms to undergo rapid evolution is likely dependent on their existing genetic variation. For example, the purple sea urchin (*Strongylocentrotus purpuratus*) that inhabits the Pacific Coast is known for its ability to adapt quickly to acidified conditions. In its larval development and morphology, the purple sea urchin shows little response to lower acidity; nevertheless, in the genome of this organism, researchers have observed substantial allelic change in a number of functional classes of proteins involving hundreds of loci. For millions of years, the upwelling of waters rich in carbon dioxide from the ocean's depths have exposed these organisms to significant highs and lows of acidity; this is the probable explanation for their chemical tolerance.

## Coastal Regions

The major culprit behind ocean acidification has been atmospheric carbon dioxide, although other factors have also contributed to the problem, especially in coastal regions. Freshwater tributaries, pollutants from surface runoff, and soil erosion can acidify coastal waters at significantly higher rates than carbon dioxide alone. In 2007, researchers at the Woods Hole Oceanographie Institution (WHOI) surveyed the waters of the eastern United States and the Gulf of Mexico to measure levels of $CO_2$ and other forms of oceanic carbon. When they compared these to the water's total alkalinity, the study revealed that the East Coast was considerably more sensitive to acidified conditions than was the Gulf of Mexico.

Regular inputs from the Mississippi River, surface runoff, and other human impacts all affect the pH of the Gulf of Mexico. These factors, coupled with the high ratio of alkalinity to dissolved inorganic carbon, help to explain why the Gulf of

Mexico has so far resisted acidification. As the WHOI researchers traveled north, they noted decreases in the ratio of alkalinity to dissolved inorganic carbon, indicating that those regions, specifically the coastline north of Georgia, would be more vulnerable if carbon dioxide levels were to increase there.

Subsistence fisheries, too, are likely to be harmed. According to a Blue Ribbon Panel Report from the state of Washington, ocean acidification is already demonstrating an impact on oyster shell growth and reproduction. Planning and resource management hold some promise for addressing the threat of acidification, but the unpredictable time scale and the variable nature of the effects remain stubborn challenges.

## Safeguarding Ocean Chemistry

Anthropogenic inputs of carbon dioxide to the atmosphere are likely to continue causing environmental damage for the foreseeable future—and not only in the air we breathe. The oceans play a significant role in sequestering carbon from the atmosphere. Indeed, they work so well as a carbon sink that until recently most scientists believed the carbon storage capacity of the oceans to be nearly limitless, thereby serving as a negative feedback mechanism for atmospheric carbon inputs. These initial hypotheses were wrong. We are now witnessing changes in ocean chemistry that will affect inorganic and organic metal speciation and could even increase the bioavailability of toxic metals. Clearly, we cannot continue to rely on the oceans to buffer the effects of our pollution indefinitely.

The effects of ocean acidification are far from uniform. Coastal regions are likely to be disproportionately affected by compounding carbon input sources such as runoff from agriculture, industry, and urban populations. Moreover, certain marine species are vulnerable to acidification whereas others are relatively resilient. Using current legislation—in particular, the U.S. Clean Water Act and the Clean Air Act—to enforce more stringent emissions standards may offset some of the harm caused by the rising acidity of the oceans. Confronting this threat will require broader public awareness, clear interpretation of data, and reasoned predictions. Ultimately, more sustainable practices, including reducing anthropogenic emissions of carbon dioxide to the atmosphere, must be adopted globally to offset the harm already done and to ensure that marine ecosystems remain viable.

## Bibliography

Bednarsek, N., et al. 2012. "Extensive dissolution of live pteropods in the Southern Ocean." *Nature Geoscience* 5; 881-885.

Feely, R. A., S. C. Doney, and S. R. Cooley 2009. "Ocean Acidification: Present conditions and future changes in a high $CO_2$ world." *Oceanography* 22:36-47.

Millero, F. J., R. Woosley, B. Ditirolio, and J. Waters. 2009. "Effect of ocean acidification on the speciation of metals in seawater." *Oceanography* 22:72-85.

NOAA Ocean Acidification Steering Committee. 2010. NOAA Ocean and Great Lakes Acidification Research Plan. NOAA Special Report. 143 pp.

# Ocean Acidification Decreases Growth and Development in American Lobster (*Homarus americanus*) Larvae

By Elise A. Keppel, Ricardo A. Scrosati, and Simon C. Courtenay
*Journal of Northwest Atlantic Fishery Science*, December 2012

## Abstract

Ocean acidification resulting from the global increase in atmospheric $CO_2$ concentration is emerging as a threat to marine species, including crustaceans. Fisheries involving the American lobster (*Homarus americanus*) are economically important in eastern Canada and the United States. Based on ocean pH levels predicted for 2100, this study examined the effects of reduced seawater pH on the growth (carapace length) and development (time to molt) of American lobster larvae throughout stages I–III until reaching stage IV (postlarvae). Each stage is reached after a corresponding molt. Larvae were reared from stage I in either acidified (pH = 7.7) or control (pH = 8.1) seawater. Organisms in acidified seawater exhibited a significantly shorter carapace length than those in control seawater after every molt. Larvae in acidified seawater also took significantly more time to reach each molt than control larvae. In nature, slowed progress through larval molts could result in greater time in the water column, where larvae are vulnerable to pelagic predators, potentially leading to reduced benthic recruitment. Evidence was also found of reduced survival when reaching the last stage under acidified conditions. Thus, from the perspective of larval ecology, it is possible that future ocean acidification may harm this important marine resource.

## Introduction

The increasing concentration of atmospheric carbon dioxide ($CO_2$) because of anthropogenic sources is driving an increase in ocean $CO_2$ concentration. This is causing a decrease in seawater pH (ocean acidification), potentially putting additional stress on marine organisms already threatened by rising ocean temperatures (Pörtner *et al.*, 2004; 2005; Raven *et al.*, 2005; Widdicombe and Spicer, 2008). Ocean acidification has been acknowledged by the Intergovernmental Panel on Climate Change to have decreased seawater pH by 0.1 units since the industrial revolution

From *Journal of Northwest Atlantic Fishery Science* 44 (December 2012): 61–66. Copyright © 2012 by *Journal of Northwest Atlantic Fishery Science*. Reprinted with permission. All rights reserved.

(Meehl *et al.*, 2007) and is predicted to result in a further decrease of 0.3-0.4 units by the end of this century (Caldeira and Wickett, 2005; Raven *et al.*, 2005).

With the increase in ocean $CO_2$ concentration, there is a concomitant decrease in carbonate saturation state (Feely *et al.*, 2004; Orr *et al.*, 2005). The outcome is lower concentration of carbonate ions available for the biosynthesis of calcium carbonate ($CaCO_3$) for building calcified body structures (*e.g.*, shells), as well as higher rates of dissolution of $CaCO_3$ from existing structures. Additionally, increased energetic costs for building and maintaining $CaCO_3$ structures may pull resources from other important biological processes such as growth and reproduction. Therefore, calcifying organisms including mollusks (Michaelidis *et al.*, 2005; Gazeau *et al.*, 2007), echinoderms (Kurihara and Shirayam, 2004), and reef-building corals (Langdon and Atkinson, 2005; Doney *et al.*, 2009) have been a strong focus of study in ocean acidification research, looking at a variety of effects on growth and reproduction (Doney *et al.*, 2009; Hendriks *et al.*, 2010; Kroeker *et al.*, 2010). One of the dominant messages coming from this research is that there is a great deal of variability in responses to decreasing pH between, and even within, taxonomic groups (Ridgwell *et al.*, 2009; Pistevos *et al.*, 2011).

American lobster (*Homarus americanus*) is a commercially important crustacean on the Atlantic coast of Canada and the United States. This species supports valuable fisheries, with annual landings of $562 million in Canada (Fisheries and Oceans Canada, 2012) and $228 million in the United States (Singer *et al.*, 2012). Thus, anticipating potential effects of ocean acidification on lobster is relevant to predicting the sustainability of this resource. Crustaceans in general have received little attention on how they may respond to acidification, and research to date has reported variable results (Whiteley, 2011). In a recent study, larvae and postlarvae of the European lobster (*Homarus gammarus*) growing in seawater at pH levels predicted for 2100 exhibited less mineralization of the carapace (Arnold *et al.*, 2009). Softer shells could put the lobster at greater risk for predation soon after molting (Factor, 1995) and may also reduce feeding ability through decreased strength of claws, which are more heavily calcified than the carapace to provide crushing strength for consuming prey (Bosselmann *et al.*, 2007). Conversely, American lobster juveniles exhibited no change in calcification rates at pH levels predicted for 2100 (Ries *et al.*, 2009). Other invertebrates, such as brittle stars (Echinodermata), have been shown to increase calcification rates with decreasing pH, but have done so at the cost of reduced energy available for other processes. In *Amphiura filiformis*, this was seen as muscle wastage (Wood *et al.*, 2008) and, in *Ophiura ophiura*, as reduced arm regeneration (Wood *et al.*, 2010). This was not tested for American lobster, but maintenance of shell mineralization may reduce energy available for important processes such as growth and molting. Some life stages may be more sensitive to lower pH than others, and the most susceptible stage is species-specific (Kurihara, 2008). In particular, lobster larvae may be most sensitive to decreases in pH due to the frequent molting required during their development. Research on the effects of ocean acidification on the various life-history stages of American lobster is necessary to understand how they may respond to future conditions. Here, we present the results of an examination of the effects of $CO_2$-induced acidification on American lobster larval growth and development at pH levels predicted for 2100. We hypothesized that larvae would exhibit reduced growth and development with reduced pH.

## Methods

We obtained stage-I larvae from the Pictou Lobster Hatchery and Museum (Pictou, Nova Scotia, Canada), where ovigerous females were supplied by local fishermen. Our experiment was carried out in June 2011, corresponding to the natural occurrence of lobster larvae in the Northumberland Strait, in the southern Gulf of St. Lawrence, Canada. Larvae were transferred from the hatchery to the Marine Ecology Lab at Saint Francis Xavier University (Antigonish, Nova Scotia) within 3 h of hatching, and randomly distributed amongst experimental containers (15 larvae per container, 6 containers per each of two pH treatments, 180 larvae in total) within minutes upon arrival to the lab. We placed 15 larvae per container to be able to have at least one organism to measure in each container at successive sampling dates, as we anticipated that mortality would occur during the experiment. Each container was supplied with 1 L of constantly aerated, filtered seawater from the Northumberland Strait (temperature ~20 °C, salinity ~31 psu). Seawater in each container was partially changed every two to three days. Molted exoskeletons and dead organisms (due to natural mortality or cannibalism) were removed as they occurred. Larvae were fed live brine shrimp (*Artemia* spp., ~5 individuals ml-1) daily.

For the experiment, we considered two levels of seawater pH (control and acidified), which were produced by bubbling either ambient air or $CO_2$-enriched air into each replicate container through diffusing stones during the entire experiment. $CO_2$ concentrations of 400 ppm and 1200 ppm were chosen to represent current conditions and year-2100 conditions (Meehl *et al.*, 2007), respectively. This approach resulted in pH values of 8.1 for the control treatment and 7.7 for the acidified treatment. The $CO_2$-enriched air was produced by mixing ambient air with $CO_2$, controlling flow rates with Sierra Instruments Smart Trak mass flow controllers (Provan Control Associates, Quebec, Canada). $CO_2$ concentration was verified daily using a Qubit S151 $CO_2$ analyzer (Qubit Systems, Ontario, Canada). Measurements of pH were recorded to the nearest 0.01 units with a pHep5 pH Tester (Hanna Instruments, Quebec, Canada) every second day for the duration of the experiment. With this setup, the two desired levels of pH remained stable during the experiment at the precision level needed for the study (0.1 units of pH).

We evaluated the effects of seawater acidification on the growth and development of American lobster larvae throughout stages I-III until reaching stage IV (postlarvae). To assess effects on growth, we measured carapace length once larvae molted to each stage (day one of the experiment for stage I). To test for effects on development, we recorded the number of days to reach each successive molt. After all larvae reached each stage in a container ($n$ = 6 containers per pH treatment), one individual was randomly selected from each container and its carapace length was measured out of the water using a dissecting microscope to the nearest 0.1

mm. Number of days to reach the molt to each stage was also recorded, using one average value per container for data analyses whenever the larvae in that container molted at different days. We identified stages using morphological characteristics previously described for this species (Factor, 1995). After carapace measurements, the measured individuals were permanently removed from the experiment. We measured carapace length for one individual per container for each molt to prevent any handling effects (due to manipulation out of the water) from occurring on the individuals that were to be measured for growth and development at later dates. The experiment was terminated after all larvae molted to stage IV (day 13), as three containers in the acidified treatment then had no organisms left because of mortality between stages III and IV. We tested for acidification effects on growth and development using Student's t-tests done with SYSTAT 13.0 (SYSTAT, 2009), wherever applicable depending on the occurrence of data variation within molts (see Results). The t-test is a statistically robust procedure, especially when sample sizes for both treatments are equal (Mead, 1991); we used the separate-variances procedure (instead of the pooled-variance procedure) to calculate t values to ensure reliable results.

## Results

### Carapace Length

Carapace length was statistically similar in both pH treatments for stage-I larvae at the beginning of the experiment ($t = 0.75$, $p = 0.472$), indicating an adequate random assignment of larvae to both treatments. Carapace length was, however, significantly lower in acidified seawater than in control seawater for each successive life-history stage: stage II ($t = 8.95$, $p < 0.001$), stage III ($t = 4.05$, $p = 0.002$), and stage IV ($t = 2.88$, $p = 0.024$). All analyses were done using data for six individuals per treatment (one random individual per container), except for stage IV (postlarvae), since six individuals reached stage IV in the control treatment (one in each of the six containers) but only three individuals reached stage IV in the acidified treatment (one in each of three containers) because of mortality between stages III and IV.

### Development

Cumulative number of days to molt to successive life-history stages was used to track development rates. Number of days to molt to stages II, III, and IV was always higher in acidified seawater. All stage-I larvae in control seawater molted to stage II at day two, while all stage-I larvae in acidified seawater molted to stage II at day five. The lack of within-treatment variation in both treatments prevented statistical tests from being done, but differences were evident, as molting in acidified conditions took more than twice the control time. All stage-II larvae in control seawater molted to stage III at day five, while stage-II larvae in acidified seawater molted to stage III at an average of 7.3 days, which was a significant difference ($t = 11.07$, $p < 0.001$). Stage-III larvae in control seawater molted to stage IV (postlarvae) at an average of 10 days, while stage-III larvae in acidified seawater molted to stage IV at an average of 12 days, which was a significant difference ($t = 2.42$, $p = 0.046$). As noted above, only three stage-III larvae (one per container) survived and molted to stage IV in acidified seawater, while the last six stage-III larvae in control water (one per container) molted to stage IV.

## Discussion

Negative species responses to ocean acidification have been commonly found in marine invertebrates. Here, it is shown that American lobster larvae exhibit reduced rates of growth and development under the lower levels of seawater pH predicted for 2100, compared with current levels. Similar responses have been observed for other marine invertebrates, such as sea stars, mussels, and corals (Fabry *et al.*, 2008). Crustacean examples include the shrimp Pandalus borealis, which displayed increased development time under acidified conditions (Bechmann *et al.*, 2011), and the spider crab Hyas araneus, which displayed both decreased growth and development rates (Walther et al., 2010), although pH levels were not always exactly the same across studies.

American lobster larvae may respond to decreased pH with reduced growth and development rates as a result of reallocation of energy to other processes. Such a response has been seen in brittlestars, which displayed muscle wastage (*Amphiura filiformis*, Wood *et al.*, 2008) or a reduced ability to regenerate lost limbs (*Ophiura ophiura*, Wood *et al.*, 2010) while maintaining growth of calcified structures in acidified seawater. This suggests that maintenance of calcified structures may occur at the cost of somatic tissue loss or alterations to other biological processes, possibly implying indirect effects on fitness and survival. In lobster larvae, additional energy may be allocated to powering proton pumps for maintenance of internal acid-base balance or mineralization of the calcified exoskeleton (Pörtner *et al.*, 2004), reducing investment in growth and delaying the energy-expensive molting process. Effects of decreased pH on calcification of the exoskeleton in American lobster larvae remain to be tested, although it was recently reported that juveniles exhibit no change in calcification rates at pH levels predicted for 2100 (Ries *et al.*, 2009). While different life-history stages of some species may respond differently to acidification (Kurihara, 2008), our results on lobster larvae fit well with results for juveniles, with reductions in larval growth possibly resulting from maintenance of calcification rates in an acidified environment. Research is required on the effects of ocean acidification on calcification in lobster larvae and on growth in juveniles to test this possibility.

The slower growth and development of American lobster larvae under acidified conditions results in delays to reaching each molt, including the key metamorphosis from stage III (last larval stage) to stage IV (postlarvae), which marks the transition from a pelagic to benthic life. A delay in this transition extends the time spent in the water column, where there is little protection from predation (Factor, 1995), which might lead to an increase in predation-related mortality. This, as well as an increase in mortality unrelated to predation between stages III and IV, as found towards the end of our experiment, might lead to reduced lobster recruitment to the seafloor and subsequent reductions in populations.

Our results differ from those for European lobster (*H. gammarus*) larvae, as their growth rate remained unaffected by acidification between stages I and IV (Arnold *et al.*, 2009). That study also found a decrease in carapace mineral content (magnesium) for stage-III larvae in acidified seawater. These results suggest an emerging pattern of differing responses to ocean acidification within taxonomic groups (Ridgwell *et al.*, 2009; Pistevos *et al.*, 2011). Larvae of *H. gammarus* might maintain growth rates at the cost of reduced carapace mineralization. Similarly, adult velvet swimming crab (*Necora puber*) was also found to decrease exoskeletal mineralization in acidified seawater due to partial dissolution of its shell to compensate for extracellular acidosis (Spicer *et al.*, 2007; Small *et al.*, 2010). Decreased calcification has also been seen in other taxonomic groups in response to acidification (*e.g.*, corals, Kleypas and Yates, 2009, and coccolithophores, Beaufort *et al.*, 2011), although tested conditions were not always identical among studies. Response differences between closely related species emphasize the need for research on a range of organisms from various geographic ranges. In doing so, it will be important to test for the same range of abiotic values to facilitate comparisons.

Overall, our results suggest that American lobster larvae may exhibit reduced performance in response to ocean acidification at pH levels predicted for 2100. It remains to be tested whether reduced growth and development would also occur in juveniles and adults. Effects on fertility and hatching also require investigation. Since some crustaceans (*e.g.*, crabs) decrease thermal tolerance at lower pH (Metzger *et al.*, 2007; Walther *et al.*, 2009), the interactive effects of acidification and rising temperature should be investigated as well. It is also unknown whether lobsters have the potential for adaptation to predicted ocean conditions to some extent. These key questions need investigation in order to best inform industry, policy-makers, and conservation programs on possible future scenarios. From the perspective of larval ecology, our study suggests that future ocean acidification may harm this important marine resource.

## Acknowledgements

We thank Christopher Harley and Jocelyn Nelson for introducing us to acidification experiments, Sean Mitchell, Julius Ellrich, and two anonymous reviewers for providing helpful comments on the manuscript, and Terry MacGrath and the Pictou Lobster Hatchery for donating larvae and offering handling advice. Research was funded by grants awarded to R.A.S. by the Canada Research Chairs program (CRC), the Canada Foundation for Innovation (CFI), and the Natural Sciences and Engineering Research Council (NSERC, Discovery Grant) and by a grant awarded to S.C.C. by Fisheries and Oceans Canada (DFO).

## Bibliography

Arnold, K. E., H. S. Findlay, J. I. Spicer, C. L. Daniels and D. Boothroyd. 2009. "Effect of $CO_2$-related acidification on aspects of the larval development of the European lobster, *Homarus gammarus* (L.)." *Biogeosciences*, 6: 1747–1754. http://dx.doi.org/10.5194/bg-6-1747-2009

Beaufort, L., I. Probert, T. de Garidel-Thoron, E. M. Bendif, D. Ruiz-Pino, N. Metzl, C. Goyet, N. Buchet, P. Coupel, M. Grelaud, B. Rost, R. E. M. Rickaby and C. De Vargas. 2011. "Sensitivity of coccolithophores to carbonate chemistry and ocean acidification." *Nature*, 476: 80–83. http://dx.doi.org/10.1038/nature10295 PMid:21814280

Bechmann, R. K., I. C. Taban, S. Westerlund, B. F. Godal, M. Arnberg, S. Vingen, A. Ingvarsdottir and T. Baussant. 2011. "Effects of ocean acidification on early life stages of shrimp (*Pandalus borealis*) and mussel (*Mytilus edulis*)." *J. Toxicol. Envir. Health*, 7: 424–438. http://dx.doi.org/10.1080/1528739.2011.550460 PMid:21391089

Bosselmann, F., P. Romano, H. Fabritius, D. Raabe and M. Epple. 2007. "The composition of the exoskeleton of two Crustacea: the American lobster *Homarus americanus* and the edible crab *Cancer pagurus*." *Thermochimica Acta*, 463: 65–68. http://dx.doi.org/10.1016/j.tca.2007.07.018

Caldeira, K. and M. E. Wickett. 2005. "Ocean model predictions of chemistry changes from carbon dioxide emissions to the atmosphere and ocean." *J. Geophys. Res.*, 110: C09S04. http://dx.doi.org/10.1029/2004JC002671

Doney, S. C., V. J. Fabry, R. A. Feely and J. A. Kleypas. 2009. "Ocean acidification: the other $CO_2$ problem." *Annu. Rev. Mar. Sci.*, 1: 169–192. http://dx.doi.org/10.1146/annurev.marine.010908.163834

Fabry, V. J., B. A. Seibel, R. A. Feely and J. C. Orr. 2008. "Impacts of ocean acidification on marine fauna and ecosystem processes." *ICES J. Mar. Sci.*, 65: 414–432. http://dx.doi.org/10.1093/icesjms/fsn048

Factor, J. R., 1995. *Biology of the lobster Homarus americanus*. San Diego, CA: Academic Press.

Feely, R. A., C. L. Sabine, K. Lee, W. Berelson, J. Kleypas, V. J. Fabry and F. J. Millero. 2004. "Impact of anthropogenic $CO_2$ on the $CaCO_3$ system in the oceans." *Science*, 305: 362–366.

Fisheries and Oceans Canada, 2012. "Commercial fisheries." Available from http://www.dfo-mpo.gc.ca/stats/commercial-eng.htm.

Gazeau, F., C. Quiblier, J. M. Jansen, J. P. Gattuso, J. J. Middelburg and C. H. R. Heip. 2007. "Impact of elevated $CO_2$ on shellfish calcification." *Geophys. Res. Lett.*, 34: L07603. http://dx.doi.org/10.1029/2006GL028554

Hendriks, I. E., C. M. Duarte and M. Álvarez. 2010. "Vulnerability of marine biodiversity to ocean acidification: a meta-analysis." *Estuar., Coast. Shelf Sci.*, 86: 157–164. http://dx.doi.org/10.1016/j.ecss.2009.11.022

Kleypas, J. A. and K. K. Yates. 2009. "Coral reefs and ocean acidification." *Oceanography*, 22: 108–117. http://dx.doi.org/10.5670/oceanog.2009.101

Kroeker, K. J., R. L. Kordas, R. N. Crim and G. G. Singh. 2010. "Meta-analysis reveals negative yet variable effects of ocean acidification on marine organisms." *Ecol.Lett.*, 13: 1419–1434. http://dx.doi.org/10.1111/j.1461-0248.2010.01518.x PMid:20958904

Kurihara, H. 2008. "Effects of $CO_2$-driven ocean acidification on the early developmental stages of invertebrates." *Mar. Ecol. Prog. Ser.*, 373: 275–284. http://dx.doi.org/10.3354/meps07802

Kurihara, H. and Y. Shirayam. 2004. "Effects of increased atmospheric $CO_2$ on sea urchin early development." *Mar. Ecol. Prog. Ser.*, 274: 161–169. http://dx.doi.org/10.3354/meps274161

Langdon, C. and M. J. Atkinson. 2005. "Effect of elevated $pCO_2$ on photosynthesis and calcification of corals and interactions with seasonal change in temperature/irradiance and nutrient enrichment." *J. Geophys. Res.*, 110: C09S07. http://dx.doi.org/10.1029/2004JC002576

Mead, R. 1991. "The design of experiments. Statistical principles for practical applications." Cambridge: Cambridge University Press.

Meehl, G. A., T. F. Stocker, W. D. Collins, P. Friedlingstein and A. T. Gaye. 2007. "Climate change 2007: the physical science basis. Contribution of working group I to the fourth assessment report of the Intergovernmental Panel on Climate Change." Cambridge: Cambridge University Press.

Metzger, R., F. J. Sartoris, M. Langenbuch and H. O. Pörtner. 2007. "Influence of elevated $CO_2$ concentrations on thermal tolerance of the edible crab *Cancer pagurus*." *J. Thermal Biol.*, 32: 144–151. http://dx.doi.org/10.1016/j.jtherbio.2007.01.010

Michaelidis, B., C. Ouzounis, A. Paleras and H. O. Pörtner. 2005. "Effects of long-term moderate hypercapnia on acid-base balance and growth rate in marine mussels (*Mytilus galloprovincialis*)." *Mar. Ecol. Prog. Ser.*, 93: 109–118. http://dx.doi.org/10.3354/meps293109

Orr, J. C., V. J. Fabry, O. Aumont and L. Bopp. 2005. "Anthropogenic ocean acidification over the twenty-first century and its impact on calcifying organisms." *Nature*, 437: 681–686. http://dx.doi.org/10.1038/nature04095 PMid:16193043

Pistevos, J. C. A., P. Calosi, S. Widdicombe and J. D. D. Bishop. 2011. "Will variation among genetic individuals influence species responses to global climate change?" *Oikos*, 120: 675–689. http://dx.doi.org/10.1111/j.1600-0706.2010.19470.x

Pörtner, H. O., M. Langenbuch and B. Michaelidis. 2005. "Synergistic effects of temperature extremes, hypoxia and increases in $CO_2$ on marine animals: from Earth history to global change." *J. Geophys. Res.*, 110: C09S10. http://dx.doi.org/10.1029/2004JC002561

Pörtner, H. O., M. Langenbuch and A. Reipschläger, 2004. "Biological impact of elevated ocean $CO_2$ concentrations: lessons from animal physiology and earth history." *J. Oceanogr.*, 60: 705–718. http://dx.doi.org/10.1007/s10872-004-5763-0

Raven, J., K. Caldeira, H. Elderfield, O. Hoegh-Guldberg, P. Liss, U. Riebesell, J. Shepherd, C. Turley and A. Watson. 2005. "Ocean acidification due to increasing atmospheric carbon dioxide." Policy document 12/05. The Royal Society, London, 57 p.

Ridgwell, A., D. N. Schmidt, C. Turley, C. Brownlee, M. T. Maldonado, P. Tortell and J. R. Young. 2009. "From laboratory manipulations to Earth system models:

scaling calcification impacts of ocean acidification." *Biogeosciences*, 6: 2611–2623. http://dx.doi. org/10.5194/bg-6-2611-2009

Ries, J. B., A. L. Cohen and D. C. McCorkle. 2009. "Marine calcifiers exhibit mixed responses to $CO_2$-induced ocean acidification." *Geology*, 37: 1131–1134. http://dx.doi.org/10.1130/G30210A.1

Singer, L. T. 2012. "Maine Department of Marine Resources, Coastal Fishery Research Priorities, Lobster (*Homarus americanus*)." Available from http://www.maine.gov/dmr/research/priorities10.

Small, D., P. Calosi, D. White, J. I. Spicer and S. Widdicombe. 2010. "Impact of medium-term exposure to $CO_2$-enriched seawater on the physiological functions of the velvet swimming crab *Necora puber*." *Aq. Biol.*, 10: 11–21.

Spicer, J. I., A. Raffo and S. Widdicombe. 2007. "Influence of $CO_2$-related seawater acidification on extracellular acid–base balance in the velvet swimming crab *Necora puber*." *Mar. Biol.*, 151: 1117–1125. http://dx.doi.org/10.1007/s00227-006-0551-6

SYSTAT. 2009. SYSTAT for Windows, Version 13.0. SYSTAT Software Inc., Richmond, California.

Walther, K., K. Anger and H. O. Pörtner. 2010. "Effects of ocean acidification and warming on the larval development of the spider crab *Hyas araneus* from different latitudes (54° vs. 79° N)." *Mar. Ecol. Prog. Ser.*, 417: 159–170. http://dx.doi.org/10.3354/meps08807

Walther, K., F. J. Sartoris, C. Bock and H. O. Pörtner. 2009. "Impact of anthropogenic ocean acidification on thermal tolerance of the spider crab *Hyas araneus*." *Biogeosciences*, 6: 2207–2215. http://dx.doi.org/10.5194/bg-6-2207-2009

Whiteley, N. M. 2011. "Physiological and ecological responses of crustaceans to ocean acidification." *Mar. Ecol. Prog. Ser.*, 430: 257–271. http://dx.doi.org/10.3354/meps09185

Widdicombe, S. and J. I. Spicer. 2008. "Predicting the impact of ocean acidification on benthic biodiversity: what can animal physiology tell us?" J. *Exp. Mar. Biol. Ecol.*, 366: 187–197. http://dx.doi.org/10.1016/j.jembe.2008.07.024

Wood, H. L., J. I. Spicer, D. M. Lowe and S. Widdicombe. 2010. "Interaction of ocean acidification and temperature: the high cost of survival in the brittlestar *Ophiura ophiura*." *Mar. Biol.*, 157: 2001–2013. http://dx.doi.org/10.1007/s00227-010-1469-6

Wood, H. L., J. I. Spicer and S. Widdicombe. 2008. "Ocean acidification may increase calcification rates, but at a cost." *Proc. Royal Soc. B*, 275: 1767–1773. http://dx.doi.org/10.1098/rspb.2008.0343 PMid:18460426 PMCid:2587798

# US Has Failed to Protect Marine Life, Say Conservationists

By Carey L. Biron
*The Guardian*, July 9, 2013

*WildEarth Guardians files petition saying US government has not put safeguards in place for 81 species.*

Environmentalists on Monday[July 2013] filed a petition with the U.S. government requesting regulatory safeguards for 81 particularly vulnerable marine wildlife species, from corals to sharks.

According to WildEarth Guardians, a conservation watchdog, U.S. officials have failed to protect ocean-dwelling species at anywhere near the rate received by animals that live on land, despite legislative and executive mandates to do so. More importantly, the group suggests, the relevant science does not support such a disparity.

For decades the United States has had federal legislation, known as the Endangered Species Act (ESA), in place to offer protections to those plants and animals officially deemed in danger of extinction. According to figures provided by WildEarth Guardians, the ESA has officially protected 2,097 species since its enactment in 1973.

Yet just 94 of these have lived in the oceans and seas. The petition's list would thus nearly double the marine species receiving federal protection.

"To date the U.S. has largely failed to protect marine species under the ESA," WildEarth Guardians stated Monday. "[This new petition] aims to begin righting this imbalance, which does not reflect the scientific reality of species at risk of extinction. The petition demonstrates that threats to marine species are no less dire or diverse than those jeopardizing terrestrial species."

The group says it wants to use the petition, listing only species that have been deemed endangered or critically endangered by widely recognized international scientific groups, to "jumpstart" the national discussion on this disparity and, more broadly, on the increasingly perilous state of marine wildlife and ecosystems.

"There's been a clear historical imbalance in terms of offering federal protections to marine species, partially because for a long time the science was stronger for terrestrial species—it was just easier to tell when they were in bad shape," Bethany Cotton, wildlife program director for WildEarth Guardians, told IPS.

"But that science has now caught up for many of these [marine] species, and their imperilment is very clear. Yet to a certain extent, the public can still deal with

From *The Guardian* (9 July 2013). Copyright © 2013 by Guardian Newspapers Ltd. Reprinted with permission. All rights reserved.

the ocean as 'out of sight, out of mind', which makes it easier for large, charismatic animals like whales to receive attention but not for smaller or lesser-known species."

She continues: "However, it is the government's responsibility to focus on the science, and it hasn't been doing that on its own."

Cotton cites current "unprecedented threats" to marine ecosystems from ocean acidification, increased pollution levels and over-fishing, particularly in international waters. She also notes that marine species are particularly vulnerable to over-exploitation by international trade.

A spokesperson for the National Marine Fisheries Service, Connie Barclay, told IPS that the department's endangered species team had not yet seen the WildEarth Guardians petition, and so could not comment on its content.

"The purpose of the Endangered Species Act is to conserve threatened and endangered species and their ecosystems. It helps guide conservation efforts and ensures that a species does not go extinct," Barclay said by e-mail, noting: "Our process for listing species under the ESA is transparent and offers opportunities for public comment."

The petition comes in the aftermath of an executive order issued in 2010 by President Barack Obama expressing concern over the deterioration of ocean ecosystems and ordering all U.S. government agencies to "use the best available science and knowledge . . . [to] protect, maintain, and restore the health and biological diversity of ocean . . . ecosystems".

That order built on recommendations by a national task force, which also led to the creation of a new comprehensive national marine policy. Three months ago, President Obama's administration published a final plan for implementation of this new National Ocean Policy.

"The Obama administration has put more focus on creating a comprehensive framework for managing our oceans," Miyoko Sakashita, oceans director for the Center for Biological Diversity, an advocacy group, told IPS.

"That said, one of the pieces that fell short was using powerful existing laws to protect the oceans, and the Endangered Species Act is an example of legislation that was probably underutilized in the National Oceans Plan."

Taking advantage of a provision within the Endangered Species Act that allows for science-based petitions from the public, the WildEarth Guardians request builds upon the assessments of two international wildlife observer groups, the International Union for the Conservation of Nature (IUCN) and the Convention on International Trade in Endangered Species of Wild Fauna and Flora (CITES), a 1973 global agreement.

All 81 species included in the new petition have been deemed endangered or critically endangered by the IUCN and CITES. As such, environmentalists see the new petition as a way to test U.S. regulators' seriousness following President Obama's 2010 order.

"If [the government] won't take action in situations as dire as those faced by these critically imperiled species," Jay Tutchton, WildEarth Guardians' general counsel, said Monday, "it signals the agency doesn't really want to do anything but talk about declining ocean health."

Importantly, the Endangered Species Act allows the U.S. government to offer protections to species not living within the country's territory. Doing so can assist in, for instance, cutting down on U.S. demand for certain wildlife products and making available funding for overseas management activities.

"There is certainly increased awareness of the significance of the threats to marine health and ocean ecosystems, but we've repeatedly seen action at the international level become stymied by politics," Bethany Cotton says.

"Just as the most politically volatile such discussions on terrestrial animals revolve around elephants, because of the money involved in the ivory trade, this is also true of the coral used in jewelry and the sharks killed for the lucrative fin trade. That's why it's particularly important that the United States, which has supported protection efforts on sharks and coral at the international level, to do whatever it can under domestic laws to protect those species."

Once the National Marine Fisheries Service has officially received the WildEarth Guardians petition, officials will have three months to decide which, if any, of the requested species warrant investigation. Thereafter, the agency will have 12 months to decide whether protections are merited and to offer proposals for draft rules.

"Oceans are tricky, as they cross a lot of jurisdictions and encounter lots of problems of the commons," the Center for Biological Diversity's Sakashita says.

"But the United States can play a very important role in this regard, both elevating the importance of protecting a particular animal and establishing itself as a leader in protecting the oceans more generally."

# Scientists Call for Global Action on Coral Reefs

By Alex Peel
*Planet Earth Online*, August 13, 2013

*Urgent cuts in carbon emissions are needed if Caribbean coral reefs are to survive past the end of the century, scientists have warned.*

A new paper, published in the journal *Current Biology*, says Caribbean reef growth is already much slower than it was 30 years ago. Its authors say that without serious action on climate change, the reefs may stop growing and begin to break down within the next 20–30 years.

"The balance between reef growth and reef erosion is changing as we alter the environment," says Dr Emma Kennedy of the University of Exeter, who led the study.

"This means that increasingly, some reefs are breaking down faster than they can replace themselves—essentially they're being worn away."

As corals grow they produce limestone skeletons which build up over time into vast reefs. They provide a natural breakwater and a complex three-dimensional habitat, making an ideal home for a vast array of marine species.

"Healthy reefs are the rainforests of the sea," says Kennedy. "They provide habitat for over a quarter of all marine species, including many colorful fish and corals."

"They also provide a range of vital benefits to humanity, like food, jobs and protection from the sea. Globally, over half a billion people rely on reef services to some extent."

In the Caribbean alone, coral reefs are thought to be worth $3.1–4.6 billion every year. But serious local and global pressures are causing corals around the world to fall into ill health.

Locally, they're suffering from nutrient pollution, overfishing and an influx of reef-smothering sediments from coastal developments.

Pacific reefs have also fallen victim to plagues of coral-eating starfish, whose larvae thrive in nitrogen washed into the sea from farms on land. Australian authorities estimate that 35 percent of the Great Barrier Reef's coral cover has been lost to crown-of-thorns starfish in the past 25 years. They're warning that a new outbreak could be on the way this year.

Carbon emissions pose a variety of dangers to corals. Rising sea levels threaten

From *Planet Earth Online* (13 August 2013). Copyright © 2013 by Natural Environment Research Council. Reprinted with permission. All rights reserved.

to leave them stranded in darker waters, starving them of the light they need to survive.

As the oceans absorb more carbon from the atmosphere, they are also becoming slightly more acidic, and less favorable to corals.

Perhaps most seriously, warming ocean temperatures are causing a breakdown in the vital give-and-take relationship between corals and the algae that live in their tissues. This leads to coral bleaching, where whole coral colonies become lighter in color or completely white, and many go on to die.

Kennedy and her team used their own observations and information from more than 300 academic papers to build computer simulations of Caribbean reef growth and erosion.

Taking over 116 different factors into account, they were able to predict the effect of various conservation measures and climate scenarios on reef health.

They found that local policies and conservation measures, like protecting key species and preventing agricultural run-off, could buy reefs an extra decade or so. But the study suggests that it's going to take global action if Caribbean reefs are to survive beyond the end of the century.

"We're all responsible for looking after our planet to a certain extent, and as individuals we can help out by trying to reduce our carbon footprint in any way we can," says Kennedy.

"But unless governments can work together at an international level, then our research suggests that the future looks grim for reefs."

"Under business-as-usual climate scenarios we found Caribbean reefs eventually all degraded well before the end of the century. At the moment, we're still following this trajectory."

## Bibliography

Kennedy EV, Perry CT, Halloran PR, Preito-Iglesias R, Schonberg CHL, Wisshak M, Form AU, Carricart-Ganivet JP, Fine M, Eakin CM, Mumby PJ, "Avoiding Coral Reef Functional Collapse Requires Local and Global Action," 2013, *Current Biology*, DOI: http://dx.doi.org/10.1016/j.cub.2013.04.020

# Arctic at Risk from Invasive Species

By Christopher Ware
*The Conversation*, November 25, 2013

More shipping is sailing through thawing Arctic waters, but while these northern routes might provide opportunities for tourism, mining and cutting down delivery times, the ships may also carry stowaways on board, introducing invasive species to pristine Arctic waters.

These findings were recently published in the journal *Diversity and Distributions*, from research by myself and colleagues at Tromsø University Museum in Norway, University of Tasmania in Australia, and Aarhus University in Denmark. The study focused on the Svalbard archipelago in the Norwegian high-Arctic—best known for being home to the northernmost post office in the world and some 3,000 polar bears.

Invasive species have traditionally been a problem at lower latitudes; this study considered whether a growing amount of human activity in the Arctic and climate change might bring about a species invasion in the far north.

## Free-Riding Travelers

Wherever humans have travelled over the past centuries they have, deliberately or accidentally, taken creatures and plants with them. Exotic grasses now grow on Antarctica, European crabs live on both North American coasts, and Australia is filled with many millions of non-native rabbits, boar, toads and camels.

By filling and discharging ballast tanks, organisms are sucked in, transported and then deposited in other parts of the world, as are creatures that live on the bottom of the ship's hull. Ships are responsible for most of the world's spread of invasive marine species.

Svalbard has experienced increased shipping over recent decades from tourism, scientific research, and mining. The ports there are far from the scale of those in Rotterdam or Singapore—there are more snow mobiles delivered to Svalbard every year than there are ships visiting—but nevertheless more than 500m tons of ballast water are discharged off Svalbard every year, from some of the 200 visiting vessels.

This means that, together with findings that Arctic oceans are warming faster than others, the region may soon lose the isolation and climatic barriers that have kept new species from invading.

From *The Conversation* (25 November 2013). Copyright © 2013 by The Conversation Trust. Reprinted with permission. All rights reserved.

Our research focused on what connections in shipping visiting Svalbard has made with the rest of the world. We assessed the environmental similarities and differences between port regions the ships had visited before arriving at Svalbard, and the potential for ships to transport known invasive species. We then repeated these steps, but with the environmental conditions predicted to occur under climate change scenarios to get a picture of how the situation could change.

## Species Invasion Warning: Rising

The results showed that the present risk posed by invasive species is relatively low due to the Svalbard's cold, 3°C seas. But a small number of ships posed a high risk due to the known invasive species in the regions they connected to Svalbard.

But under the scenarios where oceans continue to warm, the number of ships bearing invasive species will increase, and the number of species that may be able to survive in Svalbard will increase six-fold. This includes well-known invaders such as the European green crab (*Carcinus maenas*), the Japanese ghost shrimp (*Caprella mutica*), and the club sea-squirt (*Styela clava*).

## Managing the Problem

What the impact of new species on Svalbard might be is unclear, and is the subject of ongoing study. Elsewhere in the world, including in other Arctic waters, invasive species have caused severe problems, from subtle effects to threatening the collapse of fisheries

These findings give environmental managers some time to prepare barriers to potentially damaging new species. Ships in Svalbard are currently required to manage ballast water to reduce the threat of discharging non-indigenous species. Despite this, non-indigenous species are often found in samples of managed ballast water. The limitations of current management practices are acknowledged, but obstacles have prevented implementing anything better—the sooner these are overcome the better for the region.

Our results suggest that species transported on the hull are more of a threat, but removing these hull fouling organisms is more difficult. Recent guidelines developed by the International Maritime Organization go some way towards reducing this threat, but more concrete, global measures are needed.

Shipping in the Arctic is set to increase as routes become more navigable, the tourism industry grows, and resource exploration expands. As some of the most pristine environments on earth, there is the opportunity to heed the lessons of species invasion learned at lower latitudes, before it's too late.

# Our Trash Has Become a New Ocean Ecosystem Called "The Plastisphere"

By Sarah Zhang
*Gizmodo*, January 1, 2014

Sure, we all know pollution destroys ecosystems, but, for better or for worse, pollution can create ecosystems, too. The billions of tiny pieces of plastic that are now floating in our oceans are exactly that: a novel ecosystem that humans have unwittingly made by throwing away too much plastic. Microbes and insects that might have no business thriving in the middle of the ocean suddenly have found a new home amidst all that drifting plastic.

If you took a boat out to the so-called Pacific garbage patch—a swirling region of the ocean where plastic is trapped by wind and ocean currents—you won't find anything resembling a "garbage patch." The water would actually look quite pristine—until you drag a net through it to reveal floating flecks of plastic, mostly glitter-sized or smaller. The amount of plastic in the region has grown 100 fold in the last 40 years, but it still really doesn't look like much. Yet these barely visible pieces of plastic are completely remaking the ocean.

Sea skaters, for example, have found a plastic breeding ground paradise. The water insect skims across the ocean surface eating plankton and laying its eggs on the hard surfaces of flotsam, which is now in abundance as plastics have taken over our world. A 2012 study found that skater eggs increased with microplastic pieces in the ocean. Occasionally, bigger pieces of plastic will show up enveloped in thousands of sea skater eggs, like a one-gallon plastic jug covered with 70,000 of them, 15 layers thick.

The effects of a sea skater explosion will ripple out through the food chain, possibly benefitting some organisms but not others. Is it good? Is it bad? All we can say for sure is that the balance of the ocean ecosystem will likely change. The open ocean suddenly has a lot more hard, durable surfaces for organisms like the sea skater and barnacles—artificial islands of a sort for these tiny, landless creatures.

Microbes, too, have found a new home in all the plastic debris. What's more, microbes can hitch a ride on their floating plastic home, making an otherwise unlikely journey from land to the middle of the sea. A study earlier this year cataloged some of the microbes living in the plastisphere, many of them new to science; especially abundant were *Vibrio*, a group of bacteria including those that cause cholera. But scientists are still working to figure out the role of all these bacteria. "Each one of

From *Gizmodo* (1 January 2014). Copyright © 2014 by Newstex LLC. Reprinted with permission. All rights reserved.

these plastic bits is a circle of life—one microbe's waste is another microbe's dinner," one of the study's authors told the *LA Times*.

The microbes may even be breaking down the plastic, making microscopic pits that the team found in the plastic pieces. To look on the cheery side, perhaps this means we could find microbes to help degrade otherwise long-lasting plastic. But this points toward something else, too: The plastic itself is interacting with the environment.

Plastic pieces are like tiny sponges that soak up toxins such as pesticides from the water and leach them out again when broken down. Animals that eat the microplastics, like gooseneck barnacles, for example, can pass the plastics and the toxins up the food chain. A similar problem is happening in the Great Lakes, which have been contaminated by microbeads from exfoliating soap.

When it comes to individual species, though, there are winners and losers in the new plastisphere, which makes telling a tidy story about ocean plastics hard. Certainly it makes sense to stop pouring plastics into the water, but how far should we go to reverse it? Plastic-capture schemes may do more harm than good, scooping up zooplankton, an important source of food for many creatures, along with plastic. Humans might just have to learn to live with the plastisphere we've inadvertently made.

# Navy Expands Sonar Testing Despite Troubling Signs

By Julie Watson and Alicia Chang
Associated Press, December 15, 2013

The U.S. Navy plans to increase sonar testing over the next five years, even as research it funded reveals worrying signs that the loud underwater noise could disturb whales and dolphins.

Reported mass strandings of certain whale species have increased worldwide since the military started using sonar half a century ago. Scientists think the sounds scare animals into shallow waters where they can become disoriented and wash ashore, but technology capable of close monitoring has emerged only in about the last decade.

Aside from strandings, biologists are concerned marine mammals could suffer prolonged stress from changes in diving, feeding and communication.

Two recent studies off the Southern California coast found certain endangered blue whales and beaked whales stopped feeding and fled from recordings of sounds similar to military sonar.

Beaked whales are highly sensitive to sound and account for the majority of beachings near military exercises. Scientists, however, were surprised by the reaction of blue whales—the world's largest animal—long thought to be immune to the high-pitched sounds. It's unclear how the change in behavior would affect the overall population, estimated at between 5,000 and 12,000 animals.

The studies involved only a small group of tagged whales and noise levels were less intense than what's used by the Navy. Shy species, such as the Cuvier's beaked whale that can dive 3,000 feet below the surface, have taken years to find and monitor.

"This is a warning flag and deserves more research," said Stanford University biologist Jeremy Goldbogen, who led the blue whale study published this summer in the journal *Proceedings of the Royal Society B*.

Both studies were done by a team of independent scientists as part of a Navy-funded, five-year project launched in 2010 to understand how sonar affects marine mammals.

Navy officials say it's vital to national security that sailors receive sonar training in real-life conditions.

From Associated Press (15 December 2013). Copyright © 2013 by Associated Press DBA Press Association. Reprinted with permission. All rights reserved.

Environmentalists have long claimed that sonar harms marine mammals, which use acoustics to mate and forage. They want more protections and accuse the Navy of rushing to obtain five-year permits under the Marine Mammal Protection Act from the National Marine Fisheries Service to increase its sonar testing in U.S. waters without considering the latest science.

"If you deafen a marine mammal for even a short period of time, you are affecting its ability to survive," said Michael Jasny of the Natural Resources Defense Council, whose group has sued to force the Navy to add more protections.

A federal judge in September ruled marine fisheries officials did not consider the best available data when it approved permits last year for operations stretching from Northern California to the Canadian border. The agency has until August to reassess how it will protect ocean life.

The California Coastal Commission also rejected the Navy's five-year plan for exercises that would start in January off Southern California. However, the state agency does not have the power to block the drills and the Navy has ignored the agency's requested protections in the past.

The Navy estimates that its activities could inadvertently kill 186 whales and dolphins off the East Coast and 155 off Hawaii and Southern California, mostly from explosives.

It calculates more than 11,000 serious injuries off the East Coast and 2,000 off Hawaii and Southern California, along with nearly 2 million minor injuries, such as temporary hearing loss, off each coast. It also predicts marine mammals might change their behavior—such as swimming in a different direction—in 27 million instances.

Navy officials said they considered the latest research available, including the two recent studies, but none proves the activities cause significant harm to the marine populations.

Navy spokesman Kenneth Hess emphasized that the studies published this summer involved a small group of animals and some did not react, indicating the sound's distance and other context may play a role. The Navy uses simulators where possible.

"Overall, the activities we propose are very similar to the training and testing we have done in these areas for the past 60 years, and we have not seen major impacts on marine mammals from these activities," Hess said.

Until now, studies have measured animals' response based on recordings similar to military sonar or depended on the tagging of marine mammals during Navy at-sea training in which scientists could not control the distance or intensity. For the first time, researchers coordinating with the Navy are conducting experiments using mid-frequency active sonar transmissions from ships. This past summer, they tagged six whales and dolphins off the Southern California coast. Those results are still being analyzed.

Marine fisheries officials last month granted the Navy its permit for activities in the Atlantic and Gulf of Mexico, on the condition that the military review the latest science yearly. The Navy must cease exercises if mammals are spotted nearby, and establish a response plan to a mass stranding. A decision on the Pacific permit is expected to be announced this month.

Some scientists want the Navy to create safety zones that would guarantee no high-intensity sonar activity near marine sanctuaries and areas with a high concentration of blue, fin and gray whales seasonally.

"There are the ocean equivalent of deserts where sonar exercises could be conducted which would be vastly safer," said Lindy Weilgart, a biologist at Dalhousie University in Canada who doesn't receive any Navy funding.

# How Military Sonar May Be Harming Endangered Blue Whales

By Joseph Bennington-Castro
*io9*, July 3, 2013

Scientists have known for years that mid-frequency sonar can harm deep-diving toothed whales, such as by driving them from feeding grounds. Research now shows that the naval noise even elicits stark behavioral changes in blue whales, which communicate at frequencies far below sonar frequencies, suggesting that the detrimental effects of sonar may be more widespread than previously believed.

Marine mammals—whales, dolphins and porpoises in particular—rely on sound to communicate and navigate through their world. So it should come as no surprise that scientists have become increasingly concerned with the growing amounts of anthropogenic noise in the marine environment from shipping vessels, airguns (used for seismic exploration), military sonar and other sources.

The noise pollution is thought to affect animals in a number of ways, such as by interfering with communication, damaging hearing and disrupting feeding habits. But data on the overall effects of anthropogenic noise, including what type of noise is worst for individual species, is still very much lacking.

"There's so little basic scientific information about how animals respond to anthropogenic noise," says Jeremy Goldbogen, who is a biologist with Cascadia Research Collective, a Washington-based marine biology organization. "The research is very expensive and very difficult to do, especially for whales."

Research has suggested that toothed whales (Odontocetes), which include beaked, sperm and pilot whales, are particularly affected by naval sonar. In addition to driving toothed whales from feeding grounds, mid-frequency active sonar (at 1–10 kHz) has been linked to mass stranding events (beaching) and mortality of cetaceans. Indeed, a study last month in the journal *Nature* reported that there has been zero mass stranding events in the Canary Islands since the Spanish government halted all naval exercises in the area in 2004.

Just how sonar causes whale stranding is a bit of mystery, though some scientists believe the beached animals suffered from the bends (decompression sickness), Goldbogen tells *io9*. Studies have shown that stranded whales often have gas-bubble lesions inside their bodies, which likely arose from major changes in diving behavior and physiology.

Although most stranding events associated with mid-frequency sonar involved toothed whales, several cases also involved baleen whales (Mysticeti), Goldbogen

---

From *io9* (3 July 2013). Copyright © 2013 by Newstex LLC. Reprinted with permission. All rights reserved.

says. But because of the rarity of these cases, environmental reviews often discount the effects of the noise on baleen whales, sometimes also citing that the communication range of the whales are below the frequencies of military sonar exercises. So Goldbogen and his colleagues decided to find out if baleen whales do, in fact, respond in some way to mid-frequency sonar.

The team, which involved scientists from a number of organizations, including the National Oceanic and Atmospheric Administration (NOAA) and the Naval Undersea Warfare Center, began by tagging 17 blue whales off the coast of Southern California. The tags collected a whole slew of information about the whales, such as how fast they were going, how their bodies were oriented in the water and how long their multiple dives lasted.

The researchers then subjected individual whales to mid-frequency sonar or pseudorandom noise (with the same frequency) from at least 656 feet (200 meters) away. To improve safety, the sound started off at very low levels and then slowly ramped up in volume, though even the maximum volume didn't reach decibel levels used by the U.S. Navy. "They have very powerful sonar systems that can be up to 10 times louder than what we exposed [the whales] to," Goldbogen says.

The researchers found that mid-frequency sound can significantly affect whale behavior. The noise caused some whales to stop eating krill for up to an hour; other blue whales increased their swimming speed and swam away from the source of the noise.

"It's important to note that not all of the animals responded—it depended on the individual whale and on context," Goldbogen says, explaining that whales feeding on the surface tended not to care about the noise. "[But] it's significant that we did find that blue whales are able to respond to mid-frequency noise."

Feeding disruption, in particular, could prove especially detrimental to the whales' health. The researchers calculated that prior to the noise, the blue whales were eating some 19 kg (42 pounds) of krill every minute. When the mid-frequency sound caused them to stop foraging for 62 minutes, they effectively lost out on over one metric ton of krill, Goldbogen says.

The amount of uneaten krill is equal to the whales' daily metabolic demands, though the scientists don't know what long-term impacts this loss may have on the cetaceans. At this point, it's also unclear what repeated exposure to these sounds does to the whales, or what harm actual naval sonar (with its higher decibel levels) can cause.

"What's important is that this study highlights what little we know about how marine animals respond to anthropogenic sounds," Goldbogen says. Though noise from military sonar could certainly pose a problem to whales and other animals, there are a lot of other sounds polluting the marine environment. "As people concerned about the environment, I think we need to get more scientific information before we make statements about what we need to do to fix things."

# 4

# Hubris on the High Seas

© Po(PHOT) Dave Husbands/MoD/Crown Copyright/PA Wire

Discovering the 250-meter-deep canyon after leaving the Egyptian port of Safaga, the *HMS Enterprise* used her sophisticated echo sounder to create 3D images, allowing the ocean floor to be seen for the first time.

# Governing the Ocean

The 1982 United Nations Convention on the Law of the Sea (UNCLOS) is a groundbreaking set of international agreements, treaties, and laws that has played a dominant role in governing exploration, exploitation, and preservation of the marine environment into the twenty-first century. Given the ancient importance of fishing territory and oceanic travel routes, as well as the increasing importance of oceanic resources such as earth elements and petroleum, control over the sea has become one of the most crucial determinants of economic growth and development.

The model of oceanic management established by the UNCLOS is the exclusive economic zone (EEZ), a territorial division of the continental shelf determined by allowing each nation to control economic development and exploration within a portion of the sea extending from their coastal borders. The establishment of EEZs was a major advancement in regulating maritime law and it has provided a functional system for mediating territorial disputes. However, EEZ designations have also become controversial as competition for resources intensifies between world powers. In addition, issues like global conservation and the ongoing effort to control piracy in international waters transcend national boundaries and have the potential to develop into contentious debates over oceanic responsibility and management.

## The Law of the Sea

Until 1982, exploration, fishing, shipping, and the harvest of oil and marine minerals fell under an informal set of rules known as the Freedom of the Seas Doctrine, which was established in the seventeenth century and limited each nation's jurisdiction to a strip of water reaching a maximum of twelve nautical miles over the continental shelf, still known as the nation's territorial waters.

By the mid-twentieth century, competition for resources and increasing pollution levels in prominent fishing territories made it clear that new regulations were needed. In 1945, the US government, under President Harry S. Truman, extended US jurisdiction to the entire continental shelf of the United States, partially out of a desire to control oil interests off the nation's coasts. Several other nations followed a similar strategy and, by the 1960s, a host of international disputes had arisen concerning exploration and fishing rights, proposals for the establishment of oceanic nuclear weapons stations, and increasing pollution. In 1967, Arvid Pardo, United Nations ambassador from Malta, gave a speech before the United Nations assembly asking for more stringent international guidelines regarding maritime law, as an effort to combat the increasing rivalry between superpowers for control of the ocean.

The United Nations gradually developed treaties and international agreements to address the issue from a variety of perspectives. An international agreement was reached banning the use of nuclear weapons on the seabed, and a landmark treaty formally established the idea that any oceanic territory not within a specific nation's jurisdiction was to be considered the joint property of humankind. In 1973, the United Nations convened a Conference on the Law of the Sea, which met numerous times over a nine-year period and involved representatives of 160 nations. The complex series of agreements and bargains made among these representatives became the 1982 United Nations Convention on the Law of the Sea, a unique politico-legislative measure that essentially provided a framework for maritime law. The convention addressed oceanic travel and navigation, fishing, mining, oil exploration, and protection of the marine environment, and provided a framework for settling disputes.

Among the components of the UNCLOS was the establishment of exclusive economic zones—a system that provides each coastal nation with control over the portion of the continental shelf extending two hundred nautical miles from its coastline. The EEZs provide crucial access to stocks of seafood and seafloor resources, like oil and minerals. Approximately 87 percent of all known oceanic hydrocarbon reserves fall within EEZs, as do the world's most lucrative and productive fishing grounds. Under the UNCLOS, each nation has complete economic control over the EEZ, but the UNCLOS also states that international travel should not be obstructed within the portion of the EEZ lying beyond a nation's territorial waters. This provision, which has occasionally become controversial, preserves the freedom of navigation (FON) in international waters.

Each country with an EEZ also has a responsibility to protect and preserve the territory within its jurisdiction. For instance, the UNCLOS states that all EEZ nations are expected to take steps to preserve the ecological habitats and fish stocks within their territory, and to control and reduce oceanic pollution. Scientific estimates of overfishing and the depletion of ocean resources since 1994 indicate that the UNCLOS has done little to stem the tide of environmental degradation, and a number of ecological institutions have called on the United Nations to make efforts to establish more stringent international guidelines for environmental management. Ultimately, management of EEZs and oceanic navigation routes are not solely determined by the UNCLOS, but by national laws established within coastal nations. The UNCLOS provides a structure within which each nation must determine its own strategies and laws governing development, protection, and international cooperation.

## Disputes and Challenges

As competition for oceanic resources, especially seafloor oil deposits, has increased, the organization of EEZs has become increasingly disputed. The most recent formulation of the UNCLOS occurred in 1994, with the United States, China, and many other nations contending the dispensation of marine resources under the UNCLOS guidelines. For instance, the United States, while generally agreeing to the terms of the 1994 UNCLOS, refused to ratify the treaty because of the Republican Party's objection to provisions concerning the potential for future seafloor mining and petroleum development. The United States has also been involved in several other territorial and economic disputes related to EEZs, including an ongoing dispute with Canada over fishing and development rights in the Beaufort Sea.

The UNCLOS calls for a unique, compulsory method for solving disputes in which either party involved in the dispute may request international participation in settlement, through either the International Court of Justice, the International Tribunal for the Law of the Sea, or through a special tribunal created in accordance with UN principles. However, these conventions are not always sufficient in addressing international disputes and often take many years to address complex territorial issues.

One major ongoing dispute in the twenty-first century concerns the territorial ownership of the South China Sea, which is one of the world's most productive fishing territories and a crucial shipping and transportation route. The South China Sea also contains potential petroleum deposits with an estimated value of more than a trillion dollars. Ownership of the territory has been the subject of intense disagreement since the 1970s, and it has intensified after China passed domestic laws in 1992 claiming the entire South China Sea as its exclusive territory. China's disputed ownership of the sea directly affects fishing rights in Malaysia, Thailand, and the Philippines, but international powers have become involved due to Chinese interference with ships traveling through the region, thus violating FON provisions within the UNCLOS.

China has also courted international controversy due to the nation's increasing interest in the Indian Ocean. Since the 1980s, China has slowly developed ownership of, or cooperation in, a series of ports, shipping stations, and military observation outposts dotting the coast along crucial oil shipping routes that pass through the EEZs of India and several Southeast Asian countries. China has funded upgrades in ports in Malaysia, Indonesia, Myanmar, Bangladesh, Sri Lanka, and Pakistan, thus extending its influence around the southern coast of India. The United States and several other nations have referred to China's growing presence in the Indian Ocean as a "string of pearls" strategy, using ownership of key ports and military stations to dominate the shipping routes through the region.

Japan, India, the United States, and many of the nations within the Association of Southeast Asian Nations have expressed increased concern regarding China's naval presence in the Indian Ocean. Added tension has arisen from the fact that Chinese military ships have increasingly been spotted conducting maneuvers within the Indian Ocean, a development that India, the Philippines, and other neighboring governments view as potentially threatening. While China's naval buildup has been controversial, the nation's ultimate intentions remain unclear and are the subject of intense debate within the international community. The Chinese government maintains that its interest in the Indian Ocean is purely commercial, and several independent analyses have supported this assertion. However, the Chinese navy's provocative presence has complicated the issue and has the potential to destabilize crucial diplomatic agreements that affect the broader Asian environment.

## Piracy, Conservation, and the Open Ocean

Maritime security and piracy are other critical issues that complicate oceanic management and control. For instance, the twenty-first-century increase in piracy off the Horn of Africa—made famous in the United States through the hijacking of the *Maersk Alabama* cargo ship in 2009—is complicated by the ongoing civil war in Somalia and the consequent inability of the Somali government to police its territorial waters effectively. A report from the World Bank in 2013 indicated that Somali piracy costs an estimated $18 billion in losses annually. The *Maersk Alabama* incident occurred in the same year that a new coalition force, the Combined Task Force 151, was established to control piracy off the eastern coast of Africa. Combined Task Force 151 remained in operation into 2014 and was successful in reducing the frequency of pirate attacks, though piracy remains a major threat to oceanic commerce and navigation.

Laws established to combat and prevent piracy can be controversial in cases where security measures conflict with national laws or the FON through important travel routes. International disputes may also arise when a coastal nation fails to enforce law effectively within its EEZ, thus threatening international shipping and FON regulations. Piracy not only affects economic development, but also has the potential to disrupt other forms of international travel. Cruise lines and oceanic transport corporations have also pushed governments and the UN to adopt stronger measures to protect transport lanes. In some cases, piracy and consequent restrictions in oceanic passage have negatively affected the progress of scientific research and exploration. The effective regulation of the lanes connecting each nation therefore remains one of the most important issues in oceanic management.

Another issue that transcends and intersects with all laws and agreements affecting ocean management is the global issue of oceanic conservation. Any regulation, law, or territorial dispute that prohibits or limits scientific exploration and research could be critical given research that indicates rapid degradation of oceanic wildlife and ecological integrity. While each nation is responsible for establishing its own laws regarding conservation of oceanic resources, the global scale of the destruction of marine environments has increasingly made oceanic conservation a contentious international issue.

The international community must not only regulate territorial divisions and responsibilities, but must also attempt to mediate between nations demanding different measures for the protection of oceanic species and environments. The specific guidelines and laws regarding fishing, mining, and oil exploration within each nation affect not only that nation, but also the human race as a whole, through the export of oceanic products, the future availability of marine resources, and the ongoing pollution and alteration of the ocean.

—Micah Issitt

## Bibliography

Andrews, Katherine. "Governing the Exclusive Economic Zone: The Ocean Commons, Cumulative Impacts and Potential Strategies for Improved Governance." *Fulbright New Zealand*. Fulbright New Zealand, July 2008. Web. 25 Mar. 2014.

"India, Japan Join Hands to Break China's 'String of Pearls'." *Times of India*. Bennett, 30 May 2013. Web. 25 Mar. 2014.

Kimball, Lee A. *International Ocean Governance: Using International Law and Organizations to Manage Marine Resources Sustainably*. Cambridge: IUCN, 2003. Print.

"Oceans & Law of the Sea." *Division for Ocean Affairs and the Laws of the Sea*. United Nations, 22 Aug. 2013. Web. 25 Mar. 2014.

Rahman, Maseeh. "Chinese Plans in Seychelles Revive Indian Fears of Encirclement." *Guardian*. Guardian News and Media, 22 Mar. 2012. Web. 25 Mar. 2014.

Turnipseed, Mary, et al. "The Silver Anniversary of the United States' Exclusive Economic Zone: Twenty-Five Years of Ocean Use and Abuse, and the Possibility of a Blue Water Public Trust Doctrine." *Ecology Law Quarterly* 36 (2009): 1–70. Print.

"US Presses Beijing over South China Sea Dispute." *BBC News*. British Broadcasting Company, 5 Feb. 2014. Web. 25 Mar. 2014.

"What Is the EEZ?" *National Ocean Service*. Natl. Oceanic and Atmospheric Administration, 2013. Web. 25 Mar. 2014.

Yujuico, Emmanuel. "The Real Story Behind the South China Sea Dispute." *Strategic Analysis*. LSE IDEAS, 2010. Web. 25 Mar. 2014.

# China's Indian Ocean Strategy Not a Danger—Yet

By Stanley Weiss
*The Huffington Post,* July 8, 2013

When the Chinese admiral Zheng He set out on the first of seven historic voyages of exploration 608 years ago, the sails of his 317 ships blotted out the horizon. Included in the fleet were several colossal, football field-sized vessels—large enough to fit 65 of Columbus' ships end-to-end—whose holds would eventually bring home mountains of gold, ivory, and porcelain for the glory of the Ming emperor. Sailing to a dizzying array of coastal countries over the next three decades, Zheng's flotilla made its way across the modern-day Middle East, ultimately reaching the Cape of Good Hope some 4,000 miles away.

Such expeditions had never been seen before—and would not be seen again. Internal instability, Mongol threats, and high financial costs conspired to cripple China's Age of Exploration. Zheng died and was buried at sea. His magnificent ships were burned. Records of his voyages were destroyed. For nearly six centuries China turned inward, away from the ocean.

That is, until now. With its release last month of a 350-page "blue book" detailing China's strategy in the Indian Ocean, Beijing has served notice that—while insisting its interests are strictly economic—it is not content to ignore the waters to its west any longer. And India, which relies on the Indian Ocean for most of its trade and has long suspected China of pursuing a so-called "string of pearls" strategy in the region—encircling the subcontinent with a network of commercial and military facilities—is understandably wary.

Despite the blue book's conciliatory tone, it has become clear, as the journalist and geopolitical analyst Robert Kaplan observes in his book *Monsoon,* that as "China expands vertically [and] India horizontally . . . the Indian Ocean is where the rivalry between the United States and China in the Pacific interlocks with the regional rivalry between China and India." To explore Kaplan's view that "together with the contiguous Near East and Central Asia," the Indian Ocean "constitutes the new Great Game in geopolitics," I reached out to a man who has trained three generations of Indian diplomats.

Maharaja Krishna Rasgotra, a former Foreign Secretary under Indira Gandhi in the early 1980s and ambassador to six countries—a courtly Indian version of Henry Kissinger—is a keen student of this "new Great Game." Rasgotra joined India's

From *The Huffington Post* (8 July 2013). Copyright © 2013 by TheHuffingtonPost.com, Inc. Reprinted with permission. All rights reserved.

Foreign Service in 1949, just two years after India's independence, the same year the People's Republic of China was established. He has witnessed the entirety of the two Asian giants' modern relationship, from the heady years of *"Hindi-Chini bhai-bhai"*—a popular Hindi slogan meaning "Indians and Chinese are brothers"— to the brief but bitter Sino-Indian War of 1962; to the simmering border disputes that carry into the present day, including a baffling Chinese incursion into Indian territory in May that reportedly left New Delhi on the verge of crisis with Beijing.

"I look at the Indian Ocean as a projection of India's landmass—all of it vital for India's security, stability and progress," Rasgotra says. Likewise, "the Chinese have an interest in the Indian Ocean. New Delhi is watching the developments. If the Chinese get militarily interested in dominating the Indian Ocean, then India is strong enough to resist that."

Certainly, there have been developments worth watching. No sooner had the ink dried on the blue book, for instance, then China offered Iran $78 million to upgrade its Chabahar Port, which is near the Iranian border with Pakistan and a stone's throw from the Straits of Hormuz—a strategically vital chokepoint through which 20 percent of the world's oil passes. This comes amid China's $200 million investment in the Pakistani port of Gwadar, a $209 million airport in Sri Lanka, and plans to build another port on the coast of Tanzania.

While China's Ministry of National Defense has dismissed the "string of pearls" theory as "totally groundless," India has observed 22 recorded instances of Chinese nuclear submarines encroaching into the Indian Ocean—as recently as February 2013, and as close as 50 miles off Indian soil.

Still, for all China's newfound assertiveness in India's backyard, Rasgotra remains skeptical of Beijing's belligerence. The string of pearls, he tells me, "is part history, part poetry, and part mythology."

"China's strategy is motivated by two major factors," he says. "First, to project power in the Indian Ocean in rivalry not only with India but primarily with the U.S.; and second, to safeguard supplies of much-needed energy and other material sources from the Middle East and Africa." Neither is cause for hysteria, though Rasgotra feels India should do more to modernize its military. Indeed, plans are underway to spend nearly $45 billion to build 103 new warships over the next two decades while strengthening naval cooperation with friendly countries. Echoing Rasgotra, a western diplomat in Sri Lanka says confidently of the island off India's coast, "This isn't going to become India's Cuba."

Rasgotra adds that the Chinese "are beginning to realize that containing India is not a practical proposition," and sees "signs of China becoming less aggressive, even less assertive, in its dealings with India." China has seemed eager to downplay border disputes, preferring to focus on economic engagement. Trade between the two countries topped $66 billion last year, a figure China and India hope will reach $100 billion by 2015. To promote tourism, India is also considering a proposal to ease visa restrictions for Chinese citizens.

Chinese Premier Li Keqiang visited New Delhi in May, on his first trip abroad since assuming office. After several days of meetings, and signing agreements on issues ranging from urban development to religious pilgrimages, Prime Minister Li declared that "our two countries fully possess the will, wisdom and ability to together nurture a new bright spot in Asian cooperation."

Until China begins establishing military bases in Sri Lanka, Myanmar or the Maldives, Rasgotra will sleep easy. "There is a desire with China to get along, and I know there is such a desire in India," he says. "Commerce will help soften political attitudes."

As these two rising giants navigate the rocky geopolitical shoals, both countries would do well to remember the stone stele Zheng erected in Sri Lanka in 1410, not far from where a Chinese-financed shipping center now stands. Written in Chinese, Persian and Tamil, the inscription "invoked the blessings of the Hindu deities for a peaceful world built on trade." Here's hoping that out of the irritants of today's maritime maneuvering, true pearls may yet grow.

# The Road to War Is Paved with Chinese Intentions

By James Dunnigan
*StrategyPage*, January 11, 2014

China continues to aggressively confront American ships and aircraft that come close to Chinese ships in international waters. The latest incident was on December 5, when a Chinese destroyer cut in front of an American cruiser (the USS *Cowpens*) which was observing the new Chinese aircraft carrier. The Chinese ship risked a collision as it moved to within a hundred meters of the U.S. cruiser. This sort of aggressiveness has not been experienced by American warships since the Cold War when Russian warships would risk collision in what American sailors came to call "Chicken of the Sea."

The Chinese are also harassing American intelligence operations off the Chinese coast. For over a decade now the Chinese have been aggressively interfering with American intelligence gathering aircraft and ships. U.S. Navy survey ships operating in international waters often find themselves approached, especially at night, by Chinese fishing boats that deliberately get in the way. In some cases the harassment includes Chinese warships and naval patrol aircraft as well.

All this is reminiscent of Cold War incidents, usually involving Russian ships harassing American ships by moving very close, or even on a collision course. This was all for the purpose of interfering with U.S. intelligence operations, especially those off the Russian coast. Earlier in the Cold War Russian warplanes would fire on American intelligence gathering aircraft, shooting some of them down. This sort of thing declined when the U.S. quietly informed the Russians that American warships and combat aircraft would aggressively return fire. By the end of the 1960s, this aggressive activity diminished to the point where it was considered a minor nuisance and even that was eliminated by a 1972 treaty. The same pattern is playing out with the Chinese but for the last few years the Chinese have continued to protest this intelligence gathering activity so close (up to 22 kilometers from Chinese territory, an area that is considered "territorial waters").

The most troublesome intelligence gathering for the Chinese was the oceanic survey vessels. These USNS ships, with mainly civilian crews, use sonar and other sensors to study the ocean floor, and collect information on anything else going on down there (including submarines in the area). The Chinese have been very upset that the U.S. was doing this so close to their new submarine base on Hainan Island.

From *StrategyPage* (11 January 2014). Copyright © 2014 by *StrategyWorld.com*. Reprinted with permission. All rights reserved.

The U.S. has five of these USNS survey ships, and they are all spending a lot of time in the western Pacific. These ships often operate with the obvious cover of carrier aircraft or American warships, in case the Chinese forget the warnings. But this has not completely stopped the aggressive Chinese provocations.

All of this is taking place when U.S. ships and aircraft are in international waters. International law (the 1994 Law of the Sea treaty) recognizes the waters 22 kilometers from land as under the jurisdiction of the nation controlling the nearest land. That means ships cannot enter these "territorial waters" without permission. Moreover, the waters 360 kilometers from land are considered the Exclusive Economic Zone (EEZ), of the nation controlling the nearest land. The EEZ owner can control who fishes there, and extracts natural resources (mostly oil and gas) from the ocean floor. But the EEZ owner cannot prohibit free passage, or the laying of pipelines and communications cables. China has claims that USNS ships are conducting illegal espionage. But the 1994 treaty says nothing about such matters. China is simply doing what China has been doing for centuries, trying to impose its will on neighbors, or anyone venturing into what China considers areas under its control.

In July 2012 China tried a new strategy by declaring that most of the 3.5 million square kilometers South China Sea had become Sansha, the latest Chinese city. The area China claims is as part of Sansha comprises over two million square kilometers of largely open ocean and a few hundred tiny islands and reefs, many of which are only above water during low tide. Sansha is administered from one of the Paracel islands (Woody Island). The U.S. government responded by asking that China obey international law regarding territorial waters and the EEZ. In response to the American reminder, the Chinese called the U.S. a troublemaker. China has not backed down, but did not become aggressive again until November 23rd when China claimed control over large areas of international air space via an expanded ADIZ (air defense identification zone). China wants all military and commercial aircraft in these new ADIZs to ask permission from China before entering. Local nations responded by sending in military aircraft without telling China, but warning their commercial aircraft operators to cooperate because it is considered impractical to provide military air cover for all the commercial traffic. China sees this as a victory, despite the obvious intention of other nations to continue sending military aircraft through the ADIZ unannounced and despite whatever threats China makes. In response to that China has begun running combat air patrols through the ADIZ and apparently intends to try to intimidate some of the smaller countries defying the ADIZ.

All this is not some sudden Chinese effort to extend its control over large ocean areas. For over three decades China has been carrying out a long-term strategy that involves first leaving buoys (for navigation purposes, to assist Chinese fishermen) in the disputed water, followed by temporary shelters (again, for the Chinese fishermen) on islets or reefs that are above water but otherwise uninhabited. If none of the other claimants to this piece of ocean remove the buoys or shelters, China builds a more permanent structure "to aid passing Chinese fishermen". This shelter will be staffed by military personnel who will, of course, have radio, radar, and a few weapons. If no one attacks this mini-base China will expand it and warn anyone in the area that the base is Chinese territory and any attempts to remove it will be seen as an act of war. The Vietnamese tried to get physical against these Chinese bases in 1974 and 1988 and were defeated both times in brief but brutal air and sea battles. The Chinese will fight, especially if they are certain of victory. All of this could end badly, with a major war no one wants. That's how it happens.

# ASEAN Must Show Solidarity

By Alejandro Del Rosario
*Manila Standard Today,* January 22, 2014

There is safety in numbers in fighting the sea serpent that whipped up a storm in once calm and placid waters. Members of the Association of Southeast Asian Nations must show solidarity in dealing with Beijing's alternating bully tactics and appeasement approach in the South China Sea territorial dispute.

Manila read it right when it called and rejected Beijing's call for dialogue as "a ploy for a long-term scheme" to claim the entire resource-rich South China Sea.

Given China's earlier outlandish demand that fishermen of neighboring countries secure a permit from its Hainan administrative office to fish in waters outside of China's boundaries, Beijing's call for dialogue with claimant countries fly in its duplicitous face.

The Philippines has made known it would defy China and would not have its fishermen seek a permit from the Chinese. China also declared an Air Defense Identification Zone over the East China Sea to advance its claim of the Senkaku Island against Japan. Although restrained by a pacifist constitution that renounces war after its defeat in World War II, Japan is no pushover and won't be easily dislodged from Senkaku which the Chinese call Diaoyu.

US B-52 bombers flew through China's ADIZ to test how China would react. Like a bully faced with an equal force, the Chinese kept quiet. To save face, the Chinese turned to bullying its smaller and weaker neighbors again by imposing a new rule on fishing in international waters.

In the case of the Philippines, it's really fishing in its own waters, the West Philippine Sea, which is within the 200-mile exclusive economic zone under the UN Convention on the Law of the Sea.

Wu Shicun, an eminent Chinese scholar and head of the government-run Center for South China Sea Studies, wrote in a column in Beijing's English language daily *Global Times* that China has yet to establish a legal basis for demarcating the 9-dash line to claim almost the entire South China Sea also claimed in parts by Vietnam, the Philippines, Malaysia, Taiwan and Brunei.

Wu's legal opinion and the UNCLOS mandate on a 200-mile exclusive economic zone for countries with coastal lines form the core of Manila's case against Beijing at the UN international arbitration court.

China's pushing of boundaries to gain territories has alarmed the Americans.

While the US wants to avoid a clash with a rising China, it's being painted into

From *Manila Standard Today* (22 January 2014). Copyright © 2014 by *Manila Standard*. Reprinted with permission. All rights reserved.

a corner where Washington cannot be perceived by Japan, the Philippines, Taiwan and South Korea as treaty allies merely on paper. As a Pacific power, the US has to show some teeth to back up its much-ballyhooed re-balancing and pivot to Asia.

The other geo-political consideration holding back the US from taking sides is that Washington does not want a situation wherein China might return to Russia's embrace.

But can the US really afford to confront China? With $1.3 trillion in debt owed China, the US could catch a cold if China so much as sneezes. And there are some symptoms that China's economy is not that healthy despite recent GDP numbers, according to financial global guru George Soros. The Hungarian-American money man sees some troubling signs in the horizon for China.

Over-lending to the US and other cash-strapped African countries, China has also been overspending for military hardware to push its aggressive agenda in the region.

# US Navy's Indian Ocean Folly?

By James Holmes and Toshi Yoshihara
*The Diplomat,* January 4, 2011

*Maritime strategy seems increasingly focused on the Indian Ocean and Persian Gulf. It risks leaving the Navy vulnerable in the Pacific.*

Generally speaking, elected leaders and their advisers craft policy goals and, in conjunction with senior military leaders, provide strategic direction for the armed forces. As military theorist Carl von Clausewitz put it, policy shouldn't be a "tyrant," but it still "permeates" all but the more routine administrative elements of military affairs.

But what happens if political leaders fail to assert control of strategy?

Over the past decade, successive US presidential administrations have focused their energies on matters other than maritime strategy, something that often appeared remote from more immediate concerns like counterterrorism and conflicts in Iraq and Afghanistan. Enjoying the strategic holiday that began when the Soviet Navy vacated the seas leaving the US Navy unchallenged in the world's oceans and seas, it seemed that US forces just didn't need to fight anymore for command of important waters.

As a result, strategic nautical documents are typically couched in generalities and platitudes. On the Indian Ocean, for example, the 2008 National Defense Strategy, a Bush-era treatise, said: "We look to India to assume greater responsibility as a stakeholder in the international system, commensurate with its growing economic, military, and soft power." Yet concrete details of what this actually entails are scant. The 2010 National Security Strategy is equally vague.

Documents like these instead portray abstractions like "proliferation," "piracy," and "anti-access"—not living, breathing antagonists with their own capabilities, resolve, and capacity to innovate—as the principal challenges.

The 2010 Quadrennial Defense Review, for example, prophesizes that the US military will be "increasingly challenged in securing and maintaining access to the global commons and must also be prepared for operations in unfamiliar conditions and environments." It also promises to furnish "solid direction on developing capabilities that counter the proliferation of anti-access and area-denial threats, which present an increased challenge to our maritime, air, space, and cyber forces." Yet by refusing to name prospective adversaries or speculate about how such adversaries might attempt to counteract US strategy, Washington has effectively withheld actionable strategic guidance from the armed forces.

From *The Diplomat* (4 January 2011). Copyright © 2011 by *Diplomat*. Reprinted with permission. All rights reserved.

In the resulting policy vacuum, those responsible for executing national policy—the US Navy, Marine Corps, and Coast Guard—have taken to devising strategy largely free of close supervision from their political overseers. This effectively inverts the Clausewitzian principle of policy and strategy. In the triservice 2007 US Maritime Strategy *A Cooperative Strategy for 21st Century Seapower*, the uniformed service chiefs announce that the sea services will shift their center of gravity from the Atlantic and Pacific—the theaters where World War II and the Cold War unfolded—to the Pacific and Indian oceans.

The Maritime Strategy reaffirms that the US Navy will remain the two-ocean navy it has been since Congress approved the Two-Ocean Navy Act in 1940, in anticipation of a two-front war against Germany and Japan. But the second ocean is no longer the Atlantic—it's the Indian Ocean and the adjacent Persian Gulf.

No political authority seems to have ordained such a redeployment. But if policy defaults, can-do strategists might end up taking charge. The framers of the strategy vow to stage preponderant combat forces in the Western Pacific, the Indian Ocean and the Gulf for the foreseeable future, making the US Navy a squarely Asian navy. Whether the Obama administration is intellectually prepared to undertake a shift of such consequence—or even agrees that such a shift is warranted—is unclear. And parsing the language of the Maritime Strategy, it's also unclear whether the sea services are genuinely prepared to shed longstanding commitments to focus their energies on South and East Asia. US efforts at strategy-making obscure as much as they clarify.

In 1943, as war raged across the Pacific, columnist Walter Lippmann published *US Foreign Policy: Shield of the Republic*. This petite yet hard-hitting volume excoriated US presidents for assuming commitments of colossal scope in the Pacific following the Spanish-American War—notably annexing the Philippine Islands—without generating sufficient naval strength to defend them. (Theodore Roosevelt was an honorable exception to this rule.) They attempted to use a fleet designed to dominate the Caribbean Sea and the Gulf of Mexico to uphold commitments straddling half the globe. For Lippmann, this amounted to "monstrous imprudence." Letting a chasm open between policy and strategy, he maintained, sapped US policy in the Pacific of popular support while encouraging Japanese aggression and hastening the onset of war.

## Does the Strategy Really Set Priorities?

Is the United States, beset by apathy and economic malaise, again drifting toward an imprudent strategy—this time amid the vastness of the Indian Ocean? The evidence suggests so, although this time the intellectual drift is far from irreversible. At first glance, the Maritime Strategy appears to set clear geographic priorities, concentrating fleet operations in the Western Pacific, the Persian Gulf, and the Indian Ocean—in a word, in maritime Asia. The key passage:

> "Credible combat power will be continuously postured in the Western Pacific and the Arabian Gulf/Indian Ocean to protect our vital interests, assure our friends and

allies of our continuing commitment to regional security, and deter and dissuade potential adversaries and peer competitors."

But having issued a clear mandate to reposition forces to maritime Asia, the document instantly attaches a disclaimer, noting that "This combat power can be selectively and rapidly repositioned to meet contingencies that may arise elsewhere." Should some adversary attempt to disrupt or deny traffic through the maritime commons, moreover, the service chiefs reserve the right "to impose local sea control wherever necessary, ideally in concert with friends and allies, but by ourselves if we must."

The commons—the waters outside the jurisdiction of any coastal state—spans the globe. To fulfill the Maritime Strategy's directives, then, the Navy, Marines, and Coast Guard must act as a global force, able to defeat enemies wherever they may be found. To describe this as ambitious is something of an understatement.

Nor does the strategy supply clear guidance on the missions this regional-yet-global force must perform. The document lays great weight on constabulary functions. And, true to their vision of a *cooperative* strategy, the service chiefs enjoin the maritime services to fashion multinational alliances, coalitions, and partnerships to police the seas for pirates and traffickers in illicit goods, render assistance following natural disasters and humanitarian catastrophes, and above all to assure free navigation through the world's sea lanes for the merchantmen that carry raw materials and finished goods—the lifeblood of a globalized economy. The strategy portrays constabulary duty as a global, not a regional, function that will be discharged by "globally distributed, mission-tailored maritime forces" in concert with foreign navies and coast guards.

All this means that the Maritime Strategy announces with great fanfare that the United States will exercise predominant sea power in East and South Asia, only to declare that the Navy, Marine Corps, and Coast Guard must also remain capable of winning battles and policing the seas across the globe. This seemingly straightforward document induces vertigo in the close reader!

## Where to Concentrate the Fleet?

But assume Washington exercises intellectual discipline, keeping its priorities in order rather than diffusing its efforts. The sea services must still revisit a perennial debate, namely, where to station the fleet to best effect. When wrestling with complex matters, it's always helpful to consult the greats of strategic theory. Clausewitz cautions against dispersing forces and effort too widely. In the effort to do everything, everywhere, the United States risks stretching its military so thin that it proves incapable of doing much of anything anywhere. The Prussian thinker also urges commanders to shun secondary theaters or operations unless the likely gains appear "exceptionally rewarding," and unless such a diversion won't risk too much in the main theater or line of operations. In modern parlance, they should keep their eyes on the ball.

Such a focused attitude is worth cultivating. After all, even a global fleet has finite resources, and some theaters must therefore be delegated to regional powers or triaged altogether. Sea-power theorist Alfred Thayer Mahan weighs in with two related insights. Mahan supposedly counseled commanders, "never divide the fleet!" This quotation is apocryphal, but he did highlight the perils of breaking the fleet down into standing contingents weaker than likely opponents. This would subject each lesser fleet to catastrophic defeat and the US Navy to piecemeal defeat. (It should be borne in mind, of course, the context in which he was writing was the pre-Panama Canal world, where the US Navy couldn't swiftly combine Atlantic and Pacific forces; warships had to circumnavigate South America).

Far better, maintained Mahan and kindred thinkers like Theodore Roosevelt, to keep the full battle fleet on one coast and accept the risk of attack on the other coast than to leave one half-strength fleet in the Atlantic and another in the Pacific. Both fleets would be inferior to potential adversaries. In his 1897 book *The Interest of America in Sea Power, Present and Future*, accordingly, Mahan pronounces it "a broad formula" that any US fleet "must be great enough to take the sea, and to fight, with reasonable chances of success, the largest force likely to be brought against it . . ."

Later, in his 1911 work *Naval Strategy*, Mahan devised three criteria for appraising the strategic value of possible naval bases, namely "position, strength, and resources." Position referred straightforwardly enough to a site's geographic position. The best strategic positions adjoined one or more important sea lines of communication. Strength was a site's natural defenses, along with the ease with which civil engineers could augment these defenses to ward off attack. Resources meant a naval station's ability to sustain itself through foodstuffs, fuel, and other supplies, either from the surrounding country or through efficient transport infrastructure such as railways.

So how would this apply now? Take a look at the map of Asia through this Mahanian lens. The principal hubs for forward-deployed US sea power in Asia are in the Persian Gulf to the west and scattered among bases in Japan and Guam to the east. The Gulf island of Bahrain is home to a command center, while US forces routinely call at Dubai for logistical support. Forces are, as can be seen, concentrated at the opposite extremes of the vast Asian landmass. Geographic distance slows efforts to concentrate the fleet for action in either theatre. And along the way, forces bound eastward or westward depend on free passage through such narrow seas as the Strait of Hormuz, the Strait of Malacca, and the Lombok and Sunda straits. The prospect of seeing these chokepoints contested or closed altogether ought to give US naval planners pause.

But the most problematic challenges are in East Asia. In the coming years, it's entirely possible that the Japan-based Seventh Fleet may find itself inferior to the concentrated power of China's People's Liberation Army Navy, augmented by Beijing's increasingly lethal force of ballistic missiles, antiship cruise missiles, and land-based combat aircraft. If so, support from forces based in the Indian Ocean or the United States will be at a premium.

But the US Fifth Fleet is headquartered in Bahrain, in the faraway Persian Gulf theatre. Depending on events, a sizable proportion of US combat power is often within the Gulf, in effect a bay or inlet separated from the broad Indian Ocean by the chokepoint at Hormuz. To sortie for action in South Asian waters or to join the

Seventh Fleet in the Western Pacific, Fifth Fleet units must exit the Gulf through the Strait of Hormuz, passing under the shadow of Iranian antiship weaponry.

Should Tehran see fit to make mischief, Iranian forces could impede ships transiting the strait in a variety of ways. The Iranian Navy could mine this narrow sea or dispatch stealthy diesel submarines to conduct torpedo or missile attacks. Shore-based antiship missiles could strike at warships navigating the narrow channel, where they have little room to maneuver to avoid attack. In short, it's far from clear that the Persian Gulf, one of the primary regional hubs for US maritime strategy, measures up well by Mahanian principles. The Seventh Fleet could pay the price in East Asia of poor fleet dispositions in the Gulf and Indian Ocean.

It's worth asking the same hard questions about forces based in Japan, which are well within the range arc of shore-based Chinese ballistic missiles. It's clear in Japan's case that alternative basing arrangements are worth exploring.

At first glance, Singapore appears ideal for US strategic purposes, lying as it does at the interface between the South China Sea and the Indian Ocean. But the harbor is too shallow to permit big-deck aircraft carriers to berth pierside. In addition, the city-state also lies within easy striking reach of Chinese ballistic missiles, meaning that a fleet stationed there would be exposed to pre-emptive attack in port.

And it's probably useful to add a fourth criterion to Mahan's list—will a prospective host nation grant basing rights? This isn't a foregone conclusion even with close allies. Despite its alliance with the United States, Singapore cherishes its independence. Indeed, government officials have welcomed foreign warships—including aircraft carriers—of all nations to call at their seaport. This means Singapore would likely be loath to antagonize Beijing by playing host to a US Navy battle fleet over the long term. However useful for providing transient logistical support, Singapore clearly represents an unpromising candidate for a standing US naval hub.

By contrast, Australia boasts numerous advantages, occupying as it does a central position between the Indian Ocean and Western Pacific theatres, meaning forces based there could shift easily between the two oceans. For instance, Allied submarines operated from Fremantle, Western Australia, during World War II. Nor would they be forced to venture through a chokepoint to reach the high seas—a welcome contrast to the Persian Gulf hub, where all or part of the fleet could wither on the vine in wartime.

Hardened facilities along the Australian coast would also prove defensible and could be readily resupplied overland. Such seaports would likely meet the Mahanian standards of position, strength, and resources, while the Australian government—Washington's most dependable ally in Asia, alongside Tokyo—would likely prove agreeable to such an arrangement. It's certainly worth exploring.

All this means that US maritime strategy may be hurtling back to the future. As in the days of Mahan, Roosevelt, and Lippmann, the naval establishment may be placing the fleet at risk by partitioning it between two remote theatres, impeding fleet detachments' capacity for mutual support. Letting go of past commitments while refocusing tightly on the twin theatres designated in the Maritime Strategy may be the only way to achieve US strategic aims in a swiftly changing Asia.

# Military Activities in the Exclusive Economic Zones of Foreign Coastal States

By Moritaka Hayashi
*The International Journal of Marine and Coastal Law,*
December 2012

## Abstract

One disturbing element in an overall stable order built on the Law of the Sea Convention is the disagreement between some States over the use of the exclusive economic zone (EEZ) of a coastal State by another State for military purposes. While it appears to be generally accepted that military activities in the EEZ of another State are part of "the freedoms . . . of navigation and overflight and other internationally lawful uses of the sea related to these freedoms . . ." under Article 58(1), some States, notably China, hold an opposing view. The disagreement has led to several incidents involving forceful disturbance of activities of United States military vessels and aircraft in and above the EEZ of China. There is an urgent need for the States concerned and the international community to find a common understanding on the issue or some kind of practical arrangement for avoiding further serious incidents.

## Introduction

In recent years, there have been repeated incidents and disputes over military and intelligence-gathering activities conducted by military vessels or aircraft of another State in and above the exclusive economic zone (EEZ) of coastal States. In the last decade, several incidents occurred, particularly in Asian seas. Notable examples include: the protest by China against the survey/monitoring activities of the USNS *Bowditch* in the Yellow Sea in 2001 and 2002, the Indian naval headquarters' concern over the similar activities of *Bowditch* in India's EEZ in 2002 and 2003, the clash of the US Navy's EP-3 reconnaissance aircraft and a Chinese fighter jet over the EEZ off Hainan Island in 2001, the harassments by a Chinese Fisheries Bureau's patrol boat and surveillance aircraft against the US ocean surveillance ship *Victorious* in the Yellow Sea in 2009, and the harassments and threats by the Chinese navy and other vessels against the USNS *Impeccable* in China's EEZ off Hainan Island in the same year. Some of these incidents were so serious as to entail the death of a Chinese pilot and the emergency landing of the US aircraft in China.

From *The International Journal of Marine and Coastal Law* 27.4 (December 2012): 795–803. Copyright © 2012 by *The International Journal of Marine and Coastal Law*. Reprinted with permission. All rights reserved.

Behind these incidents are fundamental differences of views and positions of governments on the interpretation of international legal rules applicable to military activities, including intelligence gathering, in and above the EEZ of other States. The positions are divided most sharply between the United States and China. Some other States, including Bangladesh, Brazil, Cape Verde, India, Malaysia, Pakistan and Uruguay, have also expressed their views, which are opposed to those of the United States.[1] However, these countries have generally not asserted their positions in the form of forceful operation nor have their officials and scholars accused the other State of activities in such strong terms as those of China.

In the early years of the last decade, few materials were publicly available, at least in English, which legally defended the Chinese position against certain military activities of the United States. In recent years, however, considerable efforts have been made by Chinese authors to clarify or justify the actions taken by their government. Unfortunately, the views of such authors, as well as the government's statements, appear to only widen the division with the United States, often inviting strong rebuttal from the side of the United States.

The positions of China and the United States are divided particularly with regard to: (1) the meaning of marine scientific research (MSR) and survey activities, (2) the right to conduct intelligence-gathering activities in the EEZ, (3) the right to conduct military exercises in the EEZ, (4) the concept of the principle of peaceful uses of the ocean, and (5) certain aspects of the protection of the marine environment in the EEZ.

## Marine Scientific Research and "Survey" Activities

The Law of the Sea (LOS) Convention[2] lays down in Part XIII detailed rules on the conduct of MSR, which require other States interested in conducting MSR in the EEZ of a coastal State to obtain the latter's consent. In addition, in other parts the convention contains several provisions, such as Articles 19(2), 21(1) and 40, referring to "survey activities" or "hydrographic surveys".

The convention, however, contains no definition of MSR or "survey". From the very fact that the convention refers to "survey" separately from "research", and Part XIII regulates "research" activities only, the United States interprets MSR narrowly. The United States clearly distinguishes MSR from various other marine data collection activities such as hydrographic surveys, military surveys and surveillance, environmental monitoring, collection of meteorological data and other routine ocean observations, as well as activities related to submerged wrecks or objects of an archaeological and historical nature.[3] In the US view, the term *hydrographic survey* generally refers to the "obtaining of information for the making of navigational charts and safety of navigation,"[4] and involves collection of information about water depth, the configuration and nature of the natural bottom, the directions and force of currents, the heights and times of tides and water stages, and hazards to navigation. The data are collected for the purpose of producing nautical charts and similar products to support the safety of navigation. Hydrographic surveys are thus not the same as MSR, in that they include the collection and analysis of different types of data and have at their core a fundamentally different purpose.[5]

According to the United States, *surveys* and *surveillance* are part of *military marine data collection*, which refers to marine data collected for military purposes, and can involve oceanographic, marine geological and geophysical, chemical, biological, or acoustic data.[6] The United States' legal position on such surveys and surveillance in the EEZ of a foreign coastal State is that they are conducted as part of the freedom of navigation and "other internationally lawful uses of the sea" under Article 58 (1), and are therefore not subject to coastal State regulation.[7]

The position of China on MSR and other data collection activities in the EEZ, as explained by Chinese authors, is fundamentally different from that of the United States. It has been pointed out that if the methods of data collection and the motives or intended use of data constitute the primary distinction among MSR, hydrographic surveys and military surveys, it presents difficult questions, such as: how such motives are to be determined and who determines that; what constitutes a "scientific" or a "military" purpose and who determines that; and when does the gathering of information to make navigational charts and ensure safety of navigation become a military survey and not a hydrographic survey.[8] Chinese scholars generally consider that, if the US view is accepted, any kind of MSR operations can be conducted under the name of hydrographic or military surveys in the EEZs without any limitation by the coastal States concerned, and that it would potentially give rise to the collapse of the convention's regime on MSR.[9]

Zhang Haiwen, Deputy Director-General of the China Institute for Marine Affairs, argues that there is almost no difference between scientific instruments and equipment on board survey or surveillance vessels and those on common MSR vessels, and there is hardly any difference between marine data collected by the former and those collected by the latter.[10] He contends that, with the application of modern ocean technology and equipment, it is now difficult to distinguish between marine data collection and MSR on the basis of the types and potential uses of collectable data. Therefore, marine data collecting activities could be categorized as MSR, which is subject to the coastal State's jurisdiction under Parts V and XIII of the convention.[11]

China has incorporated the basic provisions of Part XIII on MSR in its 1998 Law on the EEZ and the Continental Shelf, with further detailed regulations in the 1996 Regulations on the Management of the Foreign-Related MSR.[12] With regard to surveying activities, however, "partially in response to the frequent appearance of US military ships conducting surveying activities in Chinese jurisdictional waters",[13] China amended its Surveying and Mapping Law of the People's Republic of China (PRC) in 2002. The amended law provides that all surveying and mapping activities conducted in the domain of China *and "other sea areas under the jurisdiction" of the PRC* shall comply with this law, and defines "surveying and mapping" broadly as referring to:

> surveying, collection and presentation of the shape, size, spatial location and properties of the natural geographic factors or the man-made facilities on the surface, as well as the activities for processing and providing of the obtained data, information and achievements. (Art. 2.)

It further provides that foreign organizations and individuals who conduct surveying and mapping in the domain of the PRC *and other sea areas under the jurisdiction* of the PRC must obtain the approval of the competent administrative department under the State Council and competent department of the armed forces (Art. 7).[14]

## Intelligence-Gathering Activities

With regard to intelligence-gathering activities, all major maritime powers traditionally have long been conducting such activities routinely as part of the exercise of freedom of the high seas without facing problems insofar as they were done on and above the high seas without violating the territorial sea of another State or its air space. The U.S. Navy holds the view that such activities are definitely part of high seas freedoms.[15] It has been also pointed out on behalf of the United States that intelligence collection is addressed in only one Article (Article 19), which relates to innocent passage, and a similar restrictive provision does not appear in Part V of the convention regarding the EEZ, and therefore such activity is permitted without coastal State consent under Article 58(1) of the convention.[16]

On the other hand, according to the Chinese scholars' views, as summarized by Judge Gao Zhiguo, intelligence-gathering activities in and above the EEZ by foreign vessels and aircraft run counter to the "peaceful purposes" or "peaceful use" principle of the convention, and constitute "military and battle field preparation in nature, and thus . . . a threat of force against the coastal State."[17] The United States, however, interprets the said principle differently, as discussed below.

## Military Exercises

With respect to military exercises or maneuvers, which have traditionally been recognized as part of the freedom of the high seas, no specific provision is included in the LOS Convention. Several coastal States, however, declared in signing or ratifying the convention that such activities, particularly those involving the use of weapons or explosives, would not be allowed in their EEZs without their consent. These States include Bangladesh, Brazil, Cape Verde, India, Malaysia, Pakistan and Uruguay.[18] Against these States, several States, including Germany, Italy, the Netherlands, and the United Kingdom, filed declarations with opposing views.[19] The United States has also taken the firm position that "military activities, such as . . . launching and landing of aircraft, . . . exercises, operations . . . [in the EEZ] are recognized historic high seas uses that are preserved by Article 58."[20]

The legal position of China on the issue of military maneuvers or exercises in the EEZ of another State does not appear to have been clearly stated in general terms. However, certain policy statements were reportedly made by government officials on the occasion of exercises conducted by the U.S. and Korean Navies, particularly those involving the nuclear-powered aircraft carrier *George Washington* in late 2010 in the Yellow Sea. In July of that year, when the joint exercise plan was disclosed, the Chinese press and army leaders commented that it would be "provocative" or pose a threat to China.[21] Such a reaction, however, was clearly of a political nature with no legal grounds indicated. Yet on 26 November 2010, the Chinese Foreign Ministry reportedly issued a statement warning against "any military activity" in China's EEZ without its permission, referring to the joint maneuvers which were to start two days later.[22] Since it was made in the context of the planned exercises, this statement implies at least that China would not recognize the freedom of military exercises in the EEZ. Beyond that, it is not clear whether China would not allow any or only some kind of military exercises. On this point, one Chinese scholar takes a flexible view, saying that each specific case of military exercise should be examined carefully according to its nature and features, and whether due regard is being paid to the rights of the coastal State, especially regarding the protection of the marine environment and management of resources.[23]

## Principle of Peaceful Uses of the Ocean

The LOS Convention makes reference to "peaceful uses" or "peaceful purposes" in several Articles, including Articles 88 and 301. Chinese authors generally argue that military hydrographic survey and intelligence-gathering activities in and above the EEZ by foreign vessels and aircraft are not considered peaceful and thus violate those provisions.[24]

In the U.S. view, on the other hand, such activities are lawful, non-aggressive military activities consistent with the UN Charter, and can be conducted in the EEZ without the coastal State's consent. It is pointed out that the convention makes a clear distinction between "threat or use of force" and other military activities, such as intelligence collection. Article 19(2)(a) repeats the wording of Article 301, and Article 19(2)(b)–(f ) restricts other military activities in the territorial sea. And Article 19(2)(c) specifically regards ships navigating the territorial seas as not innocent if they engage in "any act aimed at collecting information to the prejudice of the defense or security of the coastal state". No such provisions on information collection appear with respect to the high seas or the EEZ. Therefore, in the U.S. view, intelligence collection is not covered by the non-use-of-force provision of Article 301.[25] In the Commentary accompanying the message of President Clinton transmitting the LOS Convention to the Senate, it was underlined specifically that none of the provisions of Articles 88, 301, etc., creates new rights or obligations, imposes restrictions upon military operations, or impairs the inherent right of self-defense, and that generally military activities which are consistent with international law principles are not prohibited by any provisions of the convention.[26]

## Protection of the Marine Environment and the Obligation
## to Pay Due Regard

In March 2009, when USNS *Impeccable*, using a sonar array system, was harassed by the Chinese Navy and other vessels in China's EEZ in the South China Sea, the spokesperson of China's Foreign Ministry stated that the U.S. ship's unauthorized access into these waters for the purpose of undertaking military surveys violated the LOS Convention and Chinese laws.[27] Additionally, according to the Deputy Chief

Captain of the East China Sea Corps of the China Marine Surveillance Forces, the operations of *Impeccable*, which introduced a shielded cable into the sea and emitted sound waves in order to investigate underwater targets, conduct surveys, undertake instrument experiments, or investigate the ocean's environment, constituted "pollution of the marine environment" under the convention.[28] Thus he alleged that the United States violated the convention and was responsible for the damage caused to fishermen by such illegal activities.[29]

As discussed above, the United States takes the view that such military survey activities in the EEZ are part of the freedom of the high seas and thus the coastal States have no right to regulate. On the other hand, the Law of the Sea Convention also provides that user States of the EEZ of a coastal State shall have "due regard" to the rights and duties of the coastal State in accordance with its provisions and other rules of international law not incompatible with Part V on the EEZ (Art. 58(3)). Part V certainly recognizes the jurisdiction of the coastal State with regard to the protection and preservation of the marine environment in its EEZ. However, the jurisdiction exists only to such an extent as provided for in the convention (Art. 56(1)(b)(iii)). For the United States, e.g., it was pointed out that a warship might choose not to conduct certain operations, like a gunnery exercise targeting at whale migration, paying due regard to environmental interests of the coastal state.[30]

## Concluding Remarks

As illustrated above, the confrontation of legal positions on military uses of the EEZ between the world's greatest naval power and the world's second largest economy with a rapidly growing navy, both relying on the LOS Convention, appears to continue. It is a disturbing factor within an overall stable and solid legal structure built on the convention. The issue must be addressed urgently by the states concerned, as well as by the international community in general, with a view to finding a common position, or some mechanism or arrangement for avoiding further serious incidents.

## Notes

1. See http://www.un.org/Depts/los/convention_agreements/convention_declarations.htm.
2. United Nations Convention on the Law of the Sea, Montego Bay, 10 December 1982, in force 16 November 1994, 21 *International Legal Materials* 1261 (1982).
3. Raul Pedrozo, 'Coastal State Jurisdiction over Marine Data Collection in the Exclusive Economic Zone: U.S. Views' in P. Dutton (ed.), *Military Activities in the EEZ: A U.S.-China Dialogue on Security and International Law in the Maritime Commons* (China Maritime Studies Institute, Newport, 2010) 27.
4. *Ibid.*, p. 28.
5. *Ibid.*
6. *Ibid.*

7. J. A. Roach and R. W. Smith, *Excessive Maritime Claims* (Naval War College, Newport, 1994) 247.

8. Xue Guifang, 'Surveys and Research Activities in the EEZ: Issues and Prospects' in Dutton, *supra* note 3, p. 93.

9. Gao Zhiguo, 'China and the Law of the Sea' in M. Nordquist, T. Koh and J. N. Moore (eds.), *Freedom of Seas, Passage Rights and the 1982 Law of the Sea Convention* (Martinus Nijhoff, Leiden, 2009) 294. See also Xue Guifang, 'Marine Scientific Research and Hydrographic Survey in the EEZs: Closing Up the Legal Loopholes?' *ibid.*, p. 222 and Wu Jilu, 'The Concept of Marine Scientific Research' in Dutton, *supra* note 3, p. 65.

10. Zhang Haiwen, 'Is It Safeguarding the Freedom of Navigation or Maritime Hegemony of the United States? Comments on Raul (Pete) Pedrozo's Article on Military Activities in the EEZ' (2010) 9 *Chinese Journal of International Law* 31, para. 20.

11. *Ibid.*, para. 14. Wu, supra note 9, p. 65, also states that China's view is that hydrographic surveying is part of MSR.

12. See generally Zou Keyuan, *China's Marine Legal System and the Law of the Sea* (Martinus Nijhoff, Leiden, 2005) 277 *et seq.*

13. Xue, *supra* note 8, p. 97.

14. English translation at http://www.asianlii.org/cn/legis/cen/laws/samlotproc506/.

15. Department of the Navy, *The Commander's Handbook on the Law of Naval Operations* (Norfolk, 1995), Sections 2.4.2. and 2.4.3.

16. Pedrozo, *supra* note 3, p. 29.

17. Gao, *supra* note 9, pp. 293–294.

18. See http://www.un.org/Depts/los/convention_agreements/convention_declarations.htm.

19. *Ibid.*

20. Message from the President of the United States transmitting the United Nations Convention on the Law of the Sea and the Agreement relating to the Implementation of Part XI of the United Nations Convention on the Law of the Sea. US Senate, 103rd Congress, 2nd Session. Treaty Doc. 103–39, p. 24.

21. See *World Socialist Website*, 24 July 2010, at www.wswb.org.

22. *Want China Times* (Taiwan), 27 Nov. 2010, at www.wantchinatimes.com.

23. Ji Yongming, 'On Dissection of Disputes between China and the US over Military Activities in the EEZ by the Law of the Sea,' paper presented at the International Conference on "Security Environment of the Seas in East Asia," Singapore, 28 and 29 February 2012; available from author.

24. Gao, *supra* note 9, pp. 293–294.

25. Pedrozo, *supra* note 3, p. 30.

26. Message from the President, *supra* note 20, pp. iii and 94.

27. http://www.fmprc.gov.cn/eng/xwfw/s2510/2511/t541713.htm.

28. Yu Zhirong, 'Jurisprudential Analysis of the U.S. Navy's Military Surveys in the Exclusive Economic Zones of Coastal Countries' in Dutton, *supra* note 3, p. 42.

29. *Ibid.*, p. 43.

30. James Kraska, 'Resources Rights and Environmental Protection in the Exclusive Economic Zone: The Functional Approach to Naval Operations' in Dutton, *supra* note 3, p. 82.

# No Fishing: Row Erupts between China and US over Fishing Restrictions

By Reuters
*NewsYaps*, January 10, 2014

China defended on Friday its new fishing restrictions in disputed waters in the South China Sea against criticism from the United States, saying the rules were in accordance with international law.

The rules, approved by China's southern Hainan province, took effect on January 1 and require foreign fishing vessels to obtain approval to enter the waters, which the local government says are under its jurisdiction.

Beijing claims almost the entire oil- and gas-rich South China Sea and rejects rival claims to parts of it from the Philippines, Taiwan, Malaysia, Brunei and Vietnam.

Washington called the fishing rules "provocative and potentially dangerous", prompting a rebuttal from China's foreign ministry on Friday [January 2014].

Foreign Ministry spokeswoman Hua Chunying said the government "has the right and responsibility to regulate the relevant islands and reefs as well as non-biological resources" according to international and domestic law.

"For more than 30 years, China's relevant fisheries laws and regulations have been consistently implemented in a normal way, and have never caused any tension," Hua said at a daily news briefing.

"If someone feels the need to say that technical amendments to local fisheries regulations implemented many years ago will cause tensions in the region and pose a threat to regional stability, then I can only say that if this does not stem from a lack of basic common sense, then it must be due to an ulterior motive."

A government-affiliated fishing organization in Vietnam criticized the new rules and the Philippines said they escalate tensions in the region.

"These regulations seriously violate the freedom of navigation and the right to fish of all states in the high seas," foreign ministry spokesman Raul Hernandez said.

"We have requested China to immediately clarify the new fisheries law."

## Another Irritant

After China's announcement late last year of an air defense identification zone in the East China Sea, which drew sharp criticism from Washington, the fishing rules add another irritant to Sino-US ties.

"China has not offered any explanation or basis under international law for these

From *NewsYaps* (10 January 2014). Copyright © 2014 by *NewsYaps*. Reprinted with permission. All rights reserved.

extensive maritime claims," State Department spokeswoman Jen Psaki told a news briefing.

"Our long-standing position has been that all concerned parties should avoid any unilateral action that raises tensions and undermines the prospects for a diplomatic or other peaceful resolution of differences."

Fishermen from Vietnam and the Philippines have been caught up in heated territorial disputes with China on the seas in recent years. Last year, Vietnam accused China of opening fire on a fishing boat in the South China Sea, and later of endangering the lives of fishermen after ramming a fishing trawler.

The State Department spokeswoman gave no indication of any possible US response to the fishing zone.

## Strategic

Hainan officials were not immediately available to comment. But according to the Hainan legislature's website, foreign fishing vessels need approval to enter from the "relevant and responsible department" of the Chinese government's cabinet.

Hainan, which juts into the South China Sea from China's southern tip, is responsible for administering the country's extensive claims to the myriad islets and atolls in the sea.

It says it governs 2 million square km (770,000 square miles) of water, according to local government data issued in 2011. The South China Sea is an estimated 3.5 million square km (1.4 million square miles) in size.

The province is also home to Chinese naval facilities that include a purpose-built dock for the country's only aircraft carrier and a base for attack submarines.

The fishing rules do not outline penalties, but the requirements are similar to a 2004 national law that says boats entering Chinese territory without permission can have their catch and fishing equipment seized and face fines of up to 500,000 yuan.

Wu Shicun, head of Hainan's foreign affairs office until last May, told Reuters that offending foreign fishing vessels would be expelled if they are in waters around Hainan and the disputed Paracel Islands.

"If we can't expel them, then we'll go on board to make checks to see whether there's any illegal fishing," said Wu, now president of the National Institute for South China Sea Studies, a think-tank that advises the government on policy on the South China Sea. "We'll drag you back to be handled, confiscate (your) fishing gear, detain the vessel and fine (you). The most serious fine is 500,000 yuan."

Vietnam reiterated its claim to sovereignty over the Paracel and Spratlys islands in the South China Sea, both also claimed by Beijing.

"All foreign activities at these areas without Vietnam's acceptance are illegal and groundless," Foreign Ministry spokesman Luong Thanh Nghi said in a written response to questions about the new fishing rules.

The government-affiliated fishing organization, the Vietnam Fisheries Society, condemned the Hainan regulations.

"This action from China will directly affect Vietnamese fishermen, damage their work, their livelihoods and impact their families," said Vo Van Trac, vice chairman of the body.

Donald Rothwell, a maritime law expert at the Australian National University College of Law, said the fisheries rules were unlikely to advance China's claims on the South China Sea given the likely reaction from other countries with rival claims.

"The only way it can advance its position is if China actually seeks to enforce these laws and the enforcement mechanisms are successful and prosecutions result or it has conditions found in its favor by international courts," he said.

# China's New Fishing Regulations: An Act of State Piracy?

By Carl Thayer
*The Diplomat*, January 13, 2014

*Hainan provinces new rules about fishing complicate China's relationship with ASEAN.*

On November 29, 2013, six days after China's Ministry of National Defense announced the establishment of an Air Defense Identification Zone (ADIZ) over the East China Sea, Hainan province quietly issued new regulations on fishing in the South China Sea. These regulations were announced on December 3 and came into force on January 1, 2014.

Both of these actions were unilateral and aimed at extending the legal basis for China's claim to land features and maritime zones in the East and South China Seas. China's actions challenge the sovereignty of neighboring states, and have the potential to raise tensions and risk triggering an armed incident.

Hainan province's new fishing regulations require all foreign vessels that seek to fish or conduct surveys in waters claimed by China to obtain advance approval from the "relevant and responsible department" under the Cabinet.

Hainan province claims administrative responsibility over Hainan Island, the Xisha (Paracel) archipelago, Zhongsha (Macclesfield Bank) archipelago, the Nansha (Spratly) archipelago "and their dependent waters." These dependent waters stretch approximately two million square kilometers or roughly 57 percent of the 3.6 million square kilometers enclosed in China's nine-dash line claim over the South China Sea.

Foreign fishing boats and survey vessels that refuse to comply will be either forced out of the area or boarded, impounded and subject to a fine of up to $83,000. Hainan province authorities also assert the right to confiscate the fish catches it finds on the boats that it seizes.

China has sovereign jurisdiction over the waters and seabed included in its Exclusive Economic Zone (EEZ). Hainan provincial authorities are within their legal rights to set restrictions on foreign vessels that seek to fish in this 200 nautical miles. But Hainan authorities must respect the innocent passage of all other vessels.

China also asserts sovereign jurisdiction of the waters adjacent to the Paracel Islands. This claim is disputed by Vietnam. Both China and Vietnam, as signatories to the United Nations Convention on the Law of the Sea (UNCLOS), are obliged to refrain from taking unilateral action and are further obliged to cooperate and

From *The Diplomat* (13 January 2014). Copyright © 2014 by *Diplomat*. Reprinted with permission. All rights reserved.

refrain from the threat or use of force. These obligations have been honored in the breach in the past.

Hainan province's new regulations also cover the waters in the area where China's nine-dash line claim overlaps with the EEZs proclaimed by the Philippines and Vietnam. Any attempt to enforce Chinese jurisdiction in these waters will likely provoke resistance and could lead to armed clashes at sea.

The most contentious aspect of the new fishing regulation, however, relates to what are commonly viewed as international waters. All fishing vessels and survey ships have a right of freedom of navigation in international waters. Any Chinese attempt to interfere with these vessels could be viewed as an act of "state piracy." This could well entail international legal action against the Chinese ships involved.

It is highly unlikely that China can enforce this new edict in the vast waters claimed by Hainan province. Despite the continuing build-up of maritime enforcement capabilities, including merging several agencies into a new Coast Guard, China lacks sufficient maritime patrol aircraft and naval vessels to consistently cover this vast area. This raises the possibility that China may selectively apply these regulations against Filipino fishermen. This would serve to add pressure on Manila and raise the costs of its political defiance against China over their territorial dispute.

The new Hainan province fishing regulations also have the potential to undermine the diplomatic work put in by Chinese and Vietnamese officials to manage their territorial dispute. Last October [2013] during Premier Li Keqiang's visit to Hanoi, both sides agreed to set up a hot line between their ministries of agriculture to deal promptly with fishing incidents. They also agreed to set up a working group on maritime cooperation.

Although there continue to be isolated incidents involving Chinese state vessels and Vietnamese fishing boats, the number of incidents reported publicly as of last year appears to have declined sharply. The new fishing regulations raise the prospect of reversing this trend.

Immediately after Hainan province issued these new regulations, many of the affected countries sought clarification from China's Ministry of Foreign Affairs. The Philippines was the most vociferous in criticizing the Hainan fishing regulations. In a statement issued on January 10, the Department of Foreign Affairs stated that the new regulations "escalates tensions, unnecessarily complicates the situation in the South China Sea and threatens the peace and stability of the region."

A spokesperson for the U.S. Department of State similarly declared, "the passing of these restrictions on other countries' fishing activities in disputed portions of the South China Sea is a provocative and potentially dangerous act."

Although initially remaining silent on the manner, Vietnam finally responded to the fishing regulations a few days after Vietnam and China held their first round of consultations on the joint development of maritime resources in Beijing as a follow up to Premier Li's visit last year. A government spokesperson in Hanoi called the new regulations "illegal and invalid" and stated, "Vietnam demands that China abolish the above said erroneous acts, and practically contribute to the maintenance of peace and stability in the region."

The Chinese Foreign Ministry responded to criticism in the same manner they have dealt with complaints in the past. In China's view, the actions by government authorities were "totally normal and part of the routine for Chinese provinces bordering the sea to formulate regional rules according to the national law to regulate conservation, management and utilization of maritime biological resources."

Two question marks hang over future developments. First, will China move to create an ADIZ over the South China Sea? Last November when China's Defense Ministry announced the ADIZ over the East China Sea it also stated, "China will establish other air defense identification zones at an appropriate time after completing preparations."

The second question is what impact the fallout from this latest development will have on forthcoming consultations between China and ASEAN on a Code of Conduct in the South China Sea. In the past some members of ASEAN privately disassociated themselves from the Philippines' public criticism of China. If ASEAN cannot reach consensus on how to respond to China's new assertiveness in the South China Sea, this will play into Beijing's hands.

# A Hidden Victim of Somali Pirates: Science

By Paul Salopek
*National Geographic*, April 25, 2013

*Fear of buccaneers opens a vast "data hole" in the Indian Ocean.*

During 32 years of fieldwork in the deserts of Ethiopia, Tim White, the eminent American paleoanthropologist, has brazened through every conceivable obstacle to his research into human origins.

Flash floods have marooned his vehicles in hip-deep pools of mud. Grazing wars between groups of nomads have blocked access to promising fossil beds. And campfire visits by snakes and tarantulas are so routine they rank as minor nuisances.

Yet nothing has stymied White's pursuit of knowledge—or thwarted his scientific ambitions—like the hard-eyed men in flip-flop sandals who, valuing doubloons above Darwin, set sail hundreds of miles away in skiffs stocked with machine guns and rope ladders: Somali pirates.

"No question, it's been a serious setback," says White, who has waited years, in vain, for a research vessel to drill crucial seabed cores off Somalia that would revolutionize the dating of East Africa's spectacular hominid finds. "Piracy has stopped oceanographic work in the region. There's been no data coming out of this area for years. Zero."

White isn't alone in his frustration.

Scientists from around the globe, specializing in subjects as diverse as plate tectonics, plankton evolution, oceanography, and climate change, are decrying a growing void of research that has spread across hundreds of thousands of square miles of the Indian Ocean near the Horn of Africa—an immense, watery "data hole" swept clean of scientific research by the threat of Somali buccaneering.

Major efforts to study the dynamics of monsoons, predict global warming, or dig into seafloors to reveal humankind's prehistory have been scuttled by the same gangs of freebooters who, over the course of the past decade, have killed dozens of mariners, held thousands more hostage, and, by one World Bank estimate, fleeced the world of $18 billion a year in economic losses.

The cost to science may be less visible to the public. But it won't be borne solely by scholars.

Years of missing weather data off the Horn of Africa, for example, will affect the lives of millions of people. A scarcity of surface wind readings has already created

From *National Geographic* (25 April 2013). Copyright © 2013 by National Geographic Society. Reprinted with permission. All rights reserved.

distortions in weather models that forecast the strength, direction, and timing of rains that sustain vast farming belts on surrounding continents.

## Shelving a Rosetta Stone

"This problem has been going on a long time and with virtually no public awareness," says Sarah Feakins, a researcher at the University of Southern California whose work on paleoclimates has been hijacked by piracy fears. "All kinds of efforts are made to keep the commercial sea lanes around Somalia open. Nobody talks about the lost science."

Feakins's woes highlight the toll the pirates have exacted, albeit unwittingly, on one earth science practice in particular: seabed core sampling, which involves a miniscule global fleet of expensive research vessels that—because they stay in place to drill—are sitting ducks.

Oceanic sediment cores offer researchers a valuable archive of Earth's climate history. Ancient pollen, plankton, dust, and other clues collected from seafloors provide the bulk of what scientists know about global changes to the planet's ecosystems over time.

In 2011, Feakins devised a novel way of harnessing this technology to test one of the oldest questions of human evolution: Did our ancestors actually climb down from trees because of expanding savannas in Africa?

By poring over cores from the seas off East Africa, she would be able to peel back layers of ancient, windblown carbon isotopes associated with grasslands, settling the debate.

Her idea earned the coveted approval of the Integrated Ocean Drilling Program (IODP), an elite international scientific organization that controls the most advanced drilling platform afloat—the *JOIDES Resolution*, a gigantic, high-tech oceanographic ship topped with a 200-foot-tall drilling rig.

But when the location of her sampling became known—near the Gulf of Aden, the bull's-eye of the Somali pirate's hunting grounds—Feakins's project sank without a bubble.

"I'm using old cores from the 1970s now," she says. "It's all we've got."

The *JOIDES Resolution* is deployed in the Indian Ocean until 2016. But during the past 18 months the IODP has quietly dry-docked three major projects near Somalia.

One casualty was paleoanthropologist White's dream proposal: drilling into the Indian Ocean seabed for ashes that have wafted down from African volcanoes over the course of millions of years.

The ash, which is precisely datable under the ocean because of continuous layering, would offer a game-changing yardstick for correlating the ages of hominid fossils discovered throughout the Great Rift Valley. In effect, the clearest picture yet of the human family tree would be pulled, shimmering, from the sea.

"Rosetta," White says forlornly, referring to the Rosetta Stone, the crucial artifact that enabled 19th-century scholars to at last decipher Egyptian hieroglyphics.

## Gunboat Science

The IODP, which is funded by scientific agencies in the United States, Europe, Japan, China, and India, says it has little maneuvering room when it comes to piracy.

"We have always placed the security and safety of our staff and scientists as a number one priority," says David Divins, an IODP spokesman. "The problem is that there is some potentially pioneering science that will have to wait or find another location."

The lawless waters off Somalia, however, are unique. They offer tantalizingly rich returns on anthropological and climatological research. And even Divins admits that the wait could be long.

Research slots on the *JOIDES Resolution*—the name is an acronym for Joint Oceanographic Institutions for Deep Earth Sampling—are ferociously competitive and booked years in advance. It could be "at least another five years or so" before the vessel returns to the region, Divins says.

Some beleaguered researchers, meanwhile, have sent out an SOS to the world's navies.

Among the armadas now hunting down Somali speedboats, the Australian Navy has shown a particular willingness to shoulder scientific work. It has agreed to lower oceanographic instruments from its warships. (Some of that equipment has been retrieved pocked with bullet holes.)

Armed escorts, however, are another matter.

The only vessels afforded close naval protection are UN World Food Program cargo ships carrying relief supplies to the Horn of Africa.

Governments balk at guarding low-priority research vessels, especially when they resemble oil company drill boats—jackpot targets for pirates. The scientific agencies operating the research ships also pan the idea, saying it would sink their insurance policies.

"When I raised the military question, it caused a firestorm of anger from everybody from the U.S. State Department to the IODP," Feakins says. "I was intimidated into just dropping it."

## A Treasure Lost

The irony now is that the pirate scourge appears to have peaked off Somalia.

Statistics compiled by the International Maritime Bureau show that brigands managed to force their way aboard only 14 ships in the region in 2012, down from 31 in 2011 and 49 in 2010.

In ports such as Djibouti city, just north of Somalia, it's easy to see why.

The militarization of the area's waterways, particularly the strategic Bab-el-Mandeb Strait between Africa and Arabia, is virtually complete.

The U.S. and Europe each lead heavily armed task forces that shadow endless convoys of oil tankers and container ships past the wild shores of Somalia. Japanese corvettes sit ready at dock, their engines rumbling. Spanish, German, Turkish, and French soldiers assigned to antipiracy campaigns jam the port's hotel lobbies.

Offshore, merchant ships bob at anchor with razor wire coiled about their rails. Big placards on their hulls warn that lethal force will be used to repel attackers.

How long this martial pressure can be sustained is an open question. But for now the Somalis are outgunned.

Still, even if the oceanographic research community steams back into the Gulf of Aden tomorrow, the havoc that pirates have wreaked on science is enduring.

Writing in *EOS*, the journal of the American Geophysical Union, the meteorologists Shawn R. Smith, Mark A. Bourassa, and Michael Long point out that routine wind readings collected by ships for decades are now interrupted by a colossal blank space that gapes across 960,000 square miles (2.5 million square kilometers) of open sea.

In this case, ship captains have not simply avoided Somalia, but have refused to broadcast anything that might tip off eavesdropping buccaneers—including daily weather reports. That long radio silence has spawned a historic anomaly, or aberration, in oceanographic records.

"The data void exists in the formation region of the Somali low-level jet, a wind pattern that is one of the main drivers of the Indian summer monsoon," the *EOS* article's authors warn.

One consequence: It has become harder to predict long-term changes in a weather system that disperses rain across immense agricultural zones in Africa, the Middle East, and especially South Asia.

"For people trying to understand the science of climate change and the impact of El Niño on the Asian monsoon, I believe that this has been permanent damage," laments Peter Clift, an earth scientist at Louisiana State University in Baton Rouge.

Clift is being generous.

His own research, which explores how the Earth's geology and atmosphere interact, has been held hostage for more than a decade by the marauders off the African Horn.

He needs a drilling ship. None will come. And he says he may never complete his life's work: yet more booty stolen by the pirates of Somalia.

# 5

# Drifting Along: The Rise of the Environmental Refugee

© Andrew Biraj/Reuters/Landov

A woman looks at the River Padma from her house, under threat from erosion of the river, in Shariatpur, Bangladesh.

# Environmental Refugees in a Changing Global Climate

Since the 1950s, accumulating evidence has suggested that Earth's climate is changing at an unprecedented rate. Scientists, policymakers, and the general public continue to debate the degree to which human activities are responsible for such changes. As time goes on, the effects of global climate change are becoming increasingly pronounced and measurable. Organizations such as the United Nations Environmental Programme (UNEP) and the World Meteorological Organization (WMO) are working together to identify potential impacts of climate change. In 1988, these two organizations formed the Intergovernmental Panel on Climate Change (IPCC) to synthesize and analyze climate change data, as well as predict potential future impacts and suggest mitigating measures.

## Climate Change

In 2013 and 2014, the IPCC released portions of a multipart report on global climate change. The first part of this report, issued in September 2013, identifies several key indicators of global climate change. According to the report, the earth's average surface temperature increased significantly during the 1980s, 1990s, and 2000s; carbon dioxide levels in the atmosphere have risen steadily since 1960; and the oceans are becoming more acidic from absorbing carbon dioxide. The report concludes that human influence is at fault, primarily from the billions of tons of carbon dioxide and other greenhouse gases released into the atmosphere by industrialized nations over the past century.

The second part of the IPCC report, issued in March 2014, describes the effect of climate on the environment, agriculture, and tourism, and makes projections about what could happen over the next century. For example, much of the data shows a significant drop in crop yields over the past several decades, and analysts project a further decline of 10 percent or more. Additionally, a growing number of severe weather events such as droughts and floods, combined with steadily rising ocean levels, could displace millions of people before the end of the twenty-first century.

From an economic perspective, the report predicts that the cost of an average surface temperature increase of 3.6 degrees Fahrenheit during the twenty-first century could be as high as 2 percent of the total global gross domestic product. However, the effect of these environmental changes will not be evenly distributed throughout the world: some of the poorest countries may also experience the most disastrous consequences, so the economic repercussions could be severe.

To be sure, the concept of climate change, its cause, and its potential impacts, continue to be the subjects of debate. While few dispute that climate change is happening, some analysts believe its projected effects are exaggerated, and that humans, animals, and marine life can adapt to these changes. Additionally, some economists believe that adaptation and remedial measures will not be as expensive as initially feared. Even the IPCC's 2007 report—which received criticism from national science academies and pundits for its overreliance on prediction models and tendency toward alarmist writing—projected more severe consequences than the 2014 report.

Some even argue that climate change is a net positive: for example, during the past thirty years, satellites have identified about a 14 percent increase in greenery across the planet, as increased human-made carbon dioxide emissions and higher temperatures encourage plant growth. An analysis of the IPCC report issued by the Heartland Institute noted that increased carbon dioxide levels and warmer temperatures can be beneficial for plants, and can expand some types of habitats to the benefit of certain wildlife.

Ultimately, however, projections that the environmental and financial cost of climate change might be less severe than initially feared are of little comfort to people who are already feeling its effects.

## Rising Oceans

Regardless of the cause, there is ample proof that the ocean level is rising at an alarming rate. According to the 2007 IPCC report, the sea level has risen at a rate of about 1.7 millimeters per year over the past century. Scientists predict it could continue to rise as much as 0.44 meters by the year 2100, which would be catastrophic for low-lying coastal regions. At that rate, some towns, cities, and even entire countries could disappear into the sea.

Even if the land itself does not disappear, increased flooding due to rising sea levels can lead to severe and permanent environmental damage. Floods can cause cross-contamination of garbage and human waste with the fresh water supply, leaving the population without safe drinking water. Additionally, water containing salt or other contaminants can destroy food plants and damage fields where crops are planted, leading to famine.

Some countries are well-positioned to assist citizens displaced due to environmental hazards; for others, this task will be difficult or impossible. For example, as the permafrost under many northern Alaska towns melts, these towns could become unsafe for habitation. While leaving one's home is always difficult for logistical and emotional reasons, those who are displaced can safely and legally relocate to other locations within Alaska and the United States. By contrast, countries that are entirely located within low-lying deltas such as Bangladesh, or countries that consist entirely of small islands such as Kiribati, Tonga, and the Maldives, are running out of options.

## Displaced Persons

Any circumstance that forces people from their homes presents challenges. But when entire countries disappear, the situation becomes even more complicated.

Entire islands nations are in danger of becoming uninhabitable or literally disappearing underwater if sea levels continue to rise; indeed, increased flooding and an inability to safely settle near the coastlines has already displaced many people.

Some people from these affected areas are already fleeing their countries for higher ground and safer locations. If the most dire predictions prove true, hundreds of millions of people could need new homes by the end of the twenty-first century. However, due to international laws and regulations, they might not have anywhere to go. Many countries do not permit immigration unless the individual is sponsored by an employer, with the promise of a job upon arrival. Alternatively, one can arrive in another country unannounced and declare refugee status, but there is no guarantee of admission. In this second situation, the persons request permission to immigrate because they face persecution in their country of origin, generally due to race, religion, political affiliation, or sexual orientation.

However, the current international legal definition of *refugee* does not include displacement resulting from environmental conditions. In the few instances where people have sought refugee status under environmental claims, judges have hesitated to extend the rule to cover this situation. The issue of whether to extend refugee status to those displaced by environmental hazards is complicated; most judges believe any extension to the current definition is best addressed by an international body such as the United Nations. One critical issue is whether the climate change hazards must be permanent in order to permit someone to immigrate as a refugee, or if a one-off environmental disaster such as a hurricane or tsunami is sufficient. Another critical issue is how to assist refugees once they arrive: many will arrive with few resources of their own, and may lack the skills necessary to thrive in a new society. Countries like New Zealand, Australia, the United States, and Canada have not yet planned how to assist large numbers of displaced individuals, especially if they arrive all at once.

Some governments of endangered countries encourage their citizens not to flee as refugees. In addition to its environmental remediation efforts, the government of Kiribati also runs programs to train its residents for jobs and acquire the language skills necessary to succeed upon immigrating to another country. The United Nations and some of its member countries, including the United States, favor planned and controlled relocation, rather than extension of refugee status to those displaced for environmental reasons. Unfortunately, there is no consensus on what the plan should be, or how much time remains before the situation becomes dire. And for some, time has already run out.

## Engineering Solutions

For centuries, people used engineering and technology to counter the infrastructure damage to coastal towns caused by the sea and storms. Building sea walls to keep water away from the land, and adding fill to raise the height of existing land compared to sea level have, for some places, been effective in preventing extensive coastal damage. But these methods—though sufficient when the threat is confined to a small area—are very expensive. When expanded to the scope of entire island nations, the cost and logistics can be prohibitive. For example, in the near-term, Kiribati will need to spend nearly $1 billion just to protect its current infrastructure, including drinking water, sanitation, electricity, and roads. This price does not include ongoing maintenance, or any future damage caused by rising seas.

Another possible solution is building artificial islands where people can live, farm, and produce electricity and other necessities, in an environment protected from the rising seas. These artificial islands use technology similar to oil rigs, and allow these islands to become autonomous habitats of their own. Countries such as the Netherlands, Japan, China, and the Maldives have created similar islands for many purposes, including airports, housing, and even trash disposal. The government of Kiribati is seriously considering a $2 billion plan for such an artificial island, and architects in Bangkok, Thailand, are exploring similar options in case the city—which is largely built on marshlands—becomes overcrowded or uninhabitable over the next several decades.

However, building artificial constructs produces issues of its own. The shadows cast down into the sea from floating artificial turf could damage the sea floor and harm marine life. This is problematic because the local populations of many island nations depend on the ocean for environmental stability, food and other resources, and the economic boost to tourism. If the artificial islands cause further harm to marine ecosystems, the damage could be far-reaching and irrecoverable.

## Responsibility

Any solution to the current environmental crisis is likely to be expensive. Applying engineering solutions to existing islands or building new artificial islands can cost billions of dollars, which is no small amount for any country. And while care must be taken to choose the technical and scientific solutions that best fit each particular region, one significant issue remains: who will pay for these solutions? Many of the areas most severely affected by climate change are developing countries, and they are not economically prepared to handle the costly solutions necessary to ensure their survival. And if climate change is indeed a human-induced phenomenon due to industrialization and pollution, then these heavily affected areas might also be the smallest contributors to the problem in the first place.

It is not simply a matter of understanding the science, it is about determining who should be responsible for the potentially millions of people—many of whom may lack the resources, skills, or legal status necessary to immigrate successfully to another country—who may be displaced over the next century due to rising oceans. Should the industrialized countries with the largest contribution to environmental changes be required to bear the costs of rehabilitating damaged land? Or should they be required to offer immigration options to environmental refugees forced to flee their homes? These questions are already in need of answers, and if scientists are correct, their answers will only become more urgent over the next decades.

—Tracey M. DiLascio

## Bibliography

Black, Deborah. "Floating Islands to the Rescue in the Maldives." *Toronto Star*. Toronto Star Newspapers, 23 Aug. 2012. Web. 11 Apr. 2014.

Black, Deborah. "What Should Be Done About Climate Change Refugees?" *Toronto Star*. Toronto Star Newspapers, 11 Oct. 2013. Web. 11 Apr. 2014.

Intergovernmental Panel on Climate Change. "Climate Change 2014: Impacts, Adaptation, and Vulnerability." *IPCC WGII AR5 Technical Summary*. IPCC, 31 Mar. 2014. Web. 11 Apr. 2014.

Lakely, Jim. "Benefits of Global Warming Greatly Exceed Costs, New Study Says." *Heartland Institute Online*. Heartland Inst., 25 Mar. 2014. Web. 11 Apr. 2014.

Park, Susan. "Climate Change and the Risk of Statelessness: The Situation of Low-Lying Island States." *UNHCR Legal and Protection Policy Research Series*. UNHCR Division of Intl. Protection, May 2011. Web. 11 Apr. 2014.

Plait, Phil. "Climate Change: It's Real, and It's Us." *Slate*. Slate Group, 30 Sept. 2013. Web. 11 Apr. 2014.

Plait, Phil. "There Is No Question That We Live in a World Already Altered by Climate Change." *Slate*. Slate Group, 31 Mar 2014. Web. 11 Apr. 2014.

Ridley, Matt. "Climate Forecast: Muting the Alarm." *Wall Street Journal*. Dow Jones, 27 Mar. 2014. Web. 11 Apr. 2014.

UN Refugee Agency. "Looking After the Land." *UNHCR Website*. UNHCR, 2014. Web. 11 Apr. 2014.

# Who Will Become the World's First Climate Change Refugee?

By Robert McLeman
*The Globe and Mail,* November 17, 2013

Ioane Teitiota was not seeking fame when he moved to New Zealand, but he is now getting it. He is the first person, so far as is known, to request asylum in a common-law country on the basis of being a climate change refugee.

A native of Kiribati—a small island state in the South Pacific—Mr. Teitiota went to New Zealand several years ago as a legal guest worker, but he stayed on and his visa expired. He has now asked the New Zealand government to refrain from sending him and his family back to Kiribati, saying sea level rise is making his home island uninhabitable. A lower court has accepted as fact his evidence that high tides repeatedly breach the seawalls protecting his community, and that rising seas are killing crops, contaminating drinking water, and flooding homes. The lower court nonetheless rejected Mr. Teitiota's asylum application, finding that these reasons do not constitute grounds for protection under international law. He has appealed that decision to a higher court; the verdict is pending.

It may be that his asylum claim is simply a last-ditch attempt to avoid deportation, but it has brought considerable attention to a previously abstract concept. Studies have projected that hundreds of millions of people will be displaced this century by the impacts of climate change. At the United Nations, the Security Council has debated the subject, and decided it is best managed through the UN Framework Convention on Climate Change (UNFCCC) process. Least developed countries have been encouraged to consider the migration implications of climate change in their National Adaptation Plans, and at their 2010 Cancun meeting, UNFCCC delegates stated that migration and displacement ought to be planned for in the context of adaptation. But until Mr. Teitiota came along, no individual actually stepped forward to request international protection from the impacts of climate change.

If the New Zealand court finds him to be a refugee, expect others to make similar claims, there and elsewhere. The court will likely not do so. The internationally accepted definition of a refugee was established in a 1951 UN convention. To qualify for protection, a refugee must have a legitimate fear of persecution in his or her home country. The environment does not persecute, nor do sea levels. And so, unless humanitarian or compassionate grounds particular to his circumstances are invoked, he and his family will likely be required to return home. But even if Mr.

From *The Globe and Mail* (17 November 2013). Copyright © 2013 by Globe Information Services. Reprinted with permission. All rights reserved.

Teitiota goes away, the question of what to do about people displaced by rising sea levels will not.

The science is increasingly conclusive that human-induced climate change is causing sea levels to rise. Not by much; at present only a couple millimeters per year on average, but for atoll nations like Kiribati where the land is no more than a meter or two above the sea, even that rate of change is problematic. An atoll is a low-lying, ring-shaped island built of coral that sits upon an extinct, undersea volcano. Atolls are common in the Pacific and Indian oceans. The most populous atoll nation is the Maldives, with 340,000 people; Kiribati has a population of 100,000. Despite sea level rise, not all atolls are shrinking in area. Each atoll has its own particular underlying geology. Some are being pushed upward by tectonic activity beneath them; others are subsiding. The ones that are subsiding are at greatest risk, since sea level rise accelerates their gradual disappearance beneath the waves.

A few small islands are already in trouble, like the Carteret Islands, from which people are being relocated. The Carterets are governed by Papua New Guinea, which has plenty of land that is not in danger of being lost to rising seas. This is not the case for states like Kiribati or the Maldives; they have no high ground to which people can relocate. Seeing that the rest of the world shows little interest in curbing its greenhouse gas emissions, the government of Kiribati appears to have resigned itself to its fate. It is encouraging its citizens to migrate elsewhere, and has begun purchasing land in Fiji to provide a possible destination. The government of the Maldives is looking at building artificial islands as possible refuges.

Should the international community help by expanding the definition of a refugee so that people displaced by the impacts of climate change qualify for UN protection? This is not a good idea, and probably would not get far with policymakers. The existing refugee definition is clear and well-established. Approximately ten million people worldwide presently meet the existing definition—people like those fleeing the conflict in Syria—and the international community does a poor job helping them. There is no point in officially labeling more people as refugees if we cannot help the refugees we already have.

The number of people worldwide who might benefit from being designated 'refugees' because of sea level rise is not large—perhaps several hundred thousand over the next fifty years. This is because only a small number of states consist exclusively of low-lying islands. Refugee protection extends only to those who flee their home country. Tens of millions of people worldwide live in coastal areas exposed to sea level rise, but most are citizens of continental states or non-atoll island states, meaning they would not need to resettle in another country.

Another problem is definition and causality. Sea level rise is relatively straightforward to track, but other potential impacts of climate change are less obvious. For example, the intensity of tropical cyclones is expected to increase in coming decades. Cyclones occur naturally; human-induced climate change exacerbates them. So, does the international community want to offer guaranteed assistance to all people displaced by cyclones (something we do not do now), or only in those instances where evidence shows climate change has aggravated the harm caused? Or what if the cyclone is determined to be 'natural' but sea level rise enabled its storm surge to penetrate farther inland than it otherwise would have? Further, would we really want to guarantee protection to those who flee the storm but not to those left behind and may be in a worse predicament? What a messy can of worms we would open.

There will inevitably be people who experience harm as result of our refusal to control greenhouse gas emissions now. In cases like Kiribati, where the number of people to be harmed is relatively small, Canada and the international community can (and probably will) offer assistance on an ad hoc basis. This is not ideal from the perspective of those whose lives will be affected, but it is how we have done things in the past. Canada, for example, took ad hoc measures to facilitate the migration of people following earthquakes in Italy (1976) and Haiti (2010). Each year, Canada, Australia, New Zealand, the UK and the US collectively accept roughly 2.5 million legal permanent resident immigrants. With minor regulatory changes to their existing migration programs, these countries could easily resettle everyone displaced from small island states, obviating any need for tinkering with international refugee law.

The big challenge—the one we must start planning for now, and for which there is no simple solution—will come when coastal urban centers begin experiencing more severe tropical storms, made worse by rising sea levels. Remember the damage and harm caused by "superstorm" Sandy and hurricane Katrina? The scientific evidence points to there being more such events in the future, not less. The Chinese economic powerhouse of Shanghai, and its tens of millions of residents, sits in a sinking river delta only a few meters above rising seas, exposed to typhoons. Similar risks exist in densely populated river deltas across Asia. The costs of coastal defenses, managed retreats, and population relocations will be astronomical, and cause severe damage to the global economy. Fortunately, there is still time to plan and prepare for such contingencies through the UNFCCC process and, better yet, to reduce greenhouse gas emissions and avoid those situations altogether. But our planning will need to be done at a faster rate than has been the case until now. Mr. Teitiota can be thanked for prodding us in this direction.

# What Happens When Your Country Drowns?

By Rachel Morris
*Mother Jones,* November/December 2009

*Meet the people of Tuvalu, the world's first climate refugees.*

It's a bright, balmy Sunday afternoon and I'm driving through the western outskirts of Auckland, New Zealand, the kind of place you never see on a postcard. No majestic mountains, no improbably green pastures—just a bland tangle of shopping malls and suburbia. I follow a dead-end street, past a rubber plant, a roofing company, a drainage service, and a plastics manufacturer, until I reach a white building behind a chain-link fence. Inside is a kernel of a nation within a nation—a sneak preview of what a climate change exodus looks like.

This is the Tuvalu Christian Church, the heart of a migrant community from what may be the first country to be rendered unlivable by global warming. Tuvalu is the fourth-smallest nation on Earth: six coral atolls and three reef islands flung across 500,000 square miles of ocean, about halfway between Australia and Hawaii. It has few natural resources to export and no economy to speak of; its gross domestic product relies heavily on the sale of its desirable Internet domain suffix, which is .tv, and a modest trade in collectible stamps. Tuvalu's total land area is just 16 square miles, of which the highest point stands 16 feet above the waterline. Tuvaluans, who have a high per-capita incidence of good humor, refer to the spot as "Mount Howard," after the former Australian prime minister who refused to ratify the Kyoto Protocol.

The Intergovernmental Panel on Climate Change has warned that low-lying island nations are particularly endangered by rising seas and will also be buffeted by more frequent and more violent storms. Already, warmer ocean temperatures are eating away at the coral reefs that form Tuvalu's archipelagic spine. Tuvaluans themselves point to more tangible indicators of trouble—the "king tides" that increasingly sluice their homes, the briny water oozing up into the "grow pits" where they used to cultivate taro and other vegetables. As Julia Whitty predicted in this magazine in 2003, the prognosis has become sufficiently dire that the residents of Tuvalu and other low-lying atoll islands "are beginning to envision the wholesale abandonment of their nations." Around one-fifth of the 12,000-some inhabitants have already left, most bound for New Zealand, where the Tuvaluan community has nearly tripled since 1996.

From *Mother Jones* (November/December 2009). Copyright © 2009 by Foundation for National Progress. Reprinted with permission. All rights reserved.

Inside the church I find a vibrant scene, suggesting both the resilience of Tuvaluan culture and its ability to adapt. Rows of green plastic chairs are filled with several hundred chattering churchgoers, some in traditional lavalavas—vivid cotton skirts emblazoned with flowers—others in Western dresses and suits. A border of bright blue, yellow, and pink stars rings the upper walls—in Tuvalu these might be constructed from frangipani blossoms, but here they are woven from the plastic bands used to tether shipping cargo. As soon as I sit down, a young man in a dapper dark suit strikes up a conversation. He came here in 1997, is making good money, and hasn't been home once. "You may have heard the news about Tuvalu—with global warming, the sea is rising," he says cheerfully. "So better we come here to be safe." Tuvaluans, resigned to fielding reporters' questions about their homeland's impending doom, often offer observations like this unprompted.

After the service, the congregation drifts outside to the gravelly yard, where a group of visitors from the islands is reenacting the crucifixion of Christ on a make-shift stage draped with threadbare astroturf. Reverend Elisala Selu, a thoughtful, soft-spoken man who has worked second jobs to avoid burdening his congregants, explains that Tuvaluan politicians are reluctant to encourage the mass evacuation of their voting base, and so the church, wanting people to be prepared, has taken matters into its own hands. It instructs followers not to assume that, like Noah, they will be delivered by God from the rising waters, and hosts groups of congregants who visit New Zealand to see if they might like to relocate here. But, Selu confides, life in New Zealand isn't always easy. The Tuvaluans are one of the country's poorest, communities. Just over half the adults have found work; the median income is about $17,000 for men, $10,000 for women. There are those here illegally—overstayers, in Pacific parlance—who struggle to make ends meet; Tuvaluans on the run from debt collectors after buying cars on shady financing schemes; children left unattended for long hours because their parents work multiple jobs as cleaners or laborers or farmworkers. Then there's the jarring adjustment to urban Auckland from a place where most citizens don't pay rent or buy food, but sleep on grass mats beside the road on warm nights, go fishing or pick breadfruit when they're hungry, and where, as one jovial Tuvaluan remarked to me, "the only crime is cycling in the night without a torch [flashlight]." Selu frets about the new generation of Tuvaluan children born in New Zealand. "We try to run away from the sea rise in Tuvalu, but this is another sea-level rise," he says with a wry smile. "The next generation gets caught by two cultures. Before Tuvalu sinks physically, our identity might sink in a foreign country."

Tuvalu and other low-lying island countries like Kiribati and the Maldives are, in one sense, the starkest example of how climate change will reshape the world. But Auckland's Tuvaluan community also represents a best-case scenario—so far their migration has been orderly, and their numbers are minuscule compared with the millions of impoverished people who live in global warming hot spots like Africa's Sahel, coastal Bangladesh, and Vietnam's deltas. Koko Warner, an expert on climate change and migration at the United Nations University in Bonn, says the displacement of those populations could be "a phenomenon of a scope not experienced in human history."

Yet little has been done to prepare. In fact, our understanding of exactly how global warming will affect people—how many lives will be threatened, and what we could do to avert a succession of humanitarian disasters—remains extremely rudimentary. As Bill Gates has caustically observed, "It is interesting how often the impact of climate change is illustrated by talking about the problems the polar bears will face rather than the much greater number of poor people who will die unless significant investments are made to help them."

In June [2009], I traveled to the verdant, secluded campus of Columbia University's Earth Institute, near the New York Palisades, to find out how global warming will reconfigure the world's political geography. Earth Institute scientists, along with researchers from the United Nations University, have conducted a global study to chart how environmental change will affect vulnerable populations.

Alex de Sherbinin, one of the project's lead researchers, explained that the investigation was prompted by the realization that existing data about how many people could be uprooted by climate change had been "essentially grabbed from thin air." The most commonly cited factoid, which pops up even in authoritative sources like the British government's Stern Review on climate change, predicts 200 million "environmental refugees" by 2050—1 in every 34 people on Earth. But even the scholar who produced that number—Norman Myers, an Oxford ecologist—concedes that it required some "heroic extrapolations." None of the existing figures uses a vetted scientific methodology, and most rely instead on crude estimations, like choosing the most sensitive regions and assuming that every single inhabitant will have to leave.

De Sherbinin's project takes a more fine-grained approach. "We found that livelihood would be the main factor in how people decide to stay or go," he explained. The aim is to connect hard scientific data about glacier melt, precipitation, drought, and sea rise with knowledge of how people interact with their environment, obtained through extensive field interviews. The fieldwork is used to figure out whether there are ways to help, say, a farmer remain on his land as rainfall declines, or whether he will need to relocate to survive.

De Sherbinin gave me a quick tour of the world's prospective disaster zones by way of his laptop. He brought up a map of Tuvalu's main island of Funafuti, rendered in such detail that you could see which houses will be submerged if the sea rises by three feet. Then, the Ganges delta region of Bangladesh and India, home to 144 million people. Variegated red patches indicated population density—overlapping some of the deepest red spots were blue blotches marking the places most likely to be lost to flooding. Next: Vietnam, which de Sherbinin says is likely to lose more agricultural land (especially in the Mekong delta) to sea-level rise than any other country. Blue streaks—signifying a 6.6-foot rise—on the high end of what scientists think is possible—erased land inhabited by 14 million people. Finally, a map of the Sahel region of West Africa, where nearly half the population survives on subsistence farming, and where rainfall is projected to decline severely. Overall, the number of Africans facing water shortages is expected to double by 2050.

"For a lot of these places, prospects don't look too good—I don't want to suggest easy solutions," de Sherbinin said. But some people, he argued, have options. In

Africa, he pointed out, while desertification is a grave problem, much of the continent lacks water capture and storage systems. "There's a potential to do much more. If these countries had the wherewithal—most of them don't—they could develop in irrigation."

I heard a similar argument from Paul Kench, a geomorphologist at the University of Auckland and an expert on atoll islands. Kench looked like someone who spends a lot of time on beaches—shorts, sandals, sandy hair, golden tan. He argued that many climate scientists draw overly broad conclusions from abstract data about sea-level rise without observing the precise ways that oceanic change affects particular places. Like many New Zealanders, he has a relentlessly practical streak, and he insisted that many residents of Tuvalu and other imperiled countries could actually stay put, if only people would pay proper attention to the science.

Using data from Tuvalu, the Maldives, and Kiribati, Kench and his coauthor, Peter Cowell, are creating computer models visualizing what will happen as the sea rises. "What we've been unable to do is totally destroy an island," he said. Instead, he explained, as waves wash over these narrow slivers of land, they reshape their contours. On some islands, rising seas lifted sand from the beach and deposited it farther inland, steepening the island's plane and raising its highest point. In Tuvalu, storms shaved rubble off the reefs and welded it to nearby islands, building new outer layers "like onion skins." On other islands, seasonal tides shuffled sand from one side to another, so that in January the eastern part of the island might grow, only to recede in July as the western side extended.

Kench argued that in many Pacific atoll nations, people are clustered densely in the islands' most fragile places (in turn creating man-made environmental strains that amplify the effects of climate change). "With some careful planning, you could identify safe places to live. You could identify islands more sensitive to change than others, ones that can take more people than others. There's lots of quite sensible things we could do." The Maldives has invited Kench to research such possibilities. (Keeping its options open, the government is also considering buying land in Australia.) Right now, Kench said, in most low-lying island nations there's almost "no information to base decisions on"—even on basic questions like the relationship of valuable resources to the waterline. "That reads like stamp collecting—cataloging environmental resources and processes. But it gives you great power to make sensible decisions."

Kench's vision was appealing—the idea of a people joining hands with science and orienting their lives even more intimately around the rhythms of their environment. But it was hard to envision anyone enacting the kind of exquisitely calibrated resettlement plan that he had in mind—either local governments, starved for cash and expertise, or institutions like the World Bank, which tends to react to environmental fragility by pouring concrete. And redistributing Tuvalu's population more wisely couldn't safeguard against the projected increase of ferocious storms, the erosion of coral, or salinization of the islands' scarce arable soil.

Yet because a certain amount of environmental change is locked in no matter what negotiators at Copenhagen decide, Kench's type of thinking is sorely needed.

Thomas Fingar, the former chairman of the National Intelligence Council, conducted an assessment of the national security implications of climate change in 2008. "The international system needs to think about this, whether it's prepositioning water, tents, and so on, developing assistance programs," Fingar told me. Instead, he noted drily, when he delivered his analysis to the House committees on intelligence and global warming, it got "overshadowed by a debate over whether this topic was incredibly important or incredibly stupid." He added, "Shouldn't we start thinking about coping strategies? Stop ringing the damn alarm bell and go buy some buckets." The Obama administration is turning to these questions, but it's playing catch-up for years of lost time.

The United Nations Development Programme estimates that $86 billion will need to be spent annually by 2015 to help developing countries adapt to the effects of global warming. The UN has launched a fund for this purpose, but it has only collected $100 million so far. What's more, rich countries commonly use so-called adaptation funds as a bargaining tool to push for lower emissions from the industrializing countries of the developing world. Thus the fate of Tuvalu, which generates a tiny fraction of the world's greenhouse gases—and aims to be carbon neutral by 2020—is held hostage by the 4.3 percent produced by India, the fourth-largest emitter. "Doing a deal in Copenhagen is, to an important extent, about engaging developing countries," Yvo de Boer, the UN's top climate change official, has said. "And an important part of engaging countries is providing funds."

Even some environmental and humanitarian groups have been wary of the topic, believing that shifting the conversation to seawalls and water storage will undercut political momentum for cutting emissions. "There has been an unwitting conspiracy between strong advocates for doing something to prevent the consequences of climate change and those who deny that climate change is a problem," L. Craig Johnstone, the UN's deputy high commissioner for refugees, told me. "The one is fearful that if adaptation and disaster response are seen as the answer, people will stop trying to do anything about global warming. The others think it's all nonsense."

As a result, the notion of either adapting to climate change or migrating because of it barely figures on the agenda at international climate talks. Johnstone remarked that he was proud to have "broken new ground" by simply chairing a meeting on the subject at climate talks in Poland late last year. "A lot of times people say, 'It's interesting but we don't know how to cope with this,'" says Warner of the United Nations University. "Does it belong in Copenhagen? Or is it something different?"

Tuvaluans, meanwhile, lack the luxury of procrastinating over existential questions such as, When does a nation cease to be a nation? Can you maintain a government, let alone an identity, if your land can no longer be inhabited?

Mose Saitala has thought a lot about such dilemmas. He was the Tuvaluan secretary of finance in the 1990s, when the government became convinced that its country could disappear in 50 years. It even considered moving people to 2,000 acres of land that Tuvaluans had contemplated acquiring in Fiji, until a coup and ethnic tensions made the plan unpalatable.

Today, the genial Saitala lives in Auckland, where he helps to run a finance company that serves Pacific Islanders. When we met, I expected him to advocate for New Zealand to open its doors to more Tuvaluan migrants. (New Zealand has only allocated them 75 slots annually in a visa program for Pacific workers.) But Saitala had a more creative proposition in mind. "Tuvalu has a lot of resources—100 million in reserves," he mused. "They can easily buy a place that 10,000 people can fit into. Vanuatu, Solomons, and Papua New Guinea all have uninhabited islands. For me, I would prefer a big island off Australia, like the Norfolk Islands." In his mind, the major obstacles were legal and political ones: Could Tuvalu still earn money from fishing rights in its territorial waters if its people moved elsewhere? Would another country allow Tuvalu to remain an independent entity within its boundaries, perhaps a protectorate? And, after spending much of its savings buying a new homeland, would Tuvalu's government still be able to provide services to its people?

In numerous ways, climate change will unsettle laws and institutions shaped by the crises of a different era. The existing international system grew from the upheavals of World War II, crafted to react to violent conflicts whose existence is obvious and whose victims are reasonably easy to identify. But people displaced by environmental change fall through the cracks of that system. Refugee law only covers those who have been driven from their homeland for political reasons; because resources for such exiles are already strained, there is enormous resistance to broadening the definition. The apolitical, indeterminate effects of climate change, which require action in advance, not after the fact, may be beyond what the existing humanitarian regime can handle.

If we don't prepare, warns Walter Kälin, the UN secretary-general's representative on the human rights of internally displaced persons, "people from islands and territories will start to migrate, legally or with an irregular situation, and overall the society will slowly disintegrate. For a certain time there will be a government, but it will be a fiction. It will be a slow process of whole nations dying in the social sense in addition to the geographical sense."

On my last Saturday in Auckland, I return to the church. Tuvalu's prime minister, Apisai Ielemia, is visiting New Zealand, and he's convened a meeting with his Auckland compatriots. A small group of Tuvaluans, mostly older adults this time, files into the hall wearing formal clothing and bearing the obligatory plates of food—an easy tradition in a place where anyone can fish for free, but one the poor among Auckland's Tuvaluans struggle to maintain. Ielemia makes a brief speech and asks the attendees to voice their concerns, and after a while, the conversation inevitably turns to climate change. Ielemia deflects queries with a smile, explaining that there is no official policy to relocate more Tuvaluans. The group isn't satisfied. A short, energetic woman dressed in Lycra shorts under a denim skirt stands up and lets out an exasperated tirade in Tuvaluan and English. "When something happens, we should have a plan in place so that people know what to expect, instead of just reacting. What is the plan?" she demands. "What is the plan?" So far, no one seems to have an answer.

# Where Will We Live?

By Michael Le Page, Jeff Hecht, and Richard Fisher
*New Scientist*, March 3, 2012

Fishing boats in the North Sea bring up some strange things in their nets, from the bones of mammoths to ancient stone tools and weapons. Here and in many other places around the world, we are discovering the remains of human settlements on what is now the seabed. As the world changed after the last ice age, many of our ancestors were forced to abandon their homes. And over the next 1000 years, let alone 100,000, the world is going to change dramatically again, forcing billions of people to find a new place to live.

Some places would battle to survive even if sea level remained constant. The ancient Egyptian city of Herakleion disappeared beneath the Mediterranean Sea 2000 years ago as the soft sands of the delta it was built on subsided, and the same is happening to modern cities such as New Orleans and Shanghai. In Miami and elsewhere, seas and rivers are eroding the land that cities are built on.

With a stable climate, it might be possible to save cities like these. But as the world continues to warm, rising sea levels are going to drown many of our coastal cities, along with much farmland. The changing climate will also affect people living well above sea level, making some areas uninhabitable but creating new opportunities elsewhere.

We don't know exactly how much hotter the world will become. But let's suppose events follow the Intergovernmental Panel on Climate Change's "business as usual" scenario, with greenhouse emissions continuing to grow until 2100 and then declining rapidly. Suppose, too, that we do not attempt any kind of geoengineering.

The most likely result is that the average global temperature will rise nearly 4°C above the pre-industrial level around the year 2100, peaking at 5°C sometime in the 23rd century (though it might well get a lot hotter than this). It will stay hot, too, as it will take 3000 years or so for the planet to cool just 1°C.

That might mean that the Greenland ice sheet will be almost gone in 1000 years, with the West Antarctic ice sheet following it into the sea, raising its level by well over 10 meters. That's bad news given that coastal regions are home to much of the world's population, including many rapidly growing megacities. As the sea level rises, billions of people will be displaced.

At least this will likely be a gradual process, though there may be occasional catastrophes when storm surges overcome flood defenses. Large areas of Florida, the East and Gulf coasts of the US, the Netherlands and the UK will eventually be

From *New Scientist* 213.2854 (3 March 2012): 41–42. Copyright © 2012 by Reed Business Information Limited. Reprinted with permission. All rights reserved.

inundated. Some island nations will simply cease to exist and many of the world's greatest cities, including London, New York and Tokyo, will be partly or entirely lost beneath the waves.

And as the great ice sheet of East Antarctica slowly melts, the sea will rise even higher. For each 1°C increase in temperature, sea level could eventually rise by 5 to 20 meters. So in 5000 years' time, the sea could be well over 40 meters higher than today.

Even those living well above sea level may be forced to move. Some regions, including parts of the southern US, may become too dry to support farming or large cities. In other areas, flooding may drive people out.

Any further warming will cause catastrophic problems. A 7°C global rise will make some tropical regions so hot and humid that humans will not be able to survive without air conditioning. If the world warms by 11°C, much of the eastern US, China, Australia and South America, and the entire Indian subcontinent, will become uninhabitable.

Yet the future will open up alternative places to live. In the far north, what is now barren tundra and taiga could become fertile farmland. New land will also appear as the ice sheets melt.

A rush to exploit the resources in newly exposed bedrock in Antarctica, for instance, could encourage settlement in its coastal regions. If it stays hot enough for long enough, Antarctica will once again be a lush green continent covered in forests. Elsewhere, pockets of fresh land will rise out of the ocean in the space of hundreds of thousands of years, perhaps ripe for human settlement.

At some point our descendants could take control of the global climate. But it will take thousands of years to restore the ice sheets and get sea levels back down. By the time we are in a position to do so, some people may like life just as it is. The proud citizens of the Republic of Antarctica will fight any measure that would lead to their farms and cities being crushed by ice.

# The Rising Tide:
# Environmental Refugees

By Andrew Lam
*New America Media*, August 15, 2012

The modern world has long thought of refugees in strictly political terms, victims in a world riven by competing ideologies. But as climate change continues unabated, there is a growing population of displaced men, women and children whose homes have been rendered unlivable thanks to a wide spectrum of environmental disasters.

Despite their numbers, and their need, most nations refuse to recognize their status.

The 1951 U.N. Convention Relating to the Status of Refugees defines a refugee as a person with a genuine fear of being persecuted for membership in a particular social group or class. The environmental refugee—not necessarily persecuted, yet necessarily forced to flee—falls outside this definition.

## Not Recognized, Not Counted

Where the forest used to be, torrential rains bring barren hills of mud down on villages. Crops wither in the parched earth. Animals die. Melting glaciers and a rising sea swallow islands and low-lying nations, flooding rice fields with salt water. Factories spew toxic chemicals into rivers and oceans, killing fish and the livelihood of generations.

So people flee. Many become internally displaced, others cross any and all borders in order to survive.

Experts at last year's American Association for the Advancement of Science (AAAS) estimated their numbers would reach 50 million by 2020, due to factors such as agricultural disruption, deforestation, coastal flooding, shoreline erosion, industrial accidents and pollution.

Others say the figure will triple to 150 million by 2050.

Today, it is believed that the population of environmentally displaced has already far outstripped the number of political refugees worldwide, which according to the United Nations High Commissioner on Refugees (UNHCR) is currently at around 10.2 million.

In 1999 the International Red Cross reported some 25 million people displaced by environmental disasters. In 2009 the UNHCR estimated that number to be 36 million, 20 million of whom were listed as victims of climate change-related issues.

From *New America Media* (15 August 2012). Copyright © 2012 by *New America Media*. Reprinted with permission. All rights reserved.

More accurate statistics, however, are hard to come by.

Because the term "environmental refugee" has not been officially recognized, many countries have not bothered to count them, especially if the population is internally displaced. Other countries consider them migrants, and often undocumented immigrants, and therefore beyond the protection granted refugees.

Another factor obscuring the true scope of the population is the fact that their numbers can rise quite suddenly—such as after the Fukushima nuclear disaster last year, or Haiti's 2010 earthquake, which in a matter of hours displaced more than 3 million people.

## A "Hidden Crisis" No More

Two decades ago, noted ecologist Norman Myers predicted that humanity was slowly heading toward a "hidden crisis" in which ecosystems would fail to sustain their inhabitants, forcing people off the land to seek shelter elsewhere. With hurricanes Katrina and Rita, that crisis became painfully obvious.

Along with images of hundreds of thousands of displaced Americans scurrying across the richest nation on Earth searching for new homes came an awareness that no matter how wealthy or powerful, no country is impervious to the threat of climate related catastrophe.

Indeed, being displaced by natural disasters may very well become the central epic of the 21st century. Kiribati, the Maldives and Tuvalu are disappearing as we speak, as the sea level continues to rise. The World Bank estimates that with a 1 meter rise in sea level Bangladesh—with a population of 140 million—would lose 17.5 percent of its land mass and along with it river bank erosion, salinity intrusion, flood, damage to infrastructures, crop failure, destruction of fisheries, and loss of biodiversity.

Those that have already fled the country to neighboring India—largely because of flooding—face lives of immense misery and discrimination.

China, in particular, is a hot spot of environmental disasters as it buckles under unsustainable development, giving rise to rapid air pollution and toxic rivers. Alongside desertification, these man-made catastrophes have already left millions displaced.

John Liu, director of the Environmental Education Media Project, spent 25 years in China and witnessed the disasters there. He offered the world this unapologetic, four-alarm warning some years ago: "Every ecosystem on the planet is under threat of catastrophic collapse, and if we don't begin to acknowledge and solve them, then we will go down."

## Growing Numbers, Fewer Alternatives

When President Obama granted temporary protected status (TPS) to undocumented Haitians living in the United States in the aftermath of the earthquake in Haiti, it was a step in the right direction. After all, repatriating them back to an impoverished nation devastated by one of the worst-ever recorded disasters would be immoral at best, and at worst, a crime against humanity.

Sadly, such actions are rare and when they do come, they manage to address barely a fraction of the pressing legal and humanitarian needs of the growing population. What solutions do exist, experts agree, must recognize that the needs of environmental refugees are one and the same as those of our planet.

Policies toward climate refugees should therefore include issues of reforestation, re-habilitating degraded land and soils, and desalination of low coastal areas. And the International Court of Justice should also step up its efforts to prosecute those responsible for man-made environmental disasters such as illegal mining, deforestation and dumping of toxic waste.

"One of the marks of a global civilization is the extent to which we begin to conceive of whole-system problems and whole-system responses to those problems," noted political scientist Walt Anderson in his book *All Connected Now.*

"Events occurring in one part of the world," he argued, "are viewed as a matter of concern for the whole world in general and lead to an attempt at collective solutions."

Whether humanity can move toward that vision depends largely on how it responds to the central issue of our time.

"A rising tide lifts all boats." But in the age of melting glaciers, that tide is an ominous threat driving more refugees to flee and, if ignored, swallowing humanity itself.

# Environmental Refugees Growing in Numbers without Real Solution

By Trisha Marczak
*Mint Press News,* August 21, 2012

When the earthquake hit Haiti in 2010, it left more than 3 million people displaced, without a hope for escape. They were, for all intents and purposes, refugees.

Yet, under international law and guidelines, those very people who had lost their homes, with no hope of return, didn't meet the necessary criteria. The label "refugee" is given only to those fleeing from religious or political persecution—their situation must be caused by the direct destruction at the hand of man.

The 1951 United Nations Convention Relating to the Status of Refugees clearly defined those who fit under the category of refugee, a necessary label in order to apply for asylum in a signatory country. In this definition, a refugee is a person who is outside of his or her country and has a "well-founded" fear that, if they were to return, would face prosecution due to their religion, nationality or race.

The U.S. accepts more refugees every year than any other nation. In 2009, 60,190 refugees were resettled in America. Second to that is Canada, where that same year 10,800 refugees settled. The number of "environmental refugees" accepted that year? Zero.

Despite millions around the world who have been forced out of their homes because of environmental and climate disasters, they're not recognized as the refugees they have ultimately become. The issue surrounding the environmental refugee is not likely to go away anytime soon. According to the American Association for the Advancement of Science (AAAS), the world will see 50 million environmental refugees by 2020.

Addressing this growing phenomenon, Professor Norman Myers of Oxford University in 2005 spoke on the issue at an economic forum in Prague, highlighting the main causes of the upward trend: drought, soil erosion, desertification and deforestation.

"In their desperation, these people feel they have no alternative but to seek sanctuary elsewhere, however hazardous the attempt," Myers writes. "Not all of them have fled their countries, many being internally displaced. But all have abandoned their homelands on a semi-permanent if not permanent basis, with little hope of a foreseeable return."

From *Mint Press News* (21 August 2012). Copyright © 2012 by *Mint Press News.* Reprinted with permission. All rights reserved.

The question now is, with an increasingly dangerous threat of weather-related disasters in the world, should governments come together, as they did in the past, and draft legislation that would apply to those who are considered to be environmental refugees?

## An Environmental Refugee?

When you hear the word "refugee," an image instantly comes to mind—a malnourished, lost soul seeking political asylum and living in cramped quarters in a refugee camp. The word typically doesn't elicit images of people living in Western countries, displaced from their homes due to environmental disasters, as was the case with Hurricane Katrina.

When Hurricane Katrina hit in 2005, there was controversy over what to call those who were displaced. While they were clearly driven from their homes, with no chance of immediate return, the use of the word "refugee" was not accepted by those who pointed out the people of New Orleans, Louisiana, did not fit the U.N. description. Some even claimed using the term, as the Associated Press did, was racist, including the Rev. Jesse Jackson.

The issue of environmental refugees isn't exactly new. In 1995, there were a recorded 25 million people who fit the definition. That's compared to 27 refugees who were displaced because of religious, political and ethnic persecution, according to Myers' research. And the numbers are growing each year.

Myers points out that many of the recorded refugees were originally located in the Sub-Saharian portions of Africa. China, however, could also have been considered responsible for 6 million environmental refugees, many of whom fell victim to population rises that threatened their farmlands and agricultural plots.

Perhaps not a natural disaster, research accounts for roughly 1 million displaced people from public works projects, including large dams, taking place much of the time in China and India. And with growing accounts of extreme weather arguably related to climate change, the numbers are expected to grow.

## Recognizing the Plight

Shortly after the 2010 earthquake in Haiti, U.S. President Barack Obama issued a temporary protected status for Haitians living illegally in the United States. It wasn't necessarily refugee status, as it applied to those already living illegally in the U.S., but it did recognize that sending them home—at least within 18 months—wasn't a viable option.

While Obama signed the order, the decision didn't start with him. The Conference of Roman Catholic Bishops petitioned the administration, along with 80 Republican and Democratic congressmen, according to the *New York Times*.

The horrific nature of the hurricane touched the hearts of most Americans, as images poured out from the region, prompting action. The people who fell victim to that natural disaster were in the hearts and minds of people throughout the world just as much as any political refugee, perhaps more so. And while there were efforts from relief agencies, like UNHCR, to assist, those who were displaced from their homes with nowhere to turn were not provided an opportunity for asylum elsewhere. Had their grief been caused by humans, however, they'd have a way out.

As early as 2001, the United Nations Refugee Agency (UNHCR) released a paper, written by Richard Black of the University of Sussex, in which it addressed the issue of environmental refugees and the solutions needed to address what, even at the time, was expected to be a growing problem.

In his paper, Black addresses refugees from rising seas, relating to those migrants who are displaced due to "more dramatic and permanent changes to the environment associated with catastrophic events such as floods, volcanoes and earthquakes."

Black then goes on to address the issue of "human-induced environmental degradation," which he describes as situations caused by a failure to undertake good environmental management and sustainable development. Concluding his argument, Black states that in order for the world to make a decision regarding recognition of environmental refugees, a clear definition must be met—something he considers to be a contested process in and of itself.

Though written in 2001, Black's findings are significant now. Recently, the discussion regarding climate change hasn't so much been whether or not it exists, but what causes it—man-made or natural cycles. The world, for the most part, knows that it's coming. Now, many more scientists are linking catastrophic natural disasters with rising global temperatures.

If anything else, the world knows from this that the issue of "environmental refugees" isn't going away anytime soon. And if serious about the issue, it's one that must be addressed within the United Nations.

Black referred in 2001 to the issue as one of great importance for policy-makers at the international level. It's yet to be seen if any of the U.N.'s superpowers will step forward with some sort of proposal. However, with a global budget crisis and issue of illegal immigration front and center in Europe and the U.S., it's not the most promising of climate for those who are now suffering from climate change disasters, searching for hope outside of everything they've ever known.

# Kiribati and the Impending Climate Refugee Crisis

By Sandi Keane
*Independent Australia*, December 3, 2013

*The New Zealand courts have refused to grant asylum to a "climate refugee" from the Pacific island of Kiribati. But as Sandi Keane reports, the underlying problem is set to increase to a stupendous scale.*

Last week, the High Court of New Zealand delivered a blow to a largely ignored asylum seeker problem that has been quietly bleeding and threatening to hemorrhage into a full-scale global catastrophe within two or three decades.

A 37-year-old man from the tiny, obscure nation of Kiribati, Ioane Teitiota, stood to make history as the world's first climate refugee. He argued that global warming is a form of persecution and that those displaced by its effects should be recognized under the UN's Refugee Convention.

However, in his judgment, Justice John Priestley said it was not the High Court's place to alter the scope of the Refugee Convention by granting Mr. Teitiota's leave for appeal. The judge said the enormity and scale of the problem was a fundamental reason for his decision:

> On a broad level, were they to succeed and be adopted in other jurisdictions, at a stroke, millions of people who are facing medium-term economic deprivation, or the immediate consequences of natural disasters or warfare, or indeed presumptive hardships caused by climate change, would be entitled to protection under the Refugee Convention.

Although he has lived in New Zealand since 2007, the government has refused Mr. Teitiota and his family asylum based on the current convention which was drawn up more than 50 years ago, before rising seas started threatening the 33 low-lying equatorial islands and atolls that make up the tiny nation, just under 4,000 kilometres north-east of Brisbane.

The situation is now so dire there is no room left to bury the dead on some of the islands, let alone provide a home for the living. They are being encouraged to leave by their President, Anote Tong, who described his policy of orderly evacuation at the UN General Assembly in September as "migration with dignity."

From *Independent Australia* (3 December 2013). Copyright © 2013 by *Independent Australia*. Reprinted with permission. All rights reserved.

Fresh water—a basic human right—is the main problem. *Bloomberg Business Week* reported last week that fresh water supplies would run out before the rising seas fully submerge Kiribati.

Although aid agencies around the world have been warning governments for years about the coming tsunami of "climate refugees", the world is unprepared for Mr. Teitiota and his kind.

According to Steve Trent, chief executive of the London-based Environment Justice Foundation (EJF), governments are in denial about the effects of rising seas despite sobering statistics. The EJF, an international non-profit environment and human rights organization, has been lobbying governments and politicians for a new agreement on environmental refugees.

The EJF said that climate refugees already outnumber those people fleeing persecution by three-to-one and predicts that the number of climate refugees could climb to 150 million by 2050.

Bangladesh, one of the worst to be affected by rising seas, will be looking to house a population that already numbers 155 million. The Indian government has moved in anticipation of potential cross-border migration, erecting a 4,000 kilometre barbed-wire fence, patrolled by guards.

Mr. Trent says global policymakers can no longer ignore the plight of such vulnerable populations—estimated to be between 500 and 600 million people.

The former Victorian state Labor Minister, Tom Roper, who is now a board member of the Washington-based Climate Institute, said that a number of organizations are pushing strongly for an amended treaty to include climate refugees.

The EJF, on the other hand, believes a new legal instrument would be a more successful option as this would overcome political opposition to opening up the Geneva convention.

Following EJF's recent address to the European Parliament on a proposed alternative framework, Steve Trent reported that studies were now underway to scope out this issue. But policy is lagging well behind the pace of events, said Mr. Roper:

> It is not just sea level rise but extreme events such as droughts and floods will have a huge displacement effect as well. Entire African nations could be destroyed by desertification and droughts.

Of concern most to Australia, as a member of the Asia Pacific Forum, are its overcrowded near-neighbors Kiribati and Tuvalu. The Kiribati government is hoping to buy 2,500 hectares on Vanua Levu from the Fijian government as a potential new home for some of its 100,000-plus residents.

Tuvalu, whose capital Tarawa has more people per square kilometer than London, situated midway between Hawaii and Australia, has three times the population density of the United States. Coastal erosion has accelerated and its food and water supply is already under threat.

But neither the Australian government nor Federal Opposition appear to have any plans to deal with the building crisis in the Pacific and neither Immigration

Minister Scott Morrison nor opposition immigration spokesperson Richard Marles returned *IA*'s calls.

In April this year, the Refugee Council of Australia advised the Gillard government that it should create a new migration category for those fleeing the effects of climate change.

Yet only the Greens insist that Australia, as a major greenhouse gas emitter, should be prepared to play its part. The party's spokesperson for immigration, Senator Sarah Hanson-Young, believes the situation is urgent:

> Climate change will result in the displacement of people, creating environmental refugees and intensifying the threat of regional and global conflict. Introducing a special category of visa to take into account the worsening effects of climate change is an essential step.

EJF's Mr. Trent describes the coming crisis as a " . . . collective hot issue—one of fundamental justice and human rights."

Australia could easily resettle its near-neighbors, but he points to Bangladesh as a looming disaster: "Bangladesh will submerge and, just this morning, the BBC reported that Bangkok would go under by 2030. There is a moral obligation when the fifth-least developed country, that contributed less than 1 percent of $CO_2$, is in the frontline to be impacted first by climate change."

The EJF and Climate Institute were keenly awaiting the New Zealand decision, hoping it would set a precedent.

Mr. Teitiota's lawyer, Michael Kidd, said he will appeal the case all the way to the country's Supreme Court. He expressed surprise that Mr. Teitiota's children had been completely ignored in his original claim for asylum.

Inspired by a similarly novel argument used in Australia's historical Mabo case, in which the International Convention on the Elimination of all forms of Racial Discrimination was a reference point in a decision that granted native title to Australian Aborigines, Mr. Teitiota will appeal under UN Convention on the Rights of the Child. He will argue that sending three children, all under age six, back to Kiribati would subject them to dangerous conditions such as dwindling fresh water:

> We have quite good grounds for appeal. The UN Convention on the Rights of the Child and the Kyoto Protocol itself all influence domestic law and have to be included in the mix. Courts don't have to stick to black letter law. These arguments won't go away. They aren't just academic constructs. These are real arguments, particularly as the Immigration and Protection Tribunal completely ignored Mr. Teitiota's children and the effect on them.

The EJF has been arguing for some time that climate change should be seen through a human rights lens. Steve Trent wants to encourage policy makers globally to accept responsibility for having created the very carbon emissions that now threaten those least likely to survive global warming.

The unfolding tragedy in the Pacific was being ignored by the media. He added: "Fresh water is a basic human right . . . fingers crossed Kidd is still able to win this one."

# Threatened by Rising Seas, Small Island Nations Appeal for More Aid at UN

*UN News Centre*, September 25, 2013

On the front line of damage wrought by climate change, threatened with extinction from rising seas, leaders of some of the world's small island States took to the podium at the United Nations General Assembly today to call urgently for greater international support to mitigate the perils.

"Disastrously off course," "profound disappointment" and "moral failure" were some of the terms used by heads of Small Island Developing States, known as SIDS, to depict their situation as the 68th General Assembly prepares to draw up long-term development plans for the decades after the end in 2015 of the current cycle of the anti-poverty Millennium Development Goals (MDGs).

"The corresponding actions to address the unique and special circumstances of SIDS by the international community has been lacking," the Prime Minister of Antigua and Barbuda, Winston Baldwin Spencer, told the Assembly's annual General Debate, summing up the almost two decades since the Barbados Programme of Action was adopted at a UN conference on the sustainable development of SIDS in 1994.

"It is a recognized fact, but it is worth repeating that small island States contribute the least to the causes of climate change, yet we suffer the most from its effects. Small island States have expressed our profound disappointment at the lack of tangible action," he said referring to efforts in UN climate change talks to protect SIDS and other vulnerable countries.

"Developed countries should shoulder their moral, ethical and historical responsibilities for emitting the levels of anthropogenic greenhouse gases into the atmosphere. It is those actions which have now put the planet in jeopardy and compromised the well-being of present and future generations," the Caribbean leader stressed.

Noting uneven progress in achieving the MDGs, Prime Minister Kamla Persad-Bissessar of Trinidad and Tobago, who is also chairperson of Conference of Heads of State and Government of the Caribbean Community (CARICOM), warned that current approaches will not advance the MDG agenda by 2015 or ensure sustainable development in the post-2015 context.

"SIDS have made significantly less progress in the area of development, than other vulnerable groups of countries. In some cases SIDS are on the front lines of experiencing a reversal of many of the gains that have been achieved," she said.

"Indeed in the preparations for our participation in that upcoming discourse (on the Post-2015 Development Agenda), the recognition of the vulnerabilities of small

From *UN News Centre* (25 September 2013). Copyright © 2013 by UN Publications. Reprinted with permission. All rights reserved.

island developing States is one of the guidelines that CARICOM will apply when considering its commitments to the overall Agenda."

From the other side of the planet, Kiribati President Anote Tong, stressing the "real and existential threat" his low-lying Pacific nation faces from rising seas, called for immediate international action to mitigate climate change and rising sea levels.

"We are disastrously off course. The scientists tell us that calamity awaits—and not just for those of us on low-lying islands," he said. "What we are experiencing now on these low-lying atolls is an early warning of what will happen further down the line. No one will be spared. We cannot continue to abuse our planet in this way. For the future we want for our children and grandchildren, we need leadership.

"We need commitment. And we need action . . . now," he declared, noting that while Kiribati is taking adaptation measures to remain habitable for as long as possible, it is also looking to improve its people's skills to a level where they can compete for jobs in the international labor market with dignity if the rising ocean forces them to migrate.

"All those countries with the ability to do so must contribute to the prevention of this calamity, or be forever judged by history."

Fijian Prime Minister Josaia V. Bainimarama said an international conference next year in Samoa on the sustainable development of SIDS is a critical opportunity for the international community to renew its commitments.

"Not only are SIDS acutely vulnerable to the effects of climate change, such as sea-level rise, ocean acidification and the increased frequency of extreme weather events, but for some of us, the threat is to our very existence," added Commodore Bainimarma, current chairperson of the Group of 77 and China, a bloc of developing States established in 1964 which now comprises more than 130 countries, some two-thirds of the UN membership and over 60 percent of the world's population.

"Our response to the plight of those most at risk must therefore be characterized by a requisite sense of urgency."

President Tommy Remengesau of Palau drew on his own personal experiences and his country's flag—a yellow full moon against a blue ocean that represents nature's balance and harmony through the consistency of the rising and falling tides—to illustrate the depths of the problems stemming from climate change.

"Just before I left for this year's [General Assembly], during a full moon high tide, my back yard, which nestles against the ocean, flooded," he said. "Typhoon Usagi, just a few days later, passed through the Pacific and landed in Asia, killing many people. This was followed almost immediately by Tropical Storm Pabuk.

"Mr. President, when I was a child, my back yard did not flood—and we did not have tropical storm after tropical storm pass through our Pacific islands. It is thereof clear to me and other Pacific leaders that the full moon and the ocean are no longer metaphors for balance and harmony. Today they represent imbalance—from our past excesses."

Stressing that the primary responsibility to reduce greenhouse gasses still rests with the developed nations, he warned: "Our Global Warming doomsday is already set in stone if we fail to act."

President Emanuel Mori of the Federated States of Micronesia underlined the impossibility of separating development and the environment, noting that no country can develop its economy without degrading its natural environment to some significant degree.

"Climate change is, without question, the gravest threat to my people's welfare, livelihoods, and general security," he said. "It is the survival issue of our time. Our sustainable development is threatened by the harmful effects of excessive greenhouse gas emissions in the atmosphere, effects which poison our root crops, destroy our reef systems, and drive many of our people from their ancestral homes.

"All of us, developed and developing countries, have a stake in finding ways that minimize manmade damage to Mother Earth. Only the international community can effectively take up this cause," he added, insisting that the comprehensive climate change treaty to be adopted in 2015 must impose legally binding commitments.

The officials from small island development countries are among a host of leaders set to speak at the annual General Assembly session at which heads of State and Government and other high-level officials will present their views and comments on issues of individual national and international relevance. The debate opened yesterday and concludes on 1 October.

# "Climate Change Refugee" Fighting to Stay in New Zealand, Argues Rising Sea Levels Makes Pacific Island Home Too Dangerous

By Nick Perry
Associated Press, October 1, 2013

A man from one of the lowest-lying nations on Earth is trying to convince New Zealand judges that he's a refugee—suffering not from persecution, but from climate change.

The 37-year-old and his wife left his remote atoll in the Pacific nation of Kiribati six years ago for higher ground and better prospects in New Zealand, where their three children were born. Immigration authorities have twice rejected his argument that rising sea levels make it too dangerous for him and his family to return to Kiribati.

So on Oct. 16, the man's lawyer, Michael Kidd, plans to argue the case before New Zealand's High Court. Kidd, who specializes in human rights cases, told The Associated Press he will appeal the case all the way to the country's Supreme Court if necessary.

Legal experts consider the man's case a long shot, but it will nevertheless be closely watched and might have implications for tens of millions of residents in low-lying islands around the world. Kiribati, an impoverished string of 33 coral atolls about halfway between Hawaii and Australia, has about 103,000 people and has been identified by scientists as among the nation's most vulnerable to climate change.

In a transcript of the immigration case obtained by the AP, the Kiribati man describes extreme high tides known as king tides that he says have started to regularly breach Kiribati's defenses—killing crops, flooding homes and sickening residents. New Zealand immigration laws prevent the AP from naming him.

The man said that around 1998, king tides began regularly breaching the sea walls around his village, which was overcrowded and had no sewerage system. He said the fouled drinking water would make people vomit, and that there was no higher ground that would allow villagers to escape the knee-deep water.

He said returning to the island would endanger the lives of his two youngest children.

"There's no future for us when we go back to Kiribati," he told the tribunal, according to the transcript. "Especially for my children. There's nothing for us there."

The man's lawyer said the family is currently living and working on a New Zealand farm.

From Associated Press (1 October 2013). Copyright © 2013 by Associated Press DBA Press Association. Reprinted with permission. All rights reserved.

Last week, an international panel of climate scientists issued a report saying that it was "extremely likely" that human activity was causing global warming and predicted that oceans could rise by as much as 1 meter (3.3 feet) by the end of the century. If that were to happen, much of Kiribati would simply disappear.

Though that is a dire prospect, New Zealand's Immigration and Protection Tribunal has said it is not one that is addressed by laws dealing with refugees.

In a decision recently made public, tribunal member Bruce Burson said the legal concept of a refugee is someone who is being persecuted, which requires human interaction. He said the tribunal rejected the man's claim because nobody is persecuting him.

The tribunal found there was no evidence that the environmental conditions on Kiribati were so bad that the man and his family would face imminent danger should they return. Burson said the man's claim was also rejected because the family's predicament was no different than that faced by the wider population of Kiribati.

In his court appeal, Kidd said the fact that many people face the same threat is no grounds to dismiss a claim. He also argued that his client did suffer an indirect form of human persecution because climate change is believed to be caused by the pollution humans generate. He said his client also would face the threat of a climate-induced breakdown in law and order should he return.

Bill Hodge, a constitutional law expert and associate professor at the University of Auckland, said he applauded Kidd's "ingenious arguments" but didn't think they would succeed because his client hasn't been singled out and victimized due to something like his gender, race or political persuasion.

But Hodge added that even if the Kiribati man loses, his case might make a good argument for expanding the definition of what constitutes a refugee. He said he expected there would be increasing pressure on nations like New Zealand and Australia to help provide new homes for Pacific Islanders threatened by rising seas.

Tidal gauges indicate the world's oceans have been rising at an annual rate of 3.2 millimeters (0.1 inches) since 1970. Many scientists expect that rate to accelerate and for climate change to trigger more intense storms, which may pose an even more pressing threat to many of the world's low-lying islands.

Kiribati's government is pursuing its own strategies. It has paid a deposit for 6,000 acres in nearby Fiji, which Kiribati President Anote Tong has said will provide food security and a possible refuge for future generations. The nation has also been talking with a Japanese firm about the possibility of constructing a floating island, which would cost billions of dollars.

Rimon Rimon, a Kiribati government spokesman who said his opinions on the matter were his own, said he thought the man in New Zealand was taking the wrong approach. He said the government is working hard to train people in skills like nursing, carpentry and automotive repairs so that if they do leave Kiribati, they can be productive in their adoptive countries.

"Kiribati may be doomed by climate change in the near future," he said. "But just claiming refugee status due to climate change is the easy way out."

# Stop Using the Term "Environmental Refugee"

By Tim Kovach
*Tim Kovach*, May 13, 2013

Grist had an article last week discussing the new book *Overheated: The Human Cost of Climate Change*, from UC Berkeley's Anthony Guzman. In the book, Guzman discusses the potential socio-political consequences of 2°C warming, the threshold that the international community has set as the limit for global warming. Of course, recent research and our current emissions trajectory has us on pace to blow right past that number, but that's for another post.

Anyways, the description of the article intrigued me, so I clicked on the link. In the post, Michael C. Osbourne from Grist describes his reading of the book:

> Some of the scarier parts of the book are about the overabundance of water that's coming our way: 2 degrees warming probably equates to about a one-meter rise in sea level this century. That's enough to displace hundreds of thousands to millions of people in low-lying nations, and, as of now, there is no plan to deal with environmental refugees.

And that's where he lost me. I know that the term "environmental refugee" and its sister term, "climate refugee" have become buzzwords for environmental activists, particularly when we discuss the dire implications of climate change. In addition, they're far from new. Essam El-Hinnawi of the UN Environment Programme (UNEP) coined the term "environmental refugee" in 1985. A number of researchers and activists have bandied the term about to serve their own purposes over the years. Different reports offer a variety of wildly speculative projections on the potential number of people who will be displaced by climate change; they range from 162 million to 1 billion people displaced by 2050.

To put it succinctly, these estimates are, largely, absurd doomsday predictions that ignore the actual research on environmental migration issues. I explore the shortcomings of such projections in my previous research on climate change and national security, so I won't go relitigate the issues here. Instead, I want to point out the inaccuracy of the term "environmental refugee" itself.

The word "refugee" has an internationally recognized legal definition, which emerged from the 1951 *Convention Relating to the Status of Refugees*, the document that established the UN High Commissioner for Refugees. According to this refugee convention, a refugee is a person who:

From *Tim Kovach* (13 May 2013). Copyright © 2013 by *TimKovach.com*. Reprinted with permission. All rights reserved.

owing to well-founded fear of being persecuted for reasons of race, religion, nationality, membership of a particular social group or political opinion, is outside the country
of his nationality and is unable or, owing to such fear, is unwilling to avail himself of
the protection of that country; or who, not having a nationality and being outside the
country of his former habitual residence as a result of such events, is unable or, owing
to such fear, is unwilling to return to it.

People displaced by climatic disasters do not meet this definition. Now, if Guzman
had argued that disasters and climate change are politically constructed phenomena
and that climate change represents the single greatest environmental injustice ever
enacted on the developing world by the developed world, I would be a vocal sup-
porter. I steadfastly hold these beliefs. But that's not the argument here.

Issues surrounding migration and displacement over environmental issues are
highly complex and context-specific. Claiming that an extreme weather event will
inevitably force a poor Bangladeshi to migrate to northeastern India belies evidence
to the contrary and, more importantly, robs this hypothetical individual of his or her
personal agency. And calling people who do flee in the face of environmental stress-
es a refugee strips the term of its incredibly important political and legal weight.

All of this is not to say that people are not forcibly displaced by environmental stress and/or extreme weather events. The work of the Environmental Change
and Forced Migration (EACH-FOR) project demonstrates that environmentally induced migration and displacement are exceedingly pervasive throughout the Global
South. According to the IFRC, roughly 5,000 new people become environmentally
displaced every day. A new report from the Internal Displacement Monitoring Centre suggests that 32.4 million people were displaced by disaster events in 2012, and
some 98% of this displacement was the result of climatic disasters.

The evidence is quite robust that environmental catastrophes displace and/or
force millions of people to migrate from their homes every year. So say that. Environmentally induced migration and environmental displacement are perfectly accurate, forceful terms. I know that "refugee" carries a certain set of connotations
and a clear mandate for action, but climate hawks cannot just claim it for their own
ends. Just as people need to be aware that their actions have consequences for the
environment and the habitability of our planet, we need to learn that our words have
meaning and consequences.

# What Should Be Done about Climate Change Refugees?

By Debra Black
*Toronto Star*, October 11, 2013

*Up to 1 billion people could be displaced by climate change over the next 50 years. But many states, including Canada, prefer not to deal with it.*

A pending court case in New Zealand involving a man from the low-lying island of Kiribati could have profound implications worldwide on the future of migration due to climate change.

The 37-year-old is seeking refugee status, but not because he is being persecuted back home, one of the definitions of a refugee. Rather, he says, flooding and rising sea levels due to climate change are making it too dangerous for him, his wife and three children to return to Kiribati. The island nation, with a population of about 103,000, is made up of 33 coral atolls in the Pacific, half way between Hawaii and Australia.

The case is to go to court on Oct. 16. New Zealand immigration officials have rejected the man's previous claims, and most jurists are betting he'll lose his case in the high court. But his lawyer, Michael Kidd, told The Associated Press he will, if necessary, appeal the case all the way to the Supreme Court.

Whatever the outcome, the legal battle brings attention to a question that academics, researchers, environmentalists, politicians and diplomats have been puzzling over: what, if anything, should be done to aid the projected 200 million to 1 billion people who may be displaced by climate change over the next 50 years?

Simulations, computer models and analyses vary widely as to which cities and regions will be the worst affected. The one thing most analysts agree on, in theory, is that both developed and developing nations need to look at ways to deal with some of the migration or displacement expected because of climate change. Not all of those solutions will involve moves to other countries; they might include increased sustainable development, aid and migration within one's country, experts advise.

But many states, including Canada, would prefer not to deal with the issue at all, says Jose Rivera, senior adviser to the director of international protection at the UNHCR. "There is agreement today that climate change will result in changing weather patterns," he says. "The problem is many states have not taken climate change seriously. They haven't begun to do the forward thinking and planning for populations in harm's way."

From *Toronto Star* (11 October 2013). Copyright © 2013 by Toronto Star Newspapers Ltd. Reprinted with permission. All rights reserved.

That doesn't mean experts haven't been looking at possible solutions. Think-tanks, academics and experts on migration, human rights and the environment have all proposed ideas to deal with the waves of migration that might result from climate change.

Some would like to see a new UN convention to deal with the problem; others want the creation of a new refugee category—climate change refugees. "There are no visas for immigration or refugee status for climate change," explains Rivera. "There is no legal justification for a climate change refugee or climate change immigrant. I love polar bears and we need to worry about the effect on flora and fauna, but hey, who's thinking about human beings in all of this?"

Some believe it is important to allow those who may face displacement to stay home by creating a more sustainable economy and moving them from harm's way internally. While others suggest countries could use regulations within their current immigration laws, such as temporary protection, which the United States did after the Haitian earthquake. Or, as is the case in Canada, humanitarian grounds could be invoked to deal with the waves of displaced migrants due to climate change.

## Carbon Gas Emissions

But "the elephant in the room" in this debate is an international protocol to cut carbon gas emissions worldwide, Rivera says. Many environmentalists worry that in opening up a discussion on the displacement of people, the international focus might shift away from the negotiations to curb emissions.

However, given how much damage has already been done to the environment, mass displacement could be a very real possibility due to flooding or drought. And that needs to be planned for, many argue.

"We know people are going to be forced to leave their homes because of climate change," says Elizabeth Ferris, a senior fellow at the Brookings Institute and co-director of the Brookings-LSE Project on Internal Displacement.

But Ferris acknowledges there's not really a consensus on how many people will be on the move or where they will go. She believes it's critical to strengthen the capacity of local governments in the developing world and local communities in the developed world, such as in Canada's Arctic, to cope.

But even that may be too much. "People are just ignoring it in the United States," says Ferris. She believes the issue of migration due to climate change has slipped on the international agenda. Her sentiments were echoed by one expert, who asked not to be identified. He told the *Star* he was "disheartened" by what he heard at a recent meeting of international officials discussing slow-onset climate change and its impact on people.

Like most other nations, Canada has no separate policy when it comes to the possibility of migration due to climate change.

"Citizenship and Immigration Canada is not actively examining this issue," writes spokesperson Nancy Caron. "We are currently focused on implementing transformational changes to our immigration system to create a fast, flexible and fair system that will meet the new and emerging needs of Canada's labor market and the Canadian economy, while maintaining our traditions of family reunification and responding to current humanitarian needs."

Neither Immigration Minister Chris Alexander nor Foreign Affairs Minister John Baird would comment on the issue.

"Climate change hasn't been a high-profile issue for this government," says Daniel Scott, director of the Interdisciplinary Centre on Climate Change at the University of Waterloo. "All of the countries that are major contributors (to carbon emissions) should be actively engaged . . . Canada should be part of the dialogue to look at how we can support future climate migrants."

Scott and others fear Canada will wait until the United States or the European Union develops a policy. "As the current administration is trying to more closely align border security, passport and immigration policies with the United States," explains Scott, "until they act, it will be one more reason why Canada won't act."

Canada's inaction doesn't surprise Janet Dench, the executive director of the Canadian Council of Refugees. "I don't see any interest in the Canadian government shifting toward a policy that is looking at future international needs," she says. "The decision has been to reorient our immigration policy into what is perceived as Canada's immediate economic needs."

Dench believes Canada has a deeper responsibility to all refugees, including those affected by climate change. "It's important for us to recognize our role and responsibility in the world rather than shutting ourselves off, and environmental change is one of the areas where it's brought home to us. We can't just shut the door on the outside world and only look after ourselves."

But what action Canada and other developed countries should take is still up for grabs in Dench's mind. She falls short of calling for the creation of a separate category of "environmental refugees," suggesting the rights of all migrants should be looked at by governments around the world, rather than just adding another category for those who are forced to flee for environmental reasons.

## Nansen Initiative

Canada isn't alone in sitting on the sidelines. Other countries seem equally reluctant to put policies in place or aren't sure which policies would work. When the UNHCR was celebrating its 60th anniversary in 2011, the issue was brought up. Most signatories to the UN Convention on the Status of Refugees attending that meeting rejected dealing with the issue of climate change migration and displacement head on, agreeing only to "engage in soft dialogue and collect and share experience and practices in handling such displacement."

But out of the ashes of that meeting came an initiative by Norway and Switzerland to look at possible solutions for populations threatened with displacement because of climate change. Mexico, Costa Rica, Bangladesh, Kenya, Germany, Philippines and Australia agreed to come on board.

And in 2012 the Nansen Initiative, named partially in recognition of the first UN High Commissioner for Refugees, Fridtjof Nansen, was born. Over the next two years it is holding consultations in five regions with plans to have a report ready in 2015. Officials are hoping the consultations can kick-start global action.

"The important thing is for all governments to start to think about it, including Canada and Switzerland, my own country," says Walter Kaelin, professor of law at the University of Bern and special envoy for the Nansen Initiative. "Because it is a real challenge and challenges need to be addressed.

"If we're looking at the potential magnitude of the problem, ad hoc answers aren't enough. We need a debate about what would be a good principled approach," Kaelin says.

"We have to talk about climate change migration, forced displacement. We need a kind of tool box. We have to invest in adaptation measures so people can stay longer, prepare people for migration with dignity; invest in training people so they can compete abroad . . . In the past we've had bad experiences with relocation during the colonial period. We have to avoid past mistakes."

Most academics and researchers agree with Kaelin that preparing for possible waves of climate refugees must be multi-faceted.

For Susan Martin, developing adaptation strategies and policies that help people remain where they are, if feasible, is one avenue. Those endeavors would include working on longer-term strategies, such as researching drought-resistant seeds, new farming techniques and reforestation to deal with creeping desertification.

But she also suggests that migration itself is an adaptation strategy that must be planned for. "We tend to see it as a failure of adaptation," says Martin, a professor of international migration and director of the Institute for the Study of International Migration at Georgetown University. "But for millennia people have moved as a positive means to climate change. That's what we want to have happen . . . We don't want people to move because it's too late to do anything else, but in a manner to anticipate where things are going."

For Justin Ginnetti, senior adviser at the International Displacement Monitoring Centre in Geneva, multi-faceted preparation includes computer modeling that identifies the risks to certain populations in the developing world, including simple things such as home construction materials—concrete versus mud—and whether or not they live in a flood plain or by a river bank.

"If governments and communities address the two variables that are within their control, then they can go a long way to reducing the risk of displacement occurring in the first place," says Ginnetti. "And that's really in everyone's interest."

# Artificial Island Could Be Solution for Rising Pacific Sea Levels

By John Vidal
*The Guardian*, September 8, 2011

*Kiribati's President Anote Tong is considering the radical action of moving 100,000 people to "structures resembling oil rigs."*

Sea levels are rising so fast that the tiny Pacific state of Kiribati is seriously considering moving its 100,000 people onto artificial islands. In a speech to the 16-nation Pacific Islands Forum this week, President Anote Tong said radical action may be needed and that he had been looking at a $2 billion plan that involved "structures resembling oil rigs":

> The last time I saw the models, I was like "wow it's like science fiction, almost like something in space. So modern, I don't know if our people could live on it. But what would you do for your grandchildren? If you're faced with the option of being submerged, with your family, would you jump on an oil rig like that? And [I] think the answer is 'yes'. We are running out of options, so we are considering all of them."

Kiribati is not alone. Tuvalu, Tonga, the Maldives, the Cook and the Solomon Islands are all losing the battle against the rising seas and are finding it tough to pay for sea defenses. Kiribati faces an immediate bill of over $900 million just to protect its infrastructure.

But history shows there is no technological reason why the nation could not stay in the middle of the Pacific even if sea levels rose several feet.

The Uros people of Peru live on around 40 floating villages made of grasses in the middle of Lake Titicaca. Equally, the city of Tenochtitlan, the Aztec predecessor of Mexico City that was home to 250,000 people when the Spaniards arrived, stood on a small natural island in Lake Texcoco that was surrounded by hundreds of artificial islands.

More recently, Holland, Japan, Dubai, and Hong Kong have all built artificial islands for airports, or new housing. The mayor of London Boris Johnson has a vision of a giant international airport in the middle of the Thames estuary with five runways to replace Heathrow.

Kiribati could also take a lesson from the Maldives, where the rubbish of the capital city Male and the hundreds of tourist islands, is sent to the artificial island of Thilafushi. It's growing about one square meter per day.

From *The Guardian* (8 September 2011). Copyright © 2011 by Guardian Newspapers Ltd. Reprinted with permission. All rights reserved.

Neft Daslari, Stalin's city in the middle of the Caspian Sea, is still operational after more than 60 years. At its peak it housed over 5,000 oil workers 34 miles off the Azerbaijan coastline. It began with a single path out over the water and grew to have over 300 kilometers of streets, mainly built on the back of sunken ships.

Kiribati could emulate Spiral Island in Mexico. This was constructed by British artist Richard "Rishi" Sowa on a base of 250,000 plastic bottles. The island was destroyed by Hurricane Emily in 2005 but is being rebuilt. With millions of tons of rubbish already floating in the Pacific, and plans to collect it, Kiribati could solve two problems in one go.

But Tong's imagination has been stirred by a more futuristic vision. It's possible he's seen the "Lilypad" floating city concept by the Belgian architect Vincent Callebaut. This "ecopolis" would not only be able to produce its own energy through solar, wind, tidal and biomass but would also process $CO_2$ in the atmosphere and absorb it into its titanium dioxide skin.

Bangkok architects S+PBA have come up with the idea of a floating "wetropolis" to replace eventually the metropolis of Bangkok. They say that Bangkok is founded on marshes and with sea levels rising several centimeters a year and the population growing fast, it's cheaper and more ecologically sound to embrace the rising seas than fight them.

Stranger still could be the German architect Wolf Hilbertz's idea for a self-assembling sea city called Autopia Ampere. Hilbertz plans to use the process of electrodeposition to create an island that would build itself in the water. It would begin as a series of wire mesh armatures connected to a supply of low-voltage direct current produced by solar panels. The electrochemical reactions would draw up sea minerals over time, creating walls of calcium carbonate on the armatures.

Islands have always fascinated political utopians, and now the billionaire hedge-fund manager and technology utopian Peter Thiel, has linked with Patri Friedman, a former Google engineer and grandson of Nobel prize-winning free market economist Milton Friedman to envisage a libertarian floating country.

Their idea is to build a series of physically linked oil-rig-type platforms anchored in international waters. The new state would be built by entrepreneurs and have no regulation, laws, welfare, restrictions on weapons or moral code of ethics. Eventually, millions of "seasteading" people would live there.

Plans for a prototype are said to have been drawn up for the first diesel-powered, 12,000 ton structure with room for 270 residents. Eventually, dozens—perhaps even hundreds—of these could be linked together, says Friedman who hopes to launch a flotilla of floating offices off the San Francisco coast next year.

In the end, it depends on money, which is in short supply for poor countries. If the world puts up several billion dollars—as Tong and his people would probably prefer—it would be technically possible for Kiribati to stay where it is.

Realistically, though, Australia, New Zealand and larger Pacific states are likely to be leaned on heavily to provide land for the Kiribatians and the world can expect a series of evacuations over the next 30 years.

# Floating Islands to the Rescue in the Maldives

By Debra Black
*Toronto Star*, August 23, 2012

*Government of Maldives and a Dutch company embark on a project that many hope will be the solution to an impending environmental crisis. Dutch company is also eyeing Toronto.*

A unique series of man-made floating islands—called the 5 Lagoons Project—will begin taking shape this fall around the Maldives, a series of almost 1,300 islands in the Indian Ocean.

The floating islands are part of a joint project that many hope will be the solution to the impending environmental crisis the islands could face over the next 50 years.

Thanks to climate change and the forecast of increasing sea levels, the Maldives—which are now only one and a half meters above sea level—could one day be totally submerged.

The project is a joint venture between the Maldivian government and Dutch Docklands, a Holland-based firm that specializes in building everything from floating prisons to floating conference and hotel complexes and homes.

The 5 Lagoons Project—80 million square feet—will include: a private islands project with $10 million villas; a floating 18-hole golf course with an undersea tunnel; a conference complex and hotel; 185 $1-million waterfront homes connected along a flower-shaped quay as well as a separate floating island with homes for residents of Malé, the country's capital.

The first phase of the $1-billion project will go on sale later this year with other parts of the development to be started over the next two to five years. Privately financed, the project is a joint venture between the Maldivian government and Dutch Docklands.

Paul Van de Camp, chief executive officer of Dutch Docklands, and his company worked for two years with the Maldivian government to come up with a plan. Key to the deal was allowing foreign ownership of the high-end villas that would be constructed. In exchange Van de Camp's company would build a separate floating island with homes for the bulk of the country's population.

All of this will be done with an eye to protect the islands' natural resources and environment, said Van de Camp. The floating islands will not hurt or touch the coral

From *Toronto Star* (23 August 2012). Copyright © 2012 by Toronto Star Newspapers Ltd. Reprinted with permission. All rights reserved.

reefs and coral beds that surround the island nor the other marine life in the Indian Ocean that surrounds the Maldives.

"The Maldives are the biggest marine protected environment in the world," said Van de Camp in an interview with the *Star* during a short visit to Toronto. The government is very cautious about anything that could potentially harm the aquatic life, the environment and tourism.

The floating islands will be anchored to the seabed using cables or telescopic mooring piles. They will be stable even in storms, the company says. One of the reasons designers decided to build lots of small islands was to lessen any shadow of the seabed because it could affect wildlife.

Van de Camp and his partner, architect Koen Olthuis, have plenty of experience when it comes to designing floating things.

Since its inception a decade ago Dutch Docklands has built all kinds of floating islands and buildings in Holland, including a floating prison, a floating conference center and thousands of floating homes.

Until recently Van de Camp hadn't thought of taking his vision abroad because he had so much work in Holland. "But because of the environment issue, we decided our expertise could be exported," he said.

"As Dutch people we know as nobody else knows the fight against water is a fight you'll lose. Water is so strong you have to come up with different solutions."

With the Maldives project about to launch, Van de Camp is looking at other international possibilities. One such location could be Toronto which is ideally suited for a series of floating islands because of its location on the shores of Lake Ontario.

Van de Camp suggests that a series of floating islands would give a different dimension to the city—a new footprint that abandons the idea that the only way a city can expand is to build towers.

"We think cities shouldn't always be looking backwards and creating highrise buildings. They should also look to the water to see if they could come up with solutions on the water that would give a better shape to the city."

# America's First Climate Refugees

By Suzanne Goldenberg
*The Guardian*, May 30, 2013

*Newtok, Alaska is losing ground to the sea at a dangerous rate and for its residents, exile is inevitable.*

Sabrina Warner keeps having the same nightmare: a huge wave rearing up out of the water and crashing over her home, forcing her to swim for her life with her toddler son.

"I dream about the water coming in," she said. The landscape in winter on the Bering Sea coast seems peaceful, the tidal wave of Warner's nightmare trapped by snow and several feet of ice. But the calm is deceptive. Spring break-up will soon restore the Ninglick River to its full violent force.

In the dream, Warner climbs onto the roof of her small house. As the waters rise, she swims for higher ground: the village school which sits on 20-foot pilings.

Even that isn't high enough. By the time Warner wakes, she is clinging to the roof of the school, desperate to be saved.

Warner's vision is not far removed from a reality written by climate change. The people of Newtok, on the west coast of Alaska and about 400 miles south of the Bering Strait that separates the state from Russia, are living a slow-motion disaster that will end, very possibly within the next five years, with the entire village being washed away.

The Ninglick River coils around Newtok on three sides before emptying into the Bering Sea. It has steadily been eating away at the land, carrying off 100 feet or more some years, in a process moving at unusual speed because of climate change. Eventually all of the villagers will have to leave, becoming America's first climate change refugees.

It is not a label or a future embraced by people living in Newtok. Yup'ik Eskimo have been fishing and hunting by the shores of the Bering Sea for centuries and the villagers reject the notion they will now be forced to run in chaos from ancestral lands.

But exile is undeniable. A report by the US Army Corps of Engineers predicted that the highest point in the village—the school of Warner's nightmare—could be underwater by 2017. There was no possible way to protect the village in place, the report concluded.

If Newtok cannot move its people to the new site in time, the village will disappear. A community of 350 people, nearly all related to some degree and all intimately

From *The Guardian* (30 May 2013). Copyright © 2013 by Guardian Newspapers Ltd. Reprinted with permission. All rights reserved.

connected to the land, will cease to exist, its inhabitants scattered to the villages and towns of western Alaska, Anchorage and beyond.

It's a choice confronting more than 180 native communities in Alaska, which are flooding and losing land because of the ice melt that is part of the changing climate.

The Arctic Council, the group of countries that governs the polar regions, are gathering in Sweden today. But climate change refugees are not high on their agenda, and Obama administration officials told reporters on Friday there would be no additional money to help communities in the firing line.

On the other side of the continent, the cities and towns of the east coast are waking up to their own version of Warner's nightmare: the storm surges demonstrated by Hurricane Sandy. About half of America's population lives within 50 miles of a coastline. Those numbers are projected to grow even more in the coming decades.

What chance do any of those communities, in Alaska or on the Atlantic coast, have of a fair and secure future under climate change, if a tiny community like Newtok—just 63 houses in all—cannot be assured of survival?

But as the villagers of Newtok are discovering, recognizing the gravity of the threat posed by climate change and responding in time are two very different matters.

## Remote Location

Newtok lies 480 miles due west of Anchorage. The closest town of any size, the closest doctor, gas station, or paved road, is almost 100 miles away.

The only year-round link to the outside world is via a small propeller plane from the regional hub of Bethel.

The seven-seater plane flies over a landscape that seems pancake flat under the snow: bright white for land, slightly translucent swirls for frozen rivers. There are no trees.

The village as seen from the air is a cluster of almost identical small houses, plopped down at random on the snow. The airport is a patch of ground newly swept of snow, marked off for the pilot by a circle of orange traffic cones. The airport manager runs the luggage into the center of the village on a yellow sledge attached to his snowmobile.

Like many if not most native Alaskan villages, Newtok owes its location to a distant bureaucrat. The Yup'iks, who had lived in these parts of Alaska for hundreds of years, had traditionally used the area around present-day Newtok as a seasonal stopping-off place, convenient for late summer berry picking.

Even then, their preferred encampment, when they passed through the area, was a cluster of sod houses called Kayalavik, some miles further up river. But over the years, the authorities began pushing native Alaskans to settle in fixed locations and to send their children to school.

It was difficult for supply barges to maneuver as far up river as Kayalavik. After 1959, when Alaska became a state, the new authorities ordered villagers to move to a more convenient docking point.

That became Newtok. Current state officials admit the location—on low-lying mud flats between the river and the Bering Sea—was far from perfect. It certainly wasn't chosen with a view to future threats such as climate change.

"The places are often where they are because it was easy to unload the building materials and build the school and the post office there," said Larry Hartig, who heads the state's Commission on Environmental Conservation. "But they weren't the ideal place to be in terms of long-term stability and it's now creating a lot of problems that are exacerbated by melting permafrost and less of the seasonal sea ice that would form barriers between the winter storms and uplands."

It became clear by the 1990s that Newtok—like dozens of other remote communities in Alaska—was losing land at a dangerous rate. Almost all native Alaskan villages are located along rivers and sea coasts, and almost all are facing similar peril.

A federal government report found more than 180 other native Alaskan villages—or 86% of all native communities—were at risk because of climate change. In the case of Newtok, those effects were potentially life threatening.

A study by the US Army Corps of Engineers on the effects of climate change on native Alaskan villages, the one that predicted the school would be underwater by 2017, found no remedies for the loss of land in Newtok.

The land was too fragile and low-lying to support sea walls or other structures that could keep the water out, the report said, adding that if the village did not move, the land would eventually be overrun with water. People could die.

It was a staggering verdict for Newtok. Some of the village elders remember the upheaval of that earlier move. The villagers were adamant that they take charge of the move this time and remain an intact community—not scatter to other towns.

And so after years of poring over reports, the entire community voted to relocate to higher ground across the river. The decision was endorsed by the state authorities. In December 2007, the village held the first public meeting to plan the move.

The proposed new site for Newtok, voted on by the villagers and approved by government planners, lies only nine miles away, atop a high ridge of dark volcanic rock across the river on Nelson Island. On a good day in winter, it's a half-hour bone-shaking journey across the frozen Ninglick River by snowmobile.

But the cost of the move could run as high as $130 million, according to government estimates. For the villagers of Newtok, finding the cash, and finding their way through the government bureaucracy, is proving the challenge of their lives.

Five years on from that first public meeting, Newtok remains stuck where it was, the peeling tiles and the broken-down office furniture in the council office grown even shabbier, the dilapidated water treatment plant now shut down as a health hazard, an entire village tethered to a dangerous location by bureaucratic obstacles and lack of funds.

Village leaders hope that this coming summer, when conditions become warm enough for construction crews to get to work, could provide the big push Newtok needs by completing the first phase of basic infrastructure. And the effort needs a push. When the autumn storms blow in, the water rises fast.

## Changing Climate

Climate change remains a politically touchy subject in Alaska. The state owes its prosperity to the development of the vast Prudhoe Bay oil fields on the Arctic Coast.

Even in Newtok, there are some who believe climate change is caused by negative emotions, such as anger, hate and envy. But while some dispute the overwhelming scientific view that climate change is caused primarily by human activities, there is little argument in Alaska about its effects.

The state has warmed twice as fast as the rest of the country over the past 60 years. Freeze-up occurs later, snow is wetter and heavier. Wildfires erupt on the tundra in the summer. Rivers rush out to the sea. Moose migrate north into caribou country. Grizzlies mate with polar bear as their ranges overlap.

Even people in their 20s, like Warner and her partner Nathan Tom, can track the changes in their own lifetimes. Tom said the seasons have changed. "The snow comes in a different timing now. The snow disappears way late. That is making the geese come at the wrong time. Now they are starting to lay their eggs when there is still snow and ice and we can't go and pick them," Tom said. "It's changing a lot. It's real, global warming, it's real."

On days when the clouds move in, and the only sound is the crunch of boots on snow and the distant buzzing of snowmobiles, it's difficult to imagine a world beyond the village, let alone a threat.

But Warner has seen the river rip into land and carry off clumps of earth. "It's scary thinking about summer coming," she said. "I don't know how much more is going to erode—hopefully not as much as last year."

Warner was raised in Anchorage and Wasilla, mainly by her non-Yup'ik father. But she was introduced to Yup'ik food and Yupi'ik ways by her mother, and she has taken to village life since moving to Newtok in December 2011 to be with Tom.

Even in those short months, she said she can see the changes carved out on the land behind the family home. "When I first got here the land used to be way out there," she said, pointing towards the west. "Now that doesn't exist anymore. There is no land there anymore."

The river claims more of the village every year. Warmer temperatures are thawing the permafrost on which Newtok is built, and the land surface is no longer stable. The sea ice that protected the village from winter storms is thinning and receding, exposing Newtok to winter storms with 100 mph winds and the waves of Warner's nightmare.

When the wind blows from the east or south, the land falls away even faster. The patch of land where Warner picked last summer to practice shooting was gone, on the other side of a sharp drop-off to the river. "The summer came, 15 or 20 ft of land went just from melting, and then after we had those storms in September another 20 ft went," she said. In an average year the river swallows 83 ft of land a year, according to a report by the Government Accountability Office. Some years of course it's more.

The reddish-brown house where Tom and Warner live with their son Tyson and elderly relatives is the closest in the village to the Ninglick.

Warner fears her house will soon be swallowed up by that hungry river. "Two more years, that's what I'm guessing. About two more years until it's right up to our house," she said.

The house is now barely 200 paces away from the drop-off point. It's become a sort of tourist stop for visitors to the village, and an educational aid for teachers at the local school. Last year, one of the teachers set out stakes to mark how fast the river was rising. At least one has already been washed away.

But it won't be long before nobody in the village is safe. Other homes, once considered well back from the river, now regularly flood.

Over the years the river, in its attack on the land, engulfed a few small ponds—some fresh water, some used as raw sewage dumps—spewing human waste across the village. Last summer it almost carried off a few dumpsters filled with old fridges and computers. It swept away the barge landing, and infested the landfill.

Sometimes, though, the river gives up treasure: villagers walking newly exposed banks have discovered mammoth tusks and fossil remains.

During one storm last autumn, Warner stayed up until 4am, waiting to see if the waves would engulf the house. "I was scared because it looked so close because our window is right there. I was just looking out, and you can see these huge waves come at you," she said.

It's not easy living with that fear every day, she concedes. Anxious residents want to know that their future will be safe. They are exhausted by the years of uncertainty and fed up with a village left to decay, with leaders' energy and every scrap of funding focused on the relocation.

"Considering that our house is the closest, I would like it if they would at least let us know if we are going to have a house over there [at the new site]", said Warner. Tom's grandmother, who needs oxygen, lives with the couple. It would be tough to move her in the event of a disaster, although she claims she is not at all afraid.

The young couple go through times when they can't deal with the talk of relocation. Tom bought a big tent some time ago and the couple have talked about camping out at the site chosen for the new village, just to get away—from the stress, from the drama of village politics—until things are settled.

But the relocation keeps being put off.

"A few years ago, they said next year. And then last year they said next year. And next year, they are probably going to say next year again," said Tom. But he soon perks up. The village has sent local men, including Tom, for training as construction workers.

"It's picking up," he said. "I'm not afraid any more. The erosion is really fast. I know the state is going to deal with it pretty fast. They are not going to leave us hanging there."

# Beyond Asylum Seeker Funerals

By Andrew Hamilton
*Eureka Street,* February 25, 2011

The two Sydney funerals for the asylum seekers who died trying to reach Christmas Island was heartrending. That some of their relatives were able to gather to mourn them was some small consolation for them. From ancient times to today so many other asylum seekers have died and have lain unburied.

Ordinarily the best response to such grief would be one of silent compassion. But even in death asylum seekers open a faultline in Australian culture and society. Scott Morrison and Tony Abbott wondered aloud at the expense of bringing people from Christmas Island to an Australian funeral. They later backed down on the timing—but not the substance—of their comments.

Psychologists who work closely with asylum seekers were appalled that bereaved children should be returned to Christmas Island. They again emphasized the harm done by detention.

It would be indecent in a time of grief to speculate about what individual politicians might have meant by what they said. But the larger considerations that affect asylum seekers' lives deserve comment. Three points stand out.

First, despite all the evidence of how destructive life in detention is for children, and despite the decision of the Howard Government not to detain children, large numbers of children remain incarcerated. That is shameful. No Australian should be able to contemplate with equanimity the conscription of children, the enslavement of children, the detaining of children and other forms of child abuse.

Second, it is evident that the system of mandatory detention for adults as well as for children is unreasonable. Professor Pat McGorry's famous description of detention centers as factories for manufacturing mental illness was modest and exact.

Yet detention centers, particularly those set in remote parts of Australia with a harsh climate which are known to be most destructive, have multiplied. They come at a huge cost. Detention is a swelling economic folly. If money is an issue, it would be far more rational economically, as well as more humane, to allow asylum seekers to live in the community while their cases are being processed.

Third, the fact that arrangements involving such barbarity and such economic nonsense continue without public outcry suggests that there is strong political opposition to change. That politicians cannot agree on better arrangements suggests that the resistance to change is located deeply in Australian society.

From *Eureka Street* 21.3 (25 February 2011): 35–36. Copyright © 2011 by *Eureka Street*. Reprinted with permission. All rights reserved.

A recent conversation with a woman whose work had taken her to Christmas Island confirmed these impressions. She struck me as a decent person. On Christmas Island she had warmed to many of the asylum seekers whom she met. But she returned from the island even more convinced that they should not be admitted into Australia.

Her arguments were that Australia already had too many people, that asylum seekers would overrun the nation, that Australia was broke and could not afford to support them, and that, once admitted, even asylum seekers found not to be refugees would never leave.

She half-apologized for her views, perhaps recognizing that they stood in some tension with her habitual generosity of spirit. But she continued to argue firmly against making any concessions to children or to adults.

The most thought-provoking aspect of this conversation was to recognize that even personal contact with asylum seekers and with incarcerated children does not necessarily soften people's views. Even seeing the faces of distressed people and hearing their stories could not shake the power over the imagination exerted by the vision of a threatened, overpopulated and bankrupt nation.

It is easy to see why politicians who wish to move to a more rational and humane policy should find it so difficult, and why those who wish to further mire the murky waters should find encouragement.

If we are concerned at the way Australia treats asylum seekers, this conversation suggests that we must focus on what matters. The funerals of the asylum seekers should be the starting place, and the faces and stories of those who died and who grieve. Their humanity is salient to us.

It is also important to keep meeting arguments such as those proposed by the woman against treating asylum seekers humanely. They may be weak arguments, but they continue to attract adherents.

But the central challenge is to change the way Australians imagine asylum seekers as an obstacle to our comfort and to our wellbeing. As long as our imagination remains untouched, there will be little outrage at the suffering of children or adults. People will avert their eyes, wishing all this was not necessary, but prepared to allow others to pay the price for our comfort.

To change the public imagination is a long task, but it begins by personal conversion. There is no better place to begin than in contemplation of lonely funerals far from home.

# Bibliography

❖

Anderson, Jon. *Water Worlds: Human Geographies of the Ocean*. Farnham: Ashgate, 2014. Print.

Durand, Rodolphe, and Jean-Philippe Vergne. *The Pirate Organization: Lessons from the Fringes of Capitalism*. Boston: Harvard Business Rev., 2013. Print.

Fagan, Brian M. *The Attacking Ocean: The Past, Present, and Future of Rising Sea Levels*. New York: Bloomsbury, 2013. Print.

Garofano, John, and Andrea J. Dew. *Deep Currents and Rising Tides: The Indian Ocean and International Security*. Washington: Georgetown UP, 2013. Print.

Gershwin, Lisa-Ann, and Sylvia A. Earle. *Stung!: On Jellyfish Blooms and the Future of the Ocean*. Chicago: U of Chicago P, 2013. Print.

Griffis, Roger B, and Jennifer Howard. *Oceans and Marine Resources in a Changing Climate: A Technical Input to the 2013 National Climate Assessment*. Washington: Island, 2013. Print.

Kraska, James, and Raul A. Pedrozo. *International Maritime Security Law*. Leiden: Nijhoff, 2013. Print.

Maslo, Brooke, and Julie L. Lockwood. *Coastal Conservation*. Cambridge: Cambridge UP, 2014. Print.

McKnight, Terry, and Michael Hirsh. *Pirate Alley: Commanding Task Force 151 Off Somalia*. Annapolis: Naval Inst., 2012. Print.

Murray-Wallace, Colin V. *Quaternary Sea-Level Changes: A Global Perspective*. Cambridge: Cambridge UP, 2014. Print.

Parker, Bruce B. *The Power of the Sea: Tsunamis, Storm Surges, Rogue Waves, and Our Quest to Predict Disasters*. New York: Macmillan, 2010. Print.

Reiss, Bob. *The Eskimo and the Oil Man: The Battle at the Top of the World for America's Future*. New York: Business Plus, 2012. Print.

Shambaugh, David L. *Tangled Titans: The United States and China*. Lanham: Rowman, 2013. Print.

Sharpless, Andy, and Suzannah Evans. *The Perfect Protein: The Fish Lover's Guide to Saving the Oceans and Feeding the World*. New York: Rodale, 2013. Print.

Siedler, Gerold, Stephen M. Griffies, John Gould, and John A. Church. *Ocean Circulation and Climate: A 21st Century Perspective*. 2nd ed. Amsterdam: Academic, 2013. Print.

Till, Geoffrey. *Seapower: A Guide for the Twenty-First Century*. 3rd ed. New York: Routledge, 2013. Print.

Van, Dyke J. M, Sherry P. Broder, Seokwoo Lee and Jin-Hyun Paik. *Governing Ocean Resources: New Challenges and Emerging Regimes*. Leiden: Nijhoff, 2013. Print.

Zhexembayeva, Nadya. *Overfished Ocean Strategy: Powering Up Innovation for a Resource-Deprived World*. San Francisco: Berrett, 2014. Print.

# Websites

❖

### Alliance of Small Island States (AOSIS)

aosis.org

The forty-four-member AOSIS was formed in the late twentieth century to address the global warming crisis affecting small island nations and countries. The website hosts videos, archived published reports and newspaper articles, and global action plans related to climate change action and issues and the increasing plight of environmental refugees.

### National Ocean Council

www.whitehouse.gov/administration/eop/oceans

The National Ocean Council oversees the implementation of America's National Ocean Policy and was established after an executive order in 2010. In addition to a wealth of information regarding ocean policy on the website itself, the council maintains a web portal (www.data.gov/ocean) that provides data and tools regarding the stewardship and management of the ocean, coasts, and the Great Lakes environments.

### Natural Resources Defense Council (NRDC): Sustainable Seafood Guide

www.nrdc.org/oceans/seafoodguide

This website offers a guide to purchasing and consuming sustainable seafood, including information regarding the reading and understanding of food labels on seafood; a guide to understanding whether purchased fish was sustainably harvested; advice on how to safely purchase five popular types of seafood; and a consumer guide to understanding mercury levels in fish and other seafood.

### Ocean Preservation Society (OPS)

www.opsociety.org

Similar in nature to Surfrider, the nonprofit OPS utilizes film, photography, and media campaigns to promote ocean environmentalism and preservation. Some of the issues that can be explored through the society's website include ocean acidification, species extinction, underwater noise pollution, and whaling.

### Oceans Beyond Piracy (OBP)

oceansbeyondpiracy.org

A project sponsored by One Earth Future, OBP is focused on developing a global plan or response to combat piracy. The site provides significant data related to the occurrences and economic and human costs of maritime piracy, as well as links to relevant news stories and academic and government analysis of and reports on piracy.

### Smithsonian Ocean Portal on Deep Ocean Exploration
ocean.si.edu/deep-sea

This web portal on ocean exploration, operated by the Smithsonian National Museum of Natural History, is a treasure trove of information related to ocean life, history, and conservation. Numerous sub-portals (Ocean Life & Ecosystems, Planet Ocean, Ocean Through Time, Conservation, Human Connections) offer relevant links and news stories, blogs, slideshows, and videos on a range of issues and topics covered in this issue. A link to educator resources provides lesson plans for grade levels K–12.

### Surfrider Foundation
www.surfrider.org

With a stated focus on globally protecting oceans, waves, and beaches, the non-profit, grassroots-driven Surfrider Foundation conducts multiple environmental campaigns and programs accessible through its website. The website also offers podcasts, publications, blogs, and public service announcements detailing the foundation's efforts to protect the oceans.

# Index

❖